HOME BOOK OF
PICTURE FRAMING

HOME BOOK OF PICTURE FRAMING

Professional secrets of mounting, matting, framing, and displaying artwork, photographs, posters, collectibles, carvings, and more

Kenn Oberrecht

Stackpole Books

Published by
STACKPOLE BOOKS
Cameron and Kelker Streets
P.O. Box 1831
Harrisburg, PA 17105

Printed in the United States of America

10   9   8   7   6   5

Library of Congress Cataloging-in-Publication Data

Oberrecht, Kenn.
   Home book of picture framing: professional secrets of mounting, matting, framing, and displaying
artwork, photographs, posters, collectibles, carvings, and more / Kenn Oberrecht.
     p. cm.
   Includes index.
   ISBN 0-8117-2250-3
   1. Picture frames and framing. I. Title.
N8550.O24 1988
749'.7—dc19
                                                             88-15452
                                                               CIP

For Sam

Contents

	Safety Tips on Mounting, Matting, and Framing	9
1	Framing Basics	13
2	Mounting and Matting Materials and Tools	20
3	Basic and Conservation Mounting and Matting	34
4	Mounting Photographs and Posters	49
5	Advanced Matting Materials, Tools, and Techniques	62
6	Framing Materials and Tools	88
7	Framing with Commercial Frames and Moldings	102
8	Making Frame Moldings	112
9	Finishing Wood Frames	139
10	Glazing, Installing, and Hanging	150
11	Making Rustic Wood Frames	175
12	Making Floater Fixtures and Frames	186
13	Framing without Miters	195

14	**Framing without Frames**	203
15	**Framing Calendars**	215
16	**Framing Pegboard**	225
17	**Framing Bulletin Boards**	233
18	**Making Shadow-Box Frames**	243
19	**Building Collector Frames**	250
20	**Framing as a Business**	260
	Directory of Manufacturers and Suppliers	265
	Index	269

Safety Tips on Mounting, Matting, and Framing

Common sense can go a long way toward keeping you out of harm's way. Remember to handle tools and materials carefully and cautiously. Whether you're a beginner or veteran craftsman, you would do well to read the following tips now and review them from time to time.

1. Store matting, framing, and woodworking tools out of the reach of children, and keep children out of your work area unless you're teaching them how to frame pictures. The first framing lesson for any youngster should be one on safety.

2. When you finish using any framing tools and materials, put them away. Keep your work area free of clutter.

3. When sawing, drilling, cutting, and performing other operations, whenever possible, secure work pieces to a solid surface with clamps or a vise. This tactic not only allows you to use tools safely but also reduces the chances of errors while increasing accuracy.

4. Keep saw and knife blades, bits, and other cutting and drilling instruments clean and sharp. Any residue build-up will dull tools, and dull cutting and boring tools are dangerous. Moreover, dull bits and blades put unnecessary strain on power-tool motors.

5. Blades used in mat cutters, utility knives, and other matting and framing tools require special handling. When

they're dulled and need replacing, don't discard them as you would other trash. Keep used blades in a covered jar or can. When the container is full, discard it.

6. Before operating new tools for matting, mounting, framing, and woodworking, read the instructions that come with them. Review the instructions periodically to make sure you don't develop any bad habits. Before setting to work with any new tool, practice with it on scrap material until you develop a comfortable feel for the tool.

7. When working with power tools and hammers, always wear some sort of goggles or safety glasses. Select protective eyewear that's comfortable, and you will be more inclined to use it when you should.

8. Some noisy power tools can permanently damage your ears. When using such tools, wear approved ear protectors, available at most hardware stores and gun shops.

9. When working with abrasives, sanders, and other tools that create dust, wear a dust mask. If you suffer from any kind of respiratory ailment, consult a physician about the type of mask you should wear for maximum protection.

10. When handling glass, be careful to avoid the sharp edges and corners that can cause serious injuries. Whenever possible, wear heavy leather work gloves or use rags folded into several layers for grasping the glass near the edges.

11. When working with solvents, adhesives, and chemicals that can cause skin damage, always wear rubber or chemical-proof plastic gloves.

12. Lacquers, thinners, cleaners, solvents, and adhesives that produce toxic, flammable, or explosive fumes should be used only in a well-ventilated area, away from sources of heat or open flame. Do not use power tools around any flammable or explosive substances, as fumes might be ignited by electrical arc when the tool is switched on.

13. Read labels on all materials used in the framing process. Pay special attention to bold CAUTION and WARNING notices. When in doubt about the safe handling of any material, phone or write the manufacturer for instructions.

14. Make sure power tools are switched off before you plug them in. Always disconnect power-tool plugs before changing bits or blades or making adjustments. At the end of any work session, unplug all power tools.

15. Power tools must be properly grounded. If a tool is equipped with a three-conductor cord and three-prong plug, make sure the outlet is a proper, grounding-type receptacle. And use only the appropriate and approved extension cords with such tools.

16. Before operating any power tool, make sure power cords and extension cords are out of the way and will not interfere with tool operation.

17. Don't wear jewelry or loose-fitting clothing when operating any tools or machinery that might entangle it and cause personal injury. Remove watches, rings,

and other metal when operating any portable power tool that is not labeled "Double Insulated."

18. If a power tool stalls during operation, release the trigger or switch the machine off immediately. Then unplug the tool and work the jam loose in safety. Before resuming operation, correct the cause of the stall.

19. Always grip a portable power tool firmly before switching it on, as the torque of the motor could cause you to lose your grip. Whenever possible, grasp the tool with both hands.

20. Remove a table-saw blade guard only to make cuts that do not fully penetrate the wood, as in cutting grooves in frame molding. Immediately replace the guard after such cuts, and leave it in place for all other work. Some old-timers leave the guards off their saws, and some old-timers possess fewer than 10 fingers.

21. When miter cutting or crosscutting with a table saw or bandsaw and miter gauge, remove the fence from the saw. Never use both the fence and the miter gauge together, as this practice can lead to serious injury and saw damage.

22. When using a stationary power saw to rip broad boards into narrow stock for frame moldings, always feed the material through the saw with push blocks to keep your fingers away from the blade.

23. Maintain all tools for long life — yours and the tools'. Keep them clean, free of corrosion, and lubricated according to the manufacturers' directions.

24. Worn or damaged power cords on electrically powered tools are dangerous and should be replaced. Likewise, damaged extension cords should be repaired or discarded.

25. Keep safety in mind at all times. No matter what kind of job you're engaged in, use common sense, and concentrate on the task at hand.

1

Framing Basics

No do-it-yourself activity will save the homeowner or apartment dweller more money than the mounting, matting, and framing of artwork, photographs, posters, documents, and collectibles. Moreover, with the proper instructions, anyone can easily master professional framing techniques.

Compared with other woodworking projects, framing requires relatively few tools, and most are fairly inexpensive and easy to use, if somewhat foreign in appearance. Mounting and matting tools are also inexpensive and easily mastered. Suitable materials are abundant and readily available in most communities. And anything that can't be found locally is available from several reliable mail-order suppliers specializing in mounting, matting, and framing products.

Nevertheless, the craft seems a mystery to most, a sense perhaps perpetuated by professional framers to some extent but more likely prompted by widespread misconception and misunderstanding. To be certain, some magazine articles and books on the subject have ill served the reading public by ignoring important considerations at best and dispensing nonsense at worst. So the craft remains shrouded in mystery, while people keep paying exorbitant prices for custom matting and framing jobs that are sometimes inferior in quality and even potentially damaging to the framed work.

It's not easy for the uninitiated to look at a beautifully matted and framed work and determine all that makes it a thing of beauty, because many of the framer's secrets are concealed between glass and dust seal. And even if the work were dismantled and analyzed, it would not be readily apparent to the casual observer why certain materials were chosen in lieu of others. There are many specific guidelines, rules to be observed, rules to be broken from time to time, matters of personal preference and taste, and countless tips and tricks that make the framing of any work both functional and pleasing to the eye.

Savings Potential

I can't stress enough the practicality of do-it-yourself framing. Once you learn the basics, you can recognize substantial savings in every framing job you do. When you realize that most of the cost of a manufactured frame or custom mat-ting-and-framing job is labor, it's easier to understand why commercially made frames and custom-made mats and frames are so expensive – easier to understand but not to justify.

To provide an idea of the savings (or profits) possible, I recently made some cost comparisons, using a standard 16 x 20-inch frame as the basis. I found a com-mercially made oak frame of simple 1 x 2 molding priced at $30.85. The same frame made to order by a professional framer might cost $50 or more. I could buy the identical molding at a local home-improvement center and build the same frame for $8.58. With oak 1 x 2, however, and an extra five minutes of setup and saw time, I can make the same frame for $4.88. And that's paying retail for materials. As a professional (and any-one with a business card can call himself a professional), I can save an additional 10 to 30 percent in discounts, depending on where I buy. By going to the mill and hauling my own material, I can save up to 50 percent.

But these savings pale in comparison with the savings possible with moldings and framing systems I have devised and will cover completely in later chapters. To determine my costs in making a basic 1 x 2 molding, for example, I timed my-self. Working at a comfortable but steady pace, without rushing, I was able to turn out 200 feet of molding in one hour, at a total material cost of $10, or 5¢ a foot. Comparable commercial moldings range in price from $1.32 to $1.94 a foot, or about twenty-six to thirty-nine times as much.

Using the basic single-strip molding, I framed a pair of 20 x 22-inch prints for 40¢ each. With a double-strip molding, I framed a matted print measuring 29½ x 36½ inches for a mere $1.10. A large, limited-edition print by one of my favor-ite artists is housed in a massive 31 x 41-inch three-strip frame that set me back all of $1.75.

A local physician had that same print custom framed in a barn-siding–style molding that compares in size and ap-pearance to my own and paid $135 for the job: $75 for the frame, $35 for the mounting and matting with standard mat board, and $25 for the glass. For a total cost of about $5, I archivally mounted and double matted my own print with acid-free board I purchased at the same shop and special rice-paper hinges im-pregnated with starch paste and treated with a fungicide. Instead of having a framer cut and supply my glass, I bought mine at a glass shop for $15.

The whole job – mounting, matting, glazing, and framing – cost me about $22. Not only did mine cost $113 less than the good doctor paid, but when the acidic mats have burned the margins of his print and yellowed the highlights, mine will still look good as new. What's more, as my properly framed print increases in value, which the sold-out edition promises, his will decrease, simply because it wasn't properly matted and framed.

So the savings continue and go well beyond the dollars saved initially. The potential, in fact, is limitless. How to save those dollars at the onset and spend a few cents to protect an investment is something the average person doesn't know about—but which you are about to learn.

Consider the average modest dwelling: a three-bedroom, two-bath house, apartment, or condominium. There's a good bit of wall space to cover in any such home and a surprising number of items to be framed: perhaps a couple of colorful prints for the kitchen; several drawings, prints, or paintings for the dining room and living room; posters and photographs for children's rooms; a few favorite prints and paintings for the master bedroom; possibly some miniatures, collectibles, and three-dimensional art for the bathrooms; and a collection of family photographs for the hallway. The average person could easily have thirty, forty, or more items to be framed.

In larger homes there are walls in family rooms, hobby rooms, rec rooms, dens, libraries, and home offices. There are more hallways, stairways, and foyer space. And if someone in the home happens to be an artist or photographer, framing can become a continuous activity.

It should be clear to you by now that you can easily earn back the price of this book and more with your first framing project. Eventually, your savings can amount to hundreds or thousands of dollars. And if you're so inclined, you can turn enough of a profit on your hobby to pay for all your tools and materials, or you can even make this enjoyable hobby a full-time profession.

Types of Framables

Among the many objects suitable for framing are oil and acrylic paintings, pastels, batiks, watercolors, pencil and pen-and-ink drawings, washes, lithographs, serigraphs, engravings, etchings, diplomas, certificates, photographs, posters, three-dimensional art, and various collectibles.

Preparation of the work and the materials, tools, and techniques you use to frame it depend on the kind of work it is. Beyond that, you will be guided by convention or tradition and your own tastes and ingenuity.

Original oil and acrylic paintings are framed without mats and glass, and there's no need for a dust seal at the rear of the frame with such works. Batiks are usually framed the same way.

Some professionals insist that all prints be framed as their originals would be. So if the original was an oil painting, they say, the print should be framed as an oil painting would be. Of course, if that's what you want to do, fine, but it's ridiculous to insist you do it that way. In fact, these days, with the current popularity of limited editions, most prints are matted and framed behind glass, even if the originals were oil or acrylic paintings. Certainly, any print with potential collector's value should be archivally matted and framed behind glass, regardless of what medium the original was done in.

Prints made on canvas should be

treated the same as original oils and acrylics on canvas. They should be attached to stretcher frames, then framed without mats, glass, or dust seals. Unlimited-edition prints on paper can be framed the same way, but first should be mounted to rigid stock, such as foamboard or hardboard.

Watercolors, pastels, sketches, drawings, most prints, and other artwork on paper should be matted and framed behind glass for maximum protection and most pleasing presentation. Diplomas, certificates, and other documents should also be framed behind glass, either with or without mats, depending on personal preferences.

Photographs and posters are displayed in the widest variety of ways. Photos are often mounted and displayed without mats or frames. Some are framed without mats or glass; others are treated the same as artworks on paper, with mats and glass. And there are many specialty products available for mounting and displaying photos and posters.

Three-dimensional objects are often displayed in framed collectors' cases. Some can be mounted to a suitable background, which is then framed and displayed with or without glass. Shadow boxes are also popular for framing and displaying such objects.

Framables range in value from free to priceless. With all the cheap and free items available, and the ability to frame them expertly and inexpensively, there's no excuse for bare walls anywhere. If your tastes lean toward expensive originals, rare objects, and limited editions but your budget doesn't quite stack up, display cheaper works for now, and replace them as you can afford to. You'll not only get valuable practice matting and framing the inexpensive items, but when you replace them you should also be able to sell them for considerably more than you have invested in them. What's more, you may find some you simply don't want to part with, regardless of their worth.

Cheap and free framables are everywhere. To find them, just keep your eyes open and think framing.

Many greeting and note cards are ideal as framed miniatures, and those of a similar size often make attractive sets. Occasional cards can be framed in batches and used as seasonal decorations for Thanksgiving, Christmas, Easter, and other holidays.

Posters are often given away as part of a promotional campaign. Even those sold for profit are always considerably cheaper than original art. And the freebies can even end up being worth money. Some years ago, I found a poster in a record album I had bought. I kept it for years with the idea of maybe framing it someday or perhaps giving it to a nephew or niece. But one day during a housecleaning binge, I decided I really didn't like it all that much, so I tossed it onto the trash heap I later hauled to the dump.

As Murphy would have it, no more than a week or two later, I watched a TV program on collecting and learned that the very poster I had just discarded was relatively rare and worth several hundred bucks.

Calendars—either photographs or art reproductions—are another good source of framable material. The matching sizes of calendar pages make them ideal for framed sets.

I'm not ashamed to admit that two of

Simple notecards showing fly-fishing scenes become attractive miniatures when they are matted and framed.

my favorite prints, which many of our visitors have liked as well, are calendar art that I didn't pay a dime for. I didn't even buy the calendar; *Handyman* magazine sent it free several years ago. Two of the art reproductions in the calendar struck my fancy, so I mounted, matted, and framed them. They're the same pair of 20 x 22-inch prints I mentioned earlier that I framed for 40¢ each. So it's certainly not their monetary value that has garnered so many appreciative comments.

Garage sales and second-hand stores are also good sources for cheap framables. Look for old photographs, paintings, and prints that appeal to you but are either poorly framed or are in frames that are falling apart. These are usually slow movers that you can pick up for nearly nothing. It's amazing what new mats, glass, and frames will do for these old works.

Functions of Frame and Mat

Both frames and mats perform protective and decorative functions. To avoid undermining these purposes, you must know how to select them and match them to the works being displayed.

The right frames provide rigid encasements for works of all kinds and thereby protect them and keep them from buckling, warping, and suffering from other problems. When properly sealed and glazed, they also protect works from ambient radiation, airborne pollutants, and acid damage. Finally, they also add eye appeal to the works they contain.

The wrong frames might not only fail to protect what they hold, but can also *cause* buckling, warping, and other problems. If they're improperly sealed and glazed, they can assist in the destruction of monetarily or sentimentally valuable works. And they can be distracting, even downright ugly.

Mats add rigidity to whatever is being framed, but they also provide important separation between the work and the glass. You can cut mats to make odd-size works fit standard-size frames. You can exaggerate mat sizes and dimensions to emphasize the size or format of what you're framing, and you can select colors that match or contrast the colors in the artworks or photographs. You can use single or multiple mats and can cut mat windows in a variety of shapes and configurations.

Modern Frame Design

Over the centuries, frames have changed dramatically, from the ornate and gaudy frames made from the fifteenth to eighteenth centuries to more subdued but decorative frames of the nineteenth century and on to the stark simplicity of the mid twentieth century. Many of the early frames were complex pieces of architecture that competed with the pictures they enclosed and distracted viewers. Today, we try to keep our frames simple, their designs subtle. We want them to complement what they enclose and blend with the room's decor.

Instead of the heavy, ornamental wood frames carved in deep relief that caught the fancy of our ancestors, we prefer lighter and narrower wood frames for many applications. The gaudy gilded frames of yesteryear have largely given way to slicker, sleeker metal-section frames. Instead of silver leaf and gold leaf, we use chrome, brass plate, and anodized aluminum.

Does this mean we never use highly decorative frames, wide or massive moldings, or gilding of one kind or another? Certainly not. It means we have many options to exercise, many possibilities to choose from. And it means we can suffer a lot of confusion, especially when faced with so many design concepts that seem to contradict one another.

For example, we might be told in a book or magazine that large paintings should be framed with narrow moldings, only to turn the page and find a large painting attractively framed in a wide molding, or a small work handsomely framed with a narrow molding. Having all these options doesn't mean that there is only one best choice and all others are something less. There's no such thing as the ideal matting or framing for any picture. Many will prove suitable, and certain ones will strike you as better than others. Personal preferences and tastes play major roles in making such selections.

When it comes to designing and making your own frames and doing your own matting, the simplest and soundest advice I can offer is to do what fits the work and pleases you. But there's a chance you aren't sure about what fits any particular artwork or even about what pleases you, mainly because you haven't examined many of the options. So spend some time in art galleries and museums, looking for what pleases you. Be conscious of all the framed works around you in public buildings, offices, and other homes. Then stop by a frame shop or well-stocked home-improvement center and find out what's available. You will soon find that you have narrowed your options considerably by simply eliminating what you don't like or what doesn't seem to fit the project at hand.

And don't worry about making the wrong choice. It's rare that you will, but when you do, you can simply pick again. That's one of the advantages of doing your own matting and framing. If you paid somebody $75 to frame a picture, you would be reluctant to have it re-framed, even if you came to despise it. If you framed it yourself, however, and only spent a few dollars doing it, you wouldn't feel so bad about reframing the work when you grew tired of the original frame.

I have a number of works in this category. There's a pair of prints in matching mats and frames that looked good enough when I framed them, but I see them so often that I have grown bored with them. New mats and frames will spark them up and relieve my boredom. I have two oil paintings in frames someone else made that I never have liked, and I will soon reframe them with something more in accord with my tastes. Others that looked fine in apartments and other houses we lived in just don't fit their present environment. So they will get reframed and I will keep the old mats and frames for use with other works.

Getting into Framing

You don't have to spend four years in college, two years in a trade school, or even a year in an apprenticeship to learn all you need to know about mounting, matting, and framing. With a little time well spent and a bit of practice in the craft, you'll soon be framing as well as any professional. Before you finish this book, you should be turning out frames and mats that are every bit as fine as anything found in a professional frame shop, gallery, or museum. In fact, it won't be long before you visit museums and galleries and find the flaws in the mats and frames displayed there.

Framing is an enjoyable and rewarding hobby and something that shows results much sooner than most other do-it-yourself projects do. If you're using a pre-finished molding, you can mount, mat, glaze, and frame several items in an evening or on a casual Saturday afternoon. Even if you're making your own molding from scratch, you can turn out a batch of framed works over a single weekend.

Once you master the techniques, it's easy to turn a profit on your hobby by doing framing jobs for others. You can eventually expand this into a lucrative sideline or full-time business. And I can't think of a business that's easier to get into or one that requires less overhead or a smaller initial investment.

Whether you approach framing as a hobby or later as a business is something only you can decide. Either way, you will end up money ahead while learning a useful and rewarding craft.

2

Mounting and Matting Materials and Tools

Most works to be framed should first be mounted to a mount board of some type. Mounting keeps the work in place, and the mount board provides rigidity and prevents warping. Mounting is also a way to repair some works that are warped, curled, or even bent or torn. Many works are then sandwiched between mount boards and mats prior to framing.

Before learning the various mounting and matting techniques, you should become familiar with the materials and tools at your disposal. Some are highly specialized and used only or mainly in mounting and matting. Others are more common and widely used for other purposes as well.

Mount Boards, Mat Boards, and Backing Materials

Among the various materials suitable for mounting artwork, diplomas, certificates, documents, photographs, and posters, the most commonly used and widely available are mat board, rag board or museum board, archival corrugated board, and foamboard. Certainly, framers use a good many other materials, but the operative word here is *suitable*. Hardboard, for example, is suitable for some applications, but it is dense and heavy and adds significant weight to any framing project. It is also acidic and therefore inappropriate for conservation mounting. Although corrugated container board—the brown paper product that so-called cardboard boxes are made of—is widely used, I can't recommend it, and I never use it in any phase of mounting, matting, or framing, because it is so highly acidic and potentially damaging.

Standard mat board, a wood-pulp product, neutralized mat board, which is acid-free, and rag board, which contains no wood, come in two-ply and four-ply thicknesses. Two-ply board is about $1/32$-inch thick, and four-ply about $1/16$. The thinner board is suitable for most jobs. The thicker is sometimes used for adding rigidity to large works, but it is always at least half again as expensive as two-ply board, sometimes double in price. Also, if you plan to use a backing, two-ply should provide sufficient rigidity.

Standard mat board is acidic and should never be used as a mount board with any work of monetary or sentimental value. It can be used, however, as outer mat material in conservation mounting, matting, and framing. Both neutralized mat board and rag board are pH neutral and are suitable for all conservation applications, as either mount boards or mats. Crescent Cardboard Company, a major producer of rag and mat boards, now offers its line of standard mat board with acid-free cores and backing papers, making them suitable for most matting applications.

Archival corrugated board consists of a corrugated core faced on two sides with paper. All materials are acid-free and buffered, making this board acceptable for conservation mounting. It comes in single-wall and double-wall configurations, with respective thicknesses of $1/8$ and $1/4$ inch.

Foamboard consists of a core of ex-truded polystyrene, sandwiched between sheets of white paper. It comes in thicknesses of $1/8$, $3/16$, and $1/4$ inch, with $3/16$ being the most universally useful and probably the most widely used. An acid-free version, for conservation use, is only slightly more expensive than standard foamboard. Since it should not be used in any process requiring temperatures above 150°F, foamboard is not suitable for heat mounting. Nevertheless, it is one of the most useful materials available to the framer. Because of its light weight and rigidity, it is a superior backing material, and it is ideal for most mounting applications.

With $3/16$-inch foamboard, I am able to mount and frame all but the largest works without the need for backing material; the foamboard serves as both mount and backing. With it I can save time and money on most jobs. Foamboard is also easier to cut than mat board and rag board and doesn't seem to dull blades as fast.

All these materials are available at most frame and art-supply shops and department stores that stock products for mounting, matting, and framing. Although some stores stock the various board products in standard frame sizes, from 8 x 10 to 20 x 24 inches, most shops more commonly stock them in 32 x 40-inch sheets that you can cut to any size you need. The larger sheets are also cheaper in the long run.

Adhesives and Tapes

A number of aerosol adhesives, adhesive sheets, and dry-mounting tissues, used primarily for mounting photographs and posters, are covered fully in Chapter 4. Although they are not generally recommended for mounting valuable artwork or limited-edition prints, when such items get bent, wrinkled, or torn, some can be successfully repaired by mounting with an aerosol adhesive or an adhesive sheet.

Most household or hobby glues, pastes, and cements contain substances that are harmful to artwork and should not be used for mounting or matting, although some are suitable for frame construction and dust-seal installation. Among the most commonly found in the home are white glue and rubber cement, neither of which is suitable for mounting or matting.

Customarily, original artwork and

Ceramic tongue and acid-free linen tape are ideal for hinging mat and mount boards. Insta-Hinge kit provides a practical way to hinge artwork.

valuable reproductions on paper are mounted to mount boards with hinges made of rice paper or nonacidic tape. Rice-paper hinges are stuck to the back of the artwork and to the mount board with a paste of methyl cellulose, wheat starch, or rice starch.

Methyl cellulose is a powder you dissolve in water to make a paste. The paste is then applied to rice-paper hinges for mounting. It is easy to use, nonacidic, and reversible with water, and has an indefinite shelf life.

Although wheat-starch and rice-starch pastes are the adhesives customarily used for museum mounting, for my money they're nuisances to work with. They are indeed nonacidic but susceptible to attack by fungi, so should have a fungicide added to them. They must be mixed in water, then cooked into a paste. And leftover paste has a short shelf life. So they're impractical for the person who has only a few mounting jobs to do at any given time.

Much more practical for most of us is a product called Insta-Hinge. A kit for under $10 contains everything you need to mount up to a dozen items: paper blotters, Mylar squares, spun-nylon squares, and three 1½ x 24-inch strips of rice paper impregnated with starch paste and treated with fungicide.

Like adhesives, few general-purpose tapes are useful in mounting and matting operations. Even though some books recommend mounting watercolors and other works with masking tape, I must advise against the practice. The tape will yellow in time and is not reversible — that is, you cannot later remove the tape without pulling paper fibers from the artwork. Cellophane tape is even more harmful.

If the work you're mounting has little commercial value, you can use Scotch Magic Tape and similar so-called invisible mending tapes with good results. They aren't reversible, but they won't yellow the way other tapes do. Even if you're only using tape to temporarily hold a work in position and will remove it later, it can damage the work by removing paper fibers from it, and most leave a residue of adhesive that can harm the artwork. A nifty exception is Scotch Removable Magic Tape. I have been using this product since its introduction to temporarily hold artwork in place while I'm positioning it, and it has never lifted paper fibers or left a residue behind.

Acid-free linen tape is widely used in the framing business and is safe for conservation mounting and matting. The tape is made of linen backed with pH neutral, water-activated adhesive. It will not stain and is reversible with water. It comes in 1-inch and 1½-inch rolls from 20 to 300 yards long. The 1-inch tape will prove suitable for most jobs and can be used for making hinged mats and for hinging some works to mount boards. It is relatively thick, though, and can leave a visible impression if used to hinge works or documents on lightweight stock.

Acid-free paper tape is made of 24-pound buffered bond paper and backed with a water-activated adhesive. This lightweight tape is removable with water and is ideal for hinging artworks to mount boards, even those produced on lightweight stock. It is not substantial enough, however, for hinging mats to mount boards. It comes in 1-inch rolls of 50 to 300 yards. One 50-yard roll is enough to hinge more than 200 artworks.

Scotch Removable Magic Tape is useful for temporarily holding works in place.

Tyvek tape is a strong tape suitable for hinging mats to mount boards, but is not recommended for hinging artwork. This is a polyethylene tape backed with a pressure-sensitive adhesive and release paper, so it requires no water for use. It comes in 2¼-inch rolls 50 yards long and is a good choice for hinging large mats to mount boards.

When you're using more than one mat with any single item you're framing, the mats are easier to handle if they're stuck together. You can use double-sided tape for this, but if you will be doing much matting, I can recommend a handy tool and tape for the job. The 3M Company calls the tool a Scotch 752 ATG Adhesive Transfer Applicator. I call it a tape gun,

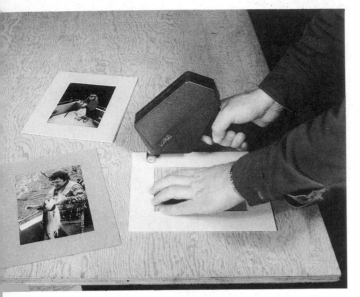

Scotch 752 ATG Adhesive Transfer Applicator in use.

and it's the fastest in the West for laying down synthetic adhesive in a continuous line or a series of patches. I originally bought mine for laminating mats, but I've put it to dozens of other uses since, including the mounting of small photographs prior to framing.

Measuring, Marking, and Positioning Instruments

For measuring and marking large sheets of mat board, foamboard, and other sheet stock, I most often use a steel tape rule. Some people prefer folding rules, so the choice is yours.

For measuring artwork, I normally use

Adhesive transfer tape inside the 752 ATG.

Useful tools for mounting and matting: aluminum T-square (with strip of masking tape on back), steel tape rule, aluminum yardstick, and thin-lead pencil.

an aluminum yardstick that I keep wiped clean with a rag dampened with denatured alcohol. I also have a 4-foot aluminum T-square that I use for some measuring and marking chores, but mostly as a guide when I'm cutting sheet stock.

Here's a tip. Whatever kind of metal straight edge you use as a cutting guide, affix a strip of masking tape to the underside for its entire length. This will help keep it from slipping as you cut.

To scribe lines on the back of a mat as guides for cutting out the mat window, you can use a carpenter's marker that's adjustable up to 6 inches or a compass set for your desired width. You won't need these tools, though, if you invest in a mat-cutting guide (such as Alto's EZ/Mat); it also serves as a marking guide and is much faster and easier to use than any other instruments.

Those who cut mats without the aid of a mat-cutting guide might want to invest in the Boyne Mat Corner Marker, available from Leichtung Workshops. This inexpensive plastic jig is quick and easy to use. Simply determine the mat width, lay the jig at each corner, mark corner lines with a pencil in the appropriate cutouts,

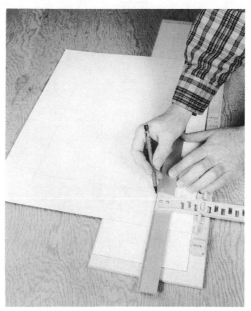

Use Alto's EZ/Mat guide to scribe guidelines.

line up the straight edge, and cut the window out with a mat cutter.

The Falcon Print Positioner was available for some time before I got around to trying one. Perhaps my curiosity was tempered by my natural skepticism about new gadgets designed to do jobs

Alto's EZ/Mat guide.

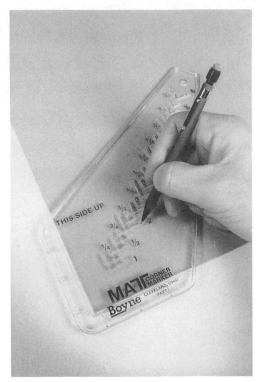

Boyne Mat Corner Marker.

this ingenious tool. Complete directions for its use are in Chapter 4.

Knives, Cutters, and Trimmers

The framer's basic cutting tool is a utility knife. You will need one for cutting mat board, rag board, foamboard, and other sheet stock. The knives come in a variety of styles with different kinds of blades. Some have fairly heavy blades that are reversible and can be honed when they become dull. Others have thin snap-off blades that are discarded when dull. Still others, such as the X-Acto knives, use replaceable blades that come from the factory as sharp as a scalpel.

If you're watching your pennies, you might prefer to sharpen your utility-knife blade, but renewing an edge to razor sharpness is a time-consuming chore and one I cannot justify. I prefer to discard a dull blade and replace it with a new one, which takes only seconds and doesn't interfere with my concentration on the task at hand.

For that reason, I use X-Acto knives and have come to favor the model with a

I've successfully seen to with old, reliable tools. Whatever my reasons, when I consider the time I've spent at the tedious task of positioning photographs and some other works for mounting, I kick myself for ignoring this amazingly simple and foolproof aid.

With the Print Positioner, there's no need to measure and scribe layout lines on the mounting board or to put guide marks on print borders. While such chores take only a few minutes with conventional tools, the entire job is reduced to seconds with the Print Positioner. And it works with any size print. For anyone who has more than a few items to mount, mat, and frame, I heartily recommend

Put old blades in a jar or can you keep for such purposes.

large screwdriver-type handle because of the additional leverage it offers when cutting through tough material or when the blade is beginning to dull. Replaceable blades come in a large array of styles and sizes. The ones I find best for all my mounting and matting work are the Dexter #3 and X-Acto #19. These same blades also happen to fit the Alto's standard mat cutter.

If you decide on a knife with replaceable blades, don't simply toss used blades into a wastebasket or trash bag where they can do damage or cause injury. Find a small can or jar with a lid, label it *Used Blades,* and put your dull blades there. Incidentally, when your knife fails to move smoothly and effortlessly through whatever you're cutting, or if it leaves a rough edge, sharpen it or replace it. A dull blade is inefficient and dangerous.

If you will be doing much mount-board and mat cutting, you might want to invest in a heavy-duty paper cutter or trimmer that will see to most of it. There are professional guillotine-style and roller-type cutters and trimmers that will easily handle mat board and other sheet stock. There are models that will accommodate widths up to 48 inches and even more, but their prices range from several hundred to more than a thousand dollars.

I got by without one of these cutters for a number of years, but as I began doing more and more mounting and matting, I decided it was time to invest in one. But I chose a 24-inch guillotine-style cutter that cost me under $100, including shipping. My guess is that it takes care of at least 75 percent of my cutting chores.

By the way, with a guillotine-style cutter, you should always cut material with the good face down on the cutter table, as the blade makes noticeable impressions on the up side.

Mat Cutters, Guides, and Straight Edges

Mat cutters that make a clean beveled cut with an angled, razor-sharp blade are about the handiest tools around for anyone with matting jobs to do. Several models are available, designed to be used with any straight edge thick enough to keep the cutter from riding up over the edge. The Dexter and X-Acto mat cutters are two examples.

There are also mat-cutting systems that range in price from more than $100 to well over $1,000. If you plan to work at matting and framing full time, perhaps you will want to check into one of these machines, but for now, and perhaps for always, you should get by most satisfactorily with something much less expensive.

For my money—literally—there's no better buy on the market than Alto's EZ/Mat system, which includes a hand-held mat cutter and an ingenious marking and

Dexter mat cutter.

Alto's EZ/Mat system includes mat cutter and guide.

Alto's EZ/Mat cutter can be used with a straight edge.

BASE

SCREWS

BLADE

WASHER

Alto's EZ/Mat cutter.

cutting guide that adjusts from 1½ to 6⅜ inches in ⅛-inch increments. The cutter guide bar is nearly 32 inches long, thus permitting a cut of almost 30 inches in a single stroke. Moreover, the system is open at both ends, permitting cuts of any length in mats of any size. With no more than five minutes' practice, anyone can be cutting beveled mats like a pro. And the whole outfit is available for under $60.

Incidentally, a friend of mine who owns a large frame shop started some years ago with the EZ/Mat system. As his business grew, rather than replace a tool that had served him so well, he simply added another. He and his employees must cut hundreds of mats a month, and they do it all with the same system I use. So I expect my Alto's EZ/Mat system to last me a lifetime.

The mat cutter that comes with the EZ/Mat system is available separately for about $10 and can be used with a straight edge. So, if your budget is tight, you can start with just the cutter and buy the entire system later. Alto's also offers a deluxe cutter that sells for about $20. Alto's oval templates are something else you might consider if you have a use for mats with oval windows.

For some reason, authors of framing books seem to feel obligated to describe the process of cutting beveled mats with a utility knife and mat cutter's straight edge, and I can't understand why. Making a clean, professional-looking cut armed only with these tools is no easy task. It takes a lot of practice to gain the needed skill, and no amount of skill will produce mats any better looking than those you can produce more quickly and efficiently with the EZ/Mat system. What's more, a mat cutter's beveled straight edge is an expensive item of limited worth. In fact, for one long enough to cut large mats, you will pay nearly as much as you would for the EZ/Mat system.

Change EZ/Mat blades with a screwdriver or nutdriver.

Alto's EZ/Mat cutter is for right-handed or left-handed use.

Alto's Deluxe Hand Cutter.

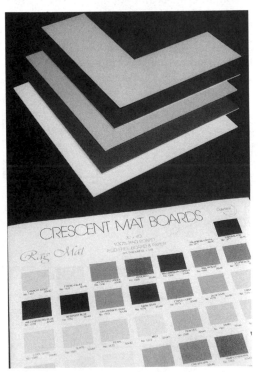

Mat-sample corners and swatches are useful in choosing the right mats.

Mat-Sample Corners and Cropping Corners

Presumably, you will be buying your sheet stock from a local frame shop, art-supply outlet, or department store where you will find color samples of mat board in the form of corner strips. When you're selecting colored mats for any piece of art, it's a good idea to take the artwork with you so you can try the various mat-sample corners with it until you find the one or ones that are just right.

As you mat various items, start making your own mat-sample corners from scraps of leftover mat board. On the back of each corner, write the brand and number of the mat board or rag board: Bainbridge #731, Crescent #1082, and such. I also include the particular shade, such as Storm Blue, Bar Harbor Gray, Moss Point Green, Inca Gold, and the like.

Before you know it, you will have accumulated quite a selection of mat-sample corners that you can use at home, and the labeling will ensure that you can duplicate exactly what you have done before. This is particularly important when you work with shades of colors that are only subtly different.

Something else you will find handy, particularly for working with photographs, is a set of cropping corners that you can make from scraps. With these, you can determine the right cropping for any photograph and thereby determine the dimensions to cut the mat window or trim the photograph.

You can make cropping corners any size you wish. Obviously, if you never work with photos any larger than 8 x 10 inches, then cropping corners need be no larger than 10 x 10 inches along the inside edges. But if you make them larger, you will be prepared for larger prints if the need ever arises. I made mine from available scraps and ended up with a pair of 20 x 26-inch corners that are black on one side, white on the other, and have seen to all my needs so far.

Cropping corners help you determine the right cropping for any photograph.

Other Useful Tools

There are a number of other tools and accessories that come in handy in the mounting and matting process. You will want to have on hand some of the things I use, and you will certainly come up with a few of your own.

I prefer pencils to pens for marking guidelines on mount and mat boards, but I like a bold black pen for making notes to myself that I can read from a distance as I'm working. So I also keep a pen and pad nearby as I work.

Spring clamps are handy for keeping big sheets of foamboard, mat board, or rag board in place during cutting operations. They are also good for clamping a

straight edge in place to keep it from moving during the cut.

Several large stainless-steel clips are useful for holding artwork in place on mount boards for marking layout lines. In their absence, you can cover the artwork with tissue paper and lay several books on top to keep everything in place, or you can cover each book with tissue paper.

Be sure to have a pack of double-edge razor blades on hand. When you slightly undercut a mat-window corner, you can slide one of these paper-thin blades into the cut line, carefully angle it with the bevel, and finish the cut by hand.

A fresh blade in your mat cutter will make beautiful, smooth, beveled cuts. A dull blade will make ragged cuts. So it stands to reason that you should discard dull blades to keep cuts clean. But you always end up cutting one too many mats

Smooth rough spots on mat edges with an emery board.

Clean mats with erasers and soft-bristled dusting brush.

with every blade, because you don't know a blade needs replacing until it starts bogging down during the cut and leaving little rough edges in its path. But no need to fret if you have a pack of emery boards on hand, fine grit on one side, medium on the other. Use the fine side to smooth out any rough areas in the bevel cut. And you'll find many other uses for both sides of these cheap and handy items.

To finely polish the beveled cut of a mat window and remove the tiniest of burrs and nicks, rub the cut with some sort of burnishing tool. You can buy a burnishing bone, actually made of highly polished bone. There are also plastic substitutes. Or you can use the back of a

comb, but if it's a comb you also use for your hair, be sure to wipe it with a cloth dampened with denatured alcohol to remove natural oils that could stain the mat.

Erasers are essential, not only for removing any noticeable pencil lines but also for cleaning away any other smudges, fingerprints, and the like. Keep an assortment on hand: a pencil eraser, ink eraser, art-gum eraser, kneadable eraser, and draftsman's film erasers of several densities.

A soft counter brush or dusting brush will whisk away most dust, lint, and eraser particles. And any canned-air product, such as Dust-Off, will blow away any other tiny bits of debris that cling to the mounted and matted work. The Black & Decker Dustbuster or similar small vacuum cleaner is also handy in the shop for cleaning mats and mounted works before framing them.

The Mounting and Matting Bench

Any stable work surface that's large enough to accommodate your projects will suffice as a mounting and matting bench, but you will probably want to take a few measures to make it the most efficient work area possible.

Although tables, workbenches, and even kitchen counters and desks will do, keep in mind that you have two important requirements for your mounting and matting bench surface. First, you must be able to keep your materials clean, which means you can't work on a grimy bench used for auto repair or on a stained and dusty woodworking bench. Also, you must cut through sheet stock with sharp knives, which means you will be gradually destroying your cutting surface. So you shouldn't use a workbench, table, or desk that you expect to remain intact.

A slab of plywood works well as a cutting surface that you will eventually replace. You can lay it atop a table, bench, or desk, in which case 1/2-inch thickness should suffice.

If you want something portable and stowable, you might consider a bench consisting of a slab of 3/4-inch plywood that rests atop a pair of folding sawhorses or fits into a Black & Decker Workmate. My own takes the latter form, and I use it

Author's 30 x 60-inch benchtop clamps into the jaws of a Workmate.

in my shop for various framing jobs and in my studio when I need a cleaner, more dust-free atmosphere.

I simply attached a length of 2 x 4 to the underside of a 30 x 60-inch piece of 3/4-inch plywood that I keep leaning against a wall in my workshop. When I need a bench, I lay the slab atop my Workmate, tighten the jaws on the 2 x 4, and there it is. I have been using the same slab for several years and it's holding up quite well. When I eventually ruin the top veneer with all the cutting I do, it will only cost me $10 or $12 to make a new bench top that will last me several more years. Quite a bargain, I think, and certainly one of my handiest mounting and matting tools.

3

Basic and Conservation Mounting and Matting

Mounting and matting are the first steps in framing and displaying most artworks on paper, as well as certain documents, photographs, and small to moderate-sized posters. Mount and mat boards also help keep works in good shape and protect them from damage if they are not going to be framed immediately. As soon as possible after you have acquired any item, try to get it mounted and matted, even if you don't have time to frame it.

Don't ever store lithographs, posters, and such in mailing tubes. If you buy an artwork by mail and it arrives in a mailing tube, remove it at once. The longer such items stay rolled up, the more difficult it is to remove the curl. Curled prints and posters are difficult to handle and are easily damaged. Immediate mounting and matting is the best solution here.

Even works that are shipped and stored flat can be damaged if their containers are potentially harmful. Never allow any work on paper to remain in contact with corrugated containerboard, cardboard, chipboard, newsprint, or any wood or paper product that you cannot identify as being acid-free and archivally safe.

If you don't have time to mount and mat an item immediately, sandwich it between two pieces of neutralized mat board, rag board, or acid-free foamboard that are at least slightly larger than the work. Tie the package together, or bind it with large rubber bands.

You also must be careful of how and where you store items waiting to be framed. Keep them in a clean, dry atmosphere where they will not be exposed to direct sunlight. A closet is ideal, or you can stack them under a bed. If you must lean them against a wall, make sure it's an interior wall. Unframed items leaned against an exterior wall are susceptible to damage by mold or fungi.

Precut Mats

Precut mats are available in sizes from 5 x 7 inches (3 x 4½-inch window) to 22 x 28 inches (15½ x 19½-inch window), and there's nothing wrong with using them whenever you wish, provided that you are aware of any potential short-comings.

The main advantage to using precut mats is that they save time, and when they're priced economically they can be quite a bargain. Of course, they come only in standard sizes and generally in far fewer colors than mat board does. But if what you're framing is of standard size and the mats available are the right price and color, by all means use them.

The mount board that comes with pre-cut mats is often made of chipboard, and the mats are made of standard mat board, which means they aren't suitable for conservation mounting. Some mount boards are made of mat board, which is less acidic than chipboard, but still not archivally safe. As a general rule, don't use precut mats on anything of significant monetary or sentimental value. Archivally safe precut mats are available from some sources, but they are expensive. And there are ways to make other precut mats and mount boards less destructive by cutting rag paper to serve as barrier sheets between the acidic boards and the artwork, but that is a time-consuming process—which defeats the purpose of using precut mats.

I don't want to discourage you from using precut mats, but rather to under-

PRE-CUT MATS
STANDARD SIZES

OUTSIDE DIMENSIONS	WINDOW DIMENSIONS
5" x 7"	3" x 4½"
5" x 7"	3¼" x 4¼"
8" x 10"	4½" x 6½"
9" x 12"	5½" x 8½"
11" x 14"	7½" x 9½"
12" x 16"	8½" x 11½"
14" x 18"	10½" x 13½"
16" x 20"	10½" x 13½"
16" x 20"	11½" x 15½"
18" x 24"	11½" x 15½"
18" x 24"	11½" x 17½"
20" x 24"	13½" x 16½"
20" x 24"	13½" x 17½"
20" x 24"	15½" x 19½"
22" x 28"	15½" x 19½"

stand where to use them and where not to. I keep a small quantity of them on hand in various sizes and use them regularly. When I find them available at good prices, I lay in a supply.

You'll find precut mats at photo-supply shops, some department stores, and at framing and art-supply outlets. Some frame shops have a better-than-average selection of colors and sizes, because they turn their matting leftovers into pre-cut mats. I have also found that these mats usually have mount boards made of mat board instead of chipboard, which makes them more broadly useful. In fact, if you can determine that the mount board is made of rag board or neutralized mat board — ask the shop owner or sales clerk — you can confidently use it to mount works of value. If it is made of mat board with acid-free core and backing, mount the work against the backing paper instead of the face paper.

Reasons for Conservation Mounting and Matting

Museum curators and top professional framers have known for years that certain materials and techniques are essential for permanence when framing works of art on paper. Moreover, paper and parchment documents and photographs require similar care. The process is known variously as museum, archival, or conservation framing.

No doubt you have noticed that newspapers begin turning brown after a few months' storage, as do the pulpy pages of some magazines and books. Even many finer papers will begin to color and turn brittle in time. What causes this is acid. Wood is naturally acidic, and most paper products are made of wood pulp. Not only will the paper products themselves discolor and deteriorate, but they will also spread the damage to any paper they touch, including nonacidic papers.

Other enemies of artworks on paper include airborne pollutants, ultraviolet radiation, moisture, mold, and fungi. What protects our watercolors, pastels, lithographs, serigraphs, posters, photo-

graphs, and paper documents from the ravages of these silent marauders are the techniques and materials we use to preserve such works.

For some reason, those who write about framing for a general audience — and many custom framers — operate under the notion that only valuable works of art should be protected with archival-quality materials and conservation techniques. Those who haven't kept abreast of the field or who simply haven't done their homework insist or imply that conservation framing is difficult, expensive, and impractical for the do-it-yourselfer. When they do broach the subject, they usually botch it. So let's put to rest, here and now, the myths and misinformation they have spread.

One expert proclaimed, "Archival framing is much more costly than temporary framing . . . [and] is often best handled by a custom framer, familiar with archival techniques and proper materials." Nonsense! It's slightly more costly initially, usually far cheaper in the long run, and the techniques couldn't be simpler.

Another insisted, "Museum board is, of course, more expensive than standard matboard and usually is available only in white and cream color, with a choice of possibly only a few other colors." Poppycock! Though once limited to white, off-white, and a few pastel colors, museum board or rag board is now available in many colors and has been for some years. It also comes in a variety of textures and patterns. Moreover, the development of a process for neutralizing the acid in pulp-based mat board has made acid-free boards available in every color that standard mat board comes in.

Any original work is potentially valuable, as are the limited-edition prints so popular these days. What's more, to most of us value means more than simple monetary worth. Many items we frame have sentimental value that goes well beyond any price tag.

For most of us who aren't serious art collectors, the value of any framable item is relative and personal. And sometimes it has absolutely nothing to do with how much something cost. For example, some years ago my wife and I took a trip to Japan, and while I was nosing around a small gallery, I found a pair of woodblock prints on handmade paper that I really liked. They were limited-edition prints from a small run, signed and numbered by the artist. I got the pair for the equivalent of five American dollars.

In those days, the dollar went a long way in Japan, so just by virtue of inflation and a weaker dollar abroad, these prints have increased in monetary value. And for all I know, the artist could have rocketed to fame by now, making the prints coveted collector's items. But frankly, I couldn't care less. I used archivally safe materials and accepted techniques when I framed them because I liked the prints and wanted them to last. To my way of thinking, if it's worth framing and displaying, it's worth preserving and protecting.

In the case of truly valuable or potentially valuable works, conservation framing is the only way to make sure they won't lose value because of how they were framed. If you owned such a work and wanted to sell it, any savvy buyer would examine the framing job. If it hasn't been properly done, he will pay you less, perhaps much less, or might even decide against buying.

Anything the artwork comes in contact

This pair of limited-edition Japanese woodblock prints on handmade paper cost only $5, but they deserve archival materials and conservation framing techniques.

with must be pH neutral if the work is to be preserved. That means the mount board and inner mat must be nonacidic, as must any adhesive, tape, or mounting hinges. And to qualify as museum quality, the mounting job must be reversible, that is, the artwork can be unmounted.

Rag board was once the only choice a framer had for conservation mounting and matting, and since rag board is about twice the price of standard mat board, conservation materials doubled the price of the job. But even at that, we're only talking about a few dollars for any one project.

Neutralized wood-pulp mat board offers lower prices than rag board. For comparison purposes, if your local supplier charges you $4 for a 32 x 40-inch sheet of standard mat board, you will probably pay $8 for rag board and $6 for neutralized mat board.

Let's say you have a print with an image size of 12 x 16 inches that you plan to mount and mat with neutralized mat board. Assume you have decided on mount and mat outside dimensions of 16 x 20 inches with a mat window of 11½ x 15½ inches. From a single 32 x 40-inch sheet, you can cut four 16 x 20-inch pieces, at a cost of $1.50 each. That means the two pieces required for a mount board and single mat will cost you a total of three bucks. Not bad, eh? But wait. When you cut the mat, you will end up with a leftover big enough to trim to 11 x 14 inches and use on another job. So, if you wanted, you could mount and triple mat your 16 x 20-inch print for $6, with enough material left over to mount and double mat an 11 x 14-inch print free.

We're not talking big bucks here at all, folks. What's more, there are ways to save even more. And the cost of hinging

materials is so low as to be nearly negligible.

Remember, I said anything that touches the artwork must be pH neutral, and what touches it are the mount board, adhesive, hinges, and inner mat. If you use only one mat, then everything must be nonacidic. In multiple matting, however, there is nothing wrong with using standard mat board for outer mats. All you need to do is seal the cut edges to keep the acidic core of the mat from contaminating the interior environment of the frame. To seal a mat, you can coat the cut edges around the periphery of the mat window with shellac applied with a small brush, or spray the whole mat with acrylic matte finish. Although the matte spray will very slightly darken the color of the mat, that's the method I always use, as it is quick, easy, cheap, and doesn't leave a shiny finish on the mat-window bevel as shellac will.

Seal standard mats with acrylic matte spray.

Some framing experts who should know better recommend using corrugated containerboard as backing material for mounted and matted works. I have seen precut mats sold with corrugated containerboard included as the mount board. I have found original watercolors, pastels, and drawings mounted on corrugated containerboard, and limited-edition prints shrink-wrapped against corrugated containerboard. Sure, this stuff is one of the cheapest paper products available (free, if you want to cut up old containerboard boxes), but it's also so acidic that it should never be used in any phase of framing. It will burn through mount boards within a matter of months and attack the artwork. It will even discolor resin-coated photographic papers and invade the trimmed edges of other heavily coated printing papers.

Although acid-free materials are a bit more expensive, the cost of conservation framing is relatively insignificant. For example, it cost me about $5 to mount and mat a limited-edition print to outside dimensions of 31 x 41 inches. Acidic materials would have cost about half what I paid, but I think the extra $2.50 was a minuscule amount to pay to protect my investment. When mounting and matting smaller works, costs are proportionately lower, so conservation materials rarely cost over a dollar or two more than standard, acidic materials. Frames, glass, dust seals, and hanging hardware cost the same either way.

Selecting Mat Material

In addition to archival considerations, you must also select mat colors and hues that fit your needs. Here, personal tastes play a more important role than in other phases of the mounting and matting process. There are hundreds of colors and shades of colors to select from — dozens of choices in white alone. Then there are textures and patterns. And if you use multiple mats, the possible combinations and permutations are infinite.

Nowhere in the entire framing process do feelings and opinions run stronger than on the subject of mat selection. And nowhere are opinions more divergent.

The author of a recent book on the subject admitted that mat color is important but insisted that white or off-white is best. In a more daring mood, he ventured, "Occasionally black or gray works well," but warned against the use of "real colors" because they "are almost always wrong." Well, that's one person's opinion. Others are adamant about avoiding the use of any colors but black or white when matting black-and-white art and photographs.

At the other extreme, you'll find electric-colored mats that are blindingly distracting. I have seen mats covered with gaudy plaids and polka dots, and some even stuffed so that they looked more like pin cushions. One frame shop I visited not long ago was owned by an artist and on display were many works, each with multiple mats that were intricately carved — dazzling scenes and motifs, all perfectly bevel-cut. The effect was overwhelming, and to this day I remember the mats well but can't recall a single piece of art displayed in them.

There are no iron-clad rules to go by, but I can offer some suggestions and recommendations. Certain principles might help you make better decisions and selections — better for *you*, because when all is said and done, you are the one who

Gray, white, and black mat corners are useful in choosing the right mats for black-and-white works.

must be happy. If you are matting and framing for others, these same principles should help you guide them toward the right selections.

Just as black mats and white mats sometimes work well with colored art-works, colored mats sometimes go with

black-and-white works. If you want to use color with a pen-and-ink or pencil drawing or similar work, you will probably find a double mat will work best, in which case the inner mat should be either black or white and the outer mat colored.

Although I have satisfactorily used color when matting black-and-white works, by and large, I use black, white, and gray mats, usually two or more in any job. I use mat-sample corners in these shades to experiment until I find the right combination and order. It's often amazing what a difference a subtle change can make.

On pen-and-ink drawings and high-contrast black-on-white prints, I most often like a black inner mat providing a narrow border around the work, usually $1/8$ or $1/4$ inch. Depending on the subject, I will then use white or gray for the outer mat, or perhaps a second mat of white and third or outer mat matching the inner one.

The combination of black inner mat and gray outer mat for these black-on-white works is a favorite of mine and one I use often. It is visually stunning, and it keeps me from having to spend time on the tedious task of matching whites. There seems to be no end to the shades of

This original cartoon by Jim Snook called for a black border, but a single black mat seemed too confining.

A black inner mat with white outer mat proved ideal for Snook's cartoon.

white and off-white used in art and printing papers, as well as in mats. Often, white mats used with black-on-white artworks appear strangely out of synch when the white of the mat and white of the paper don't match. Gray solves that problem.

Cream-colored papers are equally problematical, and here is where colored mats are decidedly more attractive than black, white, or gray. And if the ink used in the print or drawing is not quite black—dark brown is popular these days—that's all the more reason to consider colored mats.

I recently mounted and matted a fine limited-edition print by David Hagerbaumer: a low-number reproduction of a pen-and-ink drawing of a woodcock in dark-brown ink on high-grade, cream-colored stock. I matched the ink with a Crescent mat board labeled Sable. For the second mat, I used a color Crescent calls French Gray, but which, in reality, is more a shade of buff than gray. For the outer mat, Crescent's slightly darker Pewter board was perfect. The finishing touch was a very narrow, simple frame made of black-walnut molding that matched both the ink and the Sable inner mat.

The selection of mats for colored artworks is complicated by the variety of mat colors you have to choose from, but a few guidelines should make your selections a bit easier. For starters, you might want to write to Crescent Cardboard Company (a major manufacturer of mat and rag board) and ask for its mat-sample sheet, which has more than 240 swatches of mat board face papers; see directory at the back of this book for address. Then spend some time at galleries examining matted works to find

A favorite combination for many black-and-white works is a black inner mat and gray outer mat.

the effects you like most. Take a notebook with you and jot reminders that you will use later in your shop or studio.

A good book for ideas on the use of colors is *Picture Framing and Wall Display* (Lane Publishing Co., 1979), which is available at bookstores and wherever Sunset books are sold.

Something that often works well for me is to determine the main color or colors in any work and then to match my mat selection accordingly. With a double mat, I frequently pick two shades or hues of the one dominant color. For example, I might use a dark-blue inner mat and lighter blue outer mat, or dark brown and beige.

Certain kinds of art seem to lead me automatically to specific colors. Seascapes, for instance, often have me reaching for the blue mat-sample corners. Many scenic or landscape works call for natural earth tones, such as shades of brown or green. Bright flowers or fall colors will have me using similarly bright mats.

Contrasting colors can also be highly effective with some works. Crescent's Storm Blue and Bar Harbor Gray mat boards provide an arresting combination for waterfront scenes and other marine art. In a woodland scene, I effectively used Colonial Orange for the ¼-inch inner mat, Fudge Brown for the ½-inch second mat, and Suntan (medium beige) for the outer mat. The unlikely orange was a perfect match with one of the colors in the fur of two red foxes in the print.

With a little practice and some experimentation with various artworks and mat-sample corners, you'll get the hang of mat selection. Most likely, you will soon find that certain types of art naturally lead you to specific colors and color combinations.

You also must pay attention to mat textures. Some mats are smooth, some lightly textured, and some deeply impressed, embossed, or pebbled. When you're using multiple mats, there's nothing wrong with using all smooth or all lightly textured mats. But the more noticeably textured boards seem to compete with one another or provide too much of a good thing.

If I want a highly textured appearance, I might pick a mat board that simulates natural burlap to use as an outer mat and a smooth dark-brown board to make a narrow inner mat. Or I might use a linen-textured board in cream or off-white against a narrow inner mat of smooth gold.

With these few simple guidelines in mind, you should be able to examine the work of others and determine what you like most and what will best serve your needs. Mat selection really isn't all that difficult. With a little practice and experience, you will find it to be an enjoyable part of picture framing.

Basic Mounting and Matting

When you're framing items of little or no monetary value but some personal value, you should use archivally safe materials, but you needn't necessarily use those required for museum-quality jobs.

For example, for valuable or potentially valuable works, you should use a hinged or folder mat—that is, a mat hinged to the mount board—but you needn't hinge mats for items with no collector's value. You might want to, but it's your decision.

With hinged mats, both the mat and the mount board must be of equal thickness. Normally, you will also need to cut a piece of backing material to the outside dimensions of the hinged mat and use it to provide rigidity, especially in larger works. Works of little or no monetary value can be mounted to a piece of acid-free foamboard instead of a mount board and framed without need of additional backing.

In a museum-quality job, you must mount the artwork with rice-paper hinges and starch paste or with Insta-Hinges, which can be removed without damaging the work. If you aren't concerned about later removal and simply want to protect a work of personal or sentimental value, feel free to use acid-free linen tape or paper tape for the hinges.

When hinging mats, make sure mat and mount are of equal size and thickness.

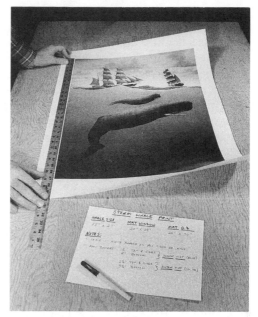

Always carefully measure the image, and double check all dimensions.

Mat windows should usually be cut ¼ inch smaller than the image size of the artwork, to overlap the image edges by ⅛ inch. With signed and numbered, limited-edition prints, it is customary to leave some of the print-border area visible to show the number and artist's signature. In such cases, exposed borders usually range from ½ to 1 inch, which means mat windows are cut 1 to 2 inches larger than image size.

Always start every mounting and matting job with a plan sheet. And remember the old do-it-yourselfer's rule that will save you a lot of grief and a pile of money: *measure twice, cut once.*

Measure the image height and width; then measure them again, and write these dimensions on your plan sheet. Now you must decide on mat-border widths. There are various rules to apply,

most of which eventually contradict one another by striking exception. The only hard-and-fast rule is this: do what pleases you.

When you're studying the work of others, compare the effects of wide and narrow mats, single and multiple mats, large and small images. Check to see if mat borders are equal or not, and determine which effect you prefer.

Mat borders are usually from 1 to 4 inches wide. Commonly, bottom borders are slightly wider, though not necessarily. To my eye, equal borders look fine on diplomas, certificates, and similar documents, and narrow borders often look good on photographs and small posters.

There was a time when framers invariably put significantly wider mat borders at the bottom of any artwork they were matting. Some still do, even though the practice is now considered passé. I have never cared for overly wide bottom borders, so I usually add no more than an inch there, depending on the size of the work and its placement on the wall. Wider bottom borders look best on low-hanging pictures.

Once you've settled on appropriate border widths, add them to the mat-window dimensions to determine outside dimensions. The print in the accompanying photos has an image size of 18 x 27 inches. I wanted a 1-inch border exposed for the signature, print number, and remarque, which meant a window of 20 x 29 inches. I added 3 inches left, right, and top, and 4 inches at the bottom for mat borders, and listed 26 x 36 inches as the outside dimensions.

At this point, the most difficult and critical part of any mounting and matting job is finished. All that's left is to cut everything out and mount the artwork.

Use an X-Acto or utility knife and straight edge to cut mats, mount board, and backing. Clamp the straight edge and board to a solid working surface with one or two spring clamps. Remember that cutting will scar the work surface, so make sure you use a piece of plywood or a benchtop especially for such purposes.

Next, scribe window guidelines on the back of the mat board with a pencil and straight edge, a compass or marking gauge set for the border width, or a mat-cutter guide. The fastest and most foolproof way to mark guidelines and cut the mat windows is with a mat cutter and guide.

To use Alto's EZ/Mat system, for example, set the guide bar for the mat-border

Use an X-Acto knife and straight edge to cut mats, mounts, and backing.

You can use a compass to scribe mat-window lines.

Use a steel tape rule to set the EZ/Mat guide bar for scribing guidelines.

width. For the inner mat in the accompanying photographs, I set the guide bar at 3 inches and scribed lines inside the left, right, and top edges. I then reset the bar at 4 inches, and scribed a line inside the bottom edge. I did the same on the back of the outer mat with the bar set for 2½ inches for top and side lines and 3½ inches for the bottom line.

If you haven't cut out beveled mat windows before, be sure to practice with the mat cutter on scraps of mat board or cardboard. The only tricky parts are stopping and starting the cut, and the only way to master the techniques is to practice. But it doesn't take long. With the EZ/Mat system, you can be cutting mats like a pro with five minutes' practice.

With the mat face down on the cutter guide, you will notice that the guide bar is ⅛ inch from the guideline. That's where it's supposed to be. Besides, the top and bottom lines are the important ones, as they indicate where to start and stop each cut.

Remember that the cutter blade is angled for the beveled cut, and it enters at an angle when you insert the blade into the back of the mat board. So put the point of the blade about ⅛ inch from the guide bar and ⅛ inch below the bottom guideline. Keeping the base of the cutter parallel with the mat-board surface, gently push the cutter down and toward the guide bar, so the cutter edge is in firm contact with the guide bar. To make the cut, push the cutter along the guide bar

Hinge mat to mount board with acid-free linen tape.

in one fluid motion, stopping the blade about ⅛ inch beyond the top guideline. Rotate the mat clockwise, and continue cutting the same way until the mat window has been cut out. This method produces slight overcuts at the corners of the mat window, but they're unnoticeable when the work is displayed. It's better to overcut the corners than undercut them. As you gain skill and confidence, you can gradually reduce the length of the overcuts until they're almost nonexistent.

If you undercut a mat-window corner, use a double-edged razor blade to complete the cut. Carefully slide it into the beveled cut, hold it at the same angle as the bevel, and slowly cut through the mat.

Hinging the mat – or in the case of multiple mats, the inner mat – to the mount board facilitates the precise positioning

of the artwork. Lay the mount board face up and the mat face down, butted top to top. Cut a piece of acid-free linen tape just slightly shorter than the mat width. Moisten the adhesive side of the tape with a damp sponge or ceramic tongue, press the tape along the seam between the two boards, and let it dry for several minutes.

There are several ways to position works on mount boards. You can scribe positioning lines on the mount board, or use the Falcon Print Positioner, which is covered in Chapter 4.

If you want to use positioning lines, start by laying a straight edge across the artwork, along the top edge of the image area. Then make a small pencil mark at the outer edges of the left and right borders. Now lay the straight edge along the left edge of the image, and make a pencil mark at the top edge of the border. Do the same along the right edge of the image area.

Scribe a horizontal line across the mount board a distance from the top edge that's ⅛ inch less than the mat's top border width. Scribe vertical lines the same way, left and right. In the case of the print in the accompanying photographs, the inner mat borders were 3 inches, top and sides, which called for guidelines 2⅞ inches from the top and side edges of the mount board. All there is to positioning the print, then, is to lay it on the mount board and align the marks at the edges of the print borders with the lines on the mount board.

Another way to position an artwork – and here's where the value of a hinged mat becomes apparent – is to lay it on the mount board and close the mat onto it. Then carefully position the work within the mat window. Wrap a book with tissue paper (two or more books for larger works), and lay it atop the artwork to hold it in place. Gently lift the mat, and make small pencil marks on the mount board at the top and side edges of the artwork. Remove the artwork, and using the pencil marks as guides, scribe guidelines parallel to the top and side edges of the mount board. Lay the work back on the mount board, align its edges with the guidelines, and double check its position with the mat in place.

Mounting artworks with hinges allows for natural expansion and contraction without causing the work to buckle or warp. If you use the Insta-Hinge kit, you will also be assured of protecting the work's collector's value.

The hinge material comes in strips that should be torn, not cut. Hinges about 3 inches long will work fine with most items. You can either fold and tear the

Attaching Insta-Hinge to artwork.

material, or for best results, moisten a small brush with water and paint a damp line across the material. Wait for about a minute until the fibers are fully moistened, and pull the hinge from the strip, leaving a frayed edge. Two hinges will suffice for most works. Large horizontal works might require three.

Attaching hinged artwork to mount board.

Make linen-tape hinges by attaching two pieces to form a *T*.

To attach an Insta-Hinge, first lay the artwork face down atop one of the blotter squares in the kit. Moisten the bottom third of the hinge's dull side with a damp brush, and attach it to the back of the artwork. Brush the hinge again to moisten it, and cover the damp portion with a spun-nylon square and blotter. Put a tissue-covered book atop the hinge, and attach another hinge near the opposite top corner. Let them stand for five minutes, or until adhesive dries.

Lay the artwork face up on the mount board. Put the tissue-covered books on it to keep it in place, and carefully position the work. Turn back the top portion of each hinge, and moisten the glossy surface with the brush. Press the hinges to the mount board, and moisten them from the top side with the damp brush. Cover each hinge with a spun-nylon

square and blotter, and put a tissue-covered book on top.

When attaching hinges to the artwork and the mount board, don't use too much water. Dampen them gradually, with only enough water on the brush to make them adhere. And let them dry completely before proceeding further.

If you're using a single mat, just fold the mat over the mounted work, and it's ready for framing. If you're using multiple mats, laminate them with double-sided tape or Scotch Adhesive Transfer Tape and tape gun.

If the work you're mounting and matting is of little or no monetary value, you might prefer to make mounting hinges with acid-free linen tape or paper tape. This is a faster and simpler process, but not acceptable for works with collector's value. Nevertheless, neither the linen nor paper tape will harm the work, which makes them fine for mounting many items that are only of personal, sentimental, or decorative value.

With either type of tape, you'll need two 3-inch strips for each hinge. To make a hinge, moisten the top inch of the adhesive side of one strip, and press it to the center of the adhesive side of another strip to form a *T*.

To mount hinges to the artwork, moisten the bottom inch of the adhesive side of the pieces forming the stems of the *T*s. Then attach each to the back of the work, just inside each top corner.

After positioning the work on the mount board, bend back the top of each hinge, and moisten the adhesive on the top part of each *T*. Then press each to the mount board, and let stand for a minute or two until adhesive dries. Then the work is ready for framing.

4

Mounting Photographs and Posters

Few areas of the framer's craft have changed as dramatically in so short a time as the mounting of photographs, posters, and similar items. Up until the mid-1970s, we either dry mounted or wet mounted them; there was no other choice.

Dry mounting, until recently the preferred method for a truly professional job, is a process that combines heat and pressure to bond a print or poster to a mount board via a special dry-mounting tissue. Although it is possible to dry mount small photographs and posters with a household iron, the best tool for the job is a dry-mounting press designed for such work. Such presses are electrically operated, thermostatically controlled, and equipped with timers. But even the best presses can ruin resin-coated photographic papers and some

coated posters. Additionally, the heat can adversely affect the dyes in color photographs and can ruin the various foam-cored products.

Wet mounting was the cheaper but messier and more tedious alternative. It was also the only safe way to handle the plastics and resins that would melt and bubble when subjected to too much heat. A variety of glues and pastes, either straight or diluted, were painted onto the back of a photo or poster, which was then laminated to a mount board of some sort and allowed to dry.

Dry mounting is still used on fiber-based photographs and posters at many photo labs, studios, and frame shops, especially those that were in business before the development of alternative equipment and methods. Some framers still use wet-mounting methods to repair

Drytac dry-mounting press.

damaged works, although vacuum mounting is quickly taking over in this area as a faster and neater process.

The development and widespread use of resin-coated photographic papers in the 1970s was probably the major force behind the introduction and refinement

The nuArc vacuum-mounting frame.

of all the dozens of mounting products and various tools and methods we use today. There is now some kind of spray adhesive, adhesive tissue, pressure-sensitive mounting board, self-adhesive foamboard, or treated hardboard to fit every conceivable need and budget. And the modern materials are a joy to work with.

Mounting Materials for Photos and Posters

The traditional photo-mounting board is pebbled mat board that's black on one side and white on the other. Of course, many other boards also serve the purpose. Selection depends on whether the work to be mounted is a black-and-white or color photograph and whether it will be flush mounted, border mounted, or matted. Framing and the display environment are other considerations.

If the work will have exposed borders or will be matted, apply the same principles of color selection you would to any other medium. Generally, use black, white, and shades of gray for black-and-white photographs and posters. Pick matching or contrasting colors for color photographs and posters, or go with subtler pastels, creams, and off-whites for more subdued treatment. And feel free to break these rules whenever it suits you.

As long as you won't be using heat, you can mount photographs and posters on foamboard, which I prefer for large posters, as it has less tendency to warp than mat board. Even more rigid than the paper-faced foamboards are those faced with plastic, such as Gatorfoam.

Hardboard (Masonite is one popular brand) is another excellent mounting material. I particularly like it for flush-mounted photographs that I display in floater frames that give the impression that the work is floating inside the frame. It's available in 24 x 24-inch to 48 x 96-inch sheets at lumber yards and home-improvement centers and comes in ⅛- and ¼-inch thicknesses, either tempered or untempered. The tempered board is less affected by moisture and is the better choice for mounting jobs.

Three-dimensional mount boards, or standouts—so called because they stand out from the wall—are favored by many photographers and decorators. They can be displayed individually or in groups, as any framed objects might be, and are often bunched into montages. Some manufacturers also offer special hangers that permit floating standouts off the wall. Using standouts in various dimensions, with and without the floater hangers, allows great breadth of creativity when displaying photographs.

All the various boards can be used in conjunction with aerosol adhesives, adhesive sheets, and adhesive cards. What's more, these and other products are available as self-adhesive boards. Some come in standard sizes; others come as sheets you cut to size. Some come both ways.

Doran Enterprises offers Gallerie-Mount sheets of adhesive Mylar film in 8 x 10, 8 x 12, 11 x 14, and 16 x 20 inches that is repositionable and can be mounted with a hand roller. (See directory at the end of this book for all addresses.)

Leonard Products Company manufactures EZ Mount, an adhesive-coated mount board for mounting photographs and small posters by hand. It comes in 8 x 10, 11 x 14, and 16 x 20 inches.

Falcon Safety Products offers an aerosol adhesive as well as Perma/Mount adhesive mounting cards that can be used with a hand roller. The cards are made slightly oversize to facilitate positioning and are available for 16 x 20-inch and smaller prints.

The 3M Company makes Super 77 Spray Adhesive and Scotch Photo Mount and Spra-Ment aerosol adhesives. I keep all three of these on hand so I will have an adhesive that will work with any material I might use. Although I don't use these or other aerosol adhesives for conservation mounting, I often use them for mounting display photographs, snapshot collages, small posters, maps, charts, and other items. Photo Mount works well on mat board and similar surfaces, but not on leather, hardboard, or certain other materials. Spra-Ment works with most materials, including cork, fabric, and various plastics. And the Super 77 Spray is an aggressive, high-tack spray that works with practically any material I use. The company also manufactures positionable Mounting Adhesive in rolls and standard-sized sheets, which can be

Aerosol adhesives from 3M Company to see to all mounting needs.

used with a squeegee for small jobs, or a press for larger items.

Pres-On Products, Inc., uses four different adhesives on five substrates to offer products to fit nearly every mounting need. Pres-On thermo adhesive is heat activated and meant for use with dry-mounting presses. Hi-Tack is formulated as both a nonrepositionable adhesive for roller-press mounting and as an acid-free adhesive for use with fabrics. Lo-Tack is a repositionable adhesive meant for mounting graphic art, photographs, posters, and such. The company offers chipboard, foamboard, Masonite, Gatorfoam, and foam-padded board, all coated with one of the adhesives. Most Pres-On products are available in standard sizes, from 5 x 7 inches to 16 x 20 inches, as well as in sheets up to 48 x 60 inches.

Coda, Inc., is a pioneer in the development of pressure-sensitive adhesives and other mounting products. The company offers a wide array of materials to fit most mounting needs. Their self-adhesive Cold-Mount products are available in rolls of standard widths and in various types of mount boards, such as single-weight and double-weight card stock, tempered ⅛-inch hardboard, foamboard, and Gatorfoam. Their own coda-Foam consists of a foam core faced with white plastic on both sides and comes in ¼-inch and ¾-inch thicknesses.

Coda also offers several interesting Cold-Mount display items. Their Stand-Outs are three-dimensional boards, available in standard sizes, from 4 x 5 inches to 20 x 24 inches. For larger works, their Mural Mounts come in sizes from 8 x 10 inches to 40 x 60 inches. Both are available edged in black, white, or wood grain.

Coda's Galerie kits are for making photo montages. They're made of self-adhesive hardboard and come with blocks of different thicknesses so they can "float" at different distances from the wall in an attractive arrangement.

Tools for Mounting Photos and Posters

For mounting small posters and photographs up to 16 x 20 inches, you won't need much in the way of tools. Depending on the type of adhesive you use, you might need no more than a clean cloth for pressing the work to a mount board. With Scotch adhesive mounting sheets, you will need a squeegee, which 3M includes with each package. A print roller is a handy item with just about every kind of adhesive, so you should invest in one. You will find them at photo-supply stores and through some mail-order outlets.

Coda, Inc., offers a unique roller with a bar attached to it that holds the print above the mount board as you attach it. It

Coda Stand-Outs make attractive photo displays.

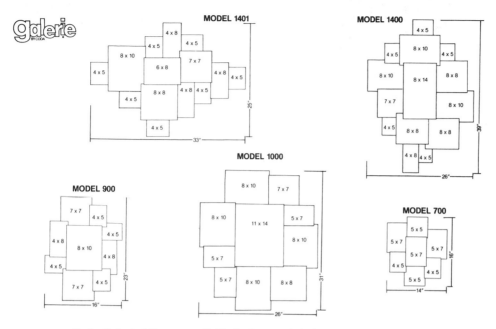

Coda Galerie kits are available in five models for "floating" photo collages.

will handle prints up to 11 x 14 inches with use of the bar, and larger ones without using the bar.

You can cut mat board and trim prints with a straight edge and utility knife. If you have much of this sort of work to do, you might want to invest in a trimmer or cutter of some kind. There are dozens of makes, models, styles, and sizes available in prices ranging from under $20 to well over $1,000.

The Falcon Print Trimmer will handle photos up to 14 inches and uses ordinary razor blades. This is a simple but accu-

Premier roller from Doran Enterprises.

Premier Gallerie Mount Applicator from Doran Enterprises.

Coda Cold-Mounter makes photo mounting easy.

Guillotine-style cutter from Doran Enterprises.

rate light-duty trimmer that will cut all weights of photographic paper as well as single-weight card stock and other lightweight mount boards. Because it's so fast and handy, I use mine for trimming all small, unmounted prints.

Of the larger, heavier-duty cutters, the

Falcon Print Trimmer in use.

guillotine-type are the least expensive. Rotary trimmers are a bit more expensive, but if you ever entertain the notion of mounting and matting professionally in high volume, you should consider the advantages such tools offer. They handle material from thin tissue to mat board with equal facility. They're fast, safe, precise machines.

Rotatrim, from The Saunders Group, is one of the most popular brands of professional rotary trimmers. Units are available through photo shops and mail-order sources for a little over $100 for the 12-inch model to about $300 for the 42-inch one.

Dry-mount, roller, and vacuum presses range in price from a few hundred to a few thousand dollars—an expense you can certainly forestall, perhaps indefinitely. If you never need to mount anything larger than a 16 x 20-inch print, you won't need a press. If you end up mounting many large items, though, you will have to consider a press, or you will have to have such mounting done for you.

Most of the photographs I mount are from 4 x 5 inches to 16 x 20 inches. I rarely have to mount a large poster, but

Three sizes of Kutrimmers from Michael Business Machines Corp.

when I do I take it to a local shop where there's a press big enough to handle it, and I pay the man his fee. Certainly, I could mount such items much more cheaply with my own press, but I would have to do a lot of mounting to save enough money to justify the initial capital outlay.

I seriously doubt that I will ever need a press, but if I do, I'm sure it will be one of the hand-operated wringer or roller-type presses for use with pressure-sensitive adhesives. There are some good buys around on such presses in moderate sizes.

Using the Falcon Print Positioner

With the Falcon Print Positioner, there's no need to measure and scribe

The floor-size Model 1110 Kutrimmer.

The Doran rotary-style trimmer.

The Rotatrim Mastercut-II from The Saunders Group.

Coda's hand-operated Cold-Mount press.

layout lines on the mount board or to even put guide marks on the item being positioned. While such chores take only a few minutes with conventional tools and techniques, the entire job is reduced to seconds with the Print Positioner. And it works with any size photograph. It's especially nice for photographs that are border-mounted—that is, where borders of the mount board will be left exposed—and have been trimmed to size, leaving nowhere to make positioning marks.

If you're going to border mount or mat a print, determine what border widths you want, and cut the mount board to the proper outside dimensions. With the print trimmed to finished dimensions, if necessary, follow these simple steps.to properly position it.

Step 1. Position the print atop the mount board in the top right corner, with top and right edges flush. Place the Positioner as shown and slide it to the left until the top left corners of the print and mount board align with corresponding horizontal numbers.

Step 2. Without moving the Positioner, slide the print to the left, against the Positioner's vertical stem, then down to the bottom edge of the mount board. Check to see how the top edge of the print aligns with the large-number scale on the stem.

Step. 3. Slide the print up along the Positioner stem until its top edge aligns with the small-number scale at a position cor-

Using the Print Positioner, Step 1.

Using the Print Positioner, Step 2.

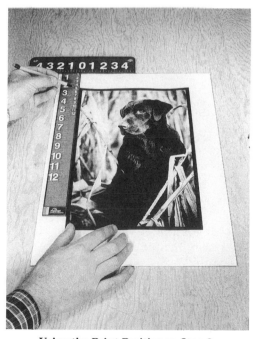

Using the Print Positioner, Step 3.

Using the Print Positioner, Step 4.

responding with the reading noted in Step 2.

Step 4. The print is now perfectly positioned on the mount board. Using the print edges as guides, lightly scribe horizontal and vertical lines at each corner. The print is now ready for mounting.

And that's all there is to it. As if by magic, this works every time with any size print. A nifty tool, and inexpensive too.

Modern Mounting Methods

Other than introducing you to the various materials and tools available, there's really little to tell you about mounting photographs and posters, except to offer a few tips to make the job easier. Any of the adhesive products you buy come with adequate instructions, and there are few differences in the way they work.

As you have no doubt surmised by now, I don't like to lay down rules and absolutes for you to work by, because there are always notable exceptions, and there are usually good reasons for breaking many rules that apply to arts and crafts. But I think one of my own rules might come in handy here.

Generally, don't plan to hand mount any print or poster larger than 16 x 20 inches. I have heard of one chap who can mount murals and posters up to 30 x 40 inches using only a hand roller, but he is an exception. Works larger than 16 x 20 inches are extremely difficult to handle, and for most of us they're impossible to mount by hand without problems. In fact, just handling them without ruining them is difficult.

If you have never mounted anything

with the modern adhesives, start with small photographs, and gradually work your way up to the 11 x 14-inch and 16 x 20-inch prints. When you have larger photos or posters to mount, take them to a shop that has a roller or vacuum press big enough to accommodate your needs.

You must keep your work area clean during any mounting or matting job, but you must be meticulous about it when mounting with adhesives. Any tiny piece of lint that ends up between the work and the mount board results in a bulge or bubble in the image surface. What's more, buildup of static electricity in some plastic products acts like a magnet to dust and lint.

When you mount with aerosol adhesives, you must guard against any potential damage from overspray. Start any such job by attaching a sheet of freezer paper to your benchtop with masking tape, and replace it as necessary. After seeing to any necessary trimming and positioning, you're ready to apply adhesive.

Lay the print or poster face down on the freezer paper. Then spray an even and complete coating of adhesive onto the back of the work. Depending on what type of adhesive you are using and the manufacturer's directions, you will either mount it immediately or let it "tack up" for a minute or so. Some porous materials require more adhesive than others, and in some cases you will need to coat both the back of the print and the surface of the mount board.

Carefully position the top corners of the print on the mount board, aligned with your guide marks, and press the top edge onto the board. Then gradually press the rest of the print onto the board, cover it with a piece of clean paper, and use a hand roller to mount it, always roll-ing from the center toward the edges, removing all bubbles.

There will be adhesive overspray on the freezer paper from your first print or poster. To protect the next work, lay a sheet of clean paper on the freezer paper and the next photo or poster on that. For prints up to 8 x 10 inches, you can use ordinary 8½ x 11-inch paper. For larger prints and posters, use freezer paper or cheaper tissue paper. There's no need to tape down these subsequent sheets of protective paper, as the overspray will keep them in place.

When working with adhesive-coated boards and adhesive sheets, you needn't worry about protecting your work sur-face, as this is a much neater process. I use the coated boards only for flush mounting and adhesive sheets for both flush mounting and border mounting, but mainly for the latter.

If I'm using adhesive boards, I prefer to mount the work first and trim it after-ward. If I'm using boards made of card stock or chipboard to flush mount 8 x 10-inch prints, for example, I simply peel away the release paper to expose the adhesive, and carefully position the top edge of the print along the top edge of the mount board. Then I gradually press the print onto the board, from top to bottom, with a clean cloth. I cover the image with a sheet of paper and use a roller to bond print to board.

On most of my 8 x 10-inch prints, the borders are ⅜ inch wide, so to end up with a flush-mounted print, I simply trim ⅜ inch from each edge. With card stock, mat board, chipboard, and such, I use my guillotine cutter to trim the prints. I first wipe the cutter table clean, then carefully lay each print face down for the

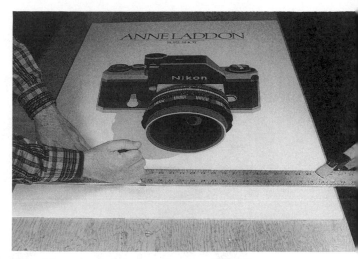

Mount large posters to oversize boards, and trim *after* mounting.

cutting, as this leaves a sharp, smooth cut edge on the image surface. What starts out as an 8 x 10-inch print with borders ends up as a flush-mounted print of 7¼ x 9¼ inches.

I don't like what the guillotine cutter does to foamboard, so when I'm mount-ing with that product, I prefer to trim it with a straight edge and utility knife, which produces a clean, smooth cut, top and bottom. In this case, I work with the print or poster face up to make it easier to see what I'm doing.

With prints and posters larger than 16 x 20 inches, I use mount boards (usually foamboard) that are slightly larger. Then, after they're mounted, I trim the excess with a straight edge and utility knife.

When I'm mounting with hardboard, however, I do the opposite. I use boards that are slightly undersized with posters and borderless prints. When the work is mounted, I lay it face down on the mat-cutting bench and very carefully use the tip of my utility knife to trim away ex-

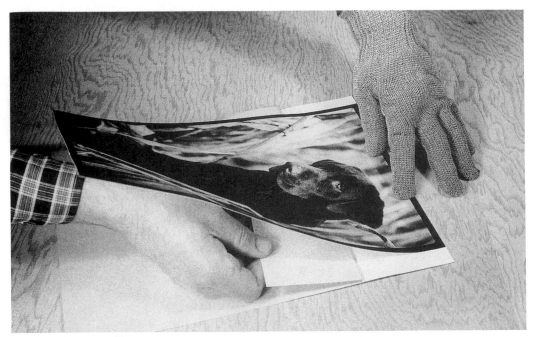

Mounting a photograph, Step 3.

Mounting a photograph, Step 5.

cess, letting the edge of the hardboard serve as a guide. A sharply pointed blade, such as the X-Acto #11, is best for this job.

Adhesive sheets or cards, coated on both sides, are ideal for border mounting prints and for mounting prints and posters that will be matted. Determine the border widths, and cut mount boards to the appropriate size. Mounting methods will vary only slightly from one make of adhesive sheet to another. But, typically, you can follow these steps with Falcon Perma/Mount adhesive cards and similar materials.

Step 1. Peel back the release paper on one side of the card about a fourth of the way, and fold it against the card.

Step 2. With the print face up, align its top edge with the top exposed edge of the adhesive card. Carefully and lightly press the print to the card.

Step 3. Grasp the folded edge of the release paper beneath the print, and slowly pull it toward the bottom of the card, allowing the print to make contact with the adhesive as you do so.

Step 4. Press the print to the adhesive by hand with a clean cloth, or use a roller, working from the center to the edges.

Step 5. Trim the print, if required, to final size with any suitable cutter or a straight edge and utility knife. If you're going to mount with mats, trim only the excess of the oversized adhesive card.

Step 6. Position the print on the mount

Mounting a photograph, Step 10.

board, and make any necessary guide marks on the board.

Step 7. Lay the print face down, peel back the release paper on the back of the print a fourth of the way, and fold it as in Step 1.

Step 8. With the print face up, align its top corners with the guide marks on the mount board, and lightly press it in place.

Step 9. Slowly pull the release paper away, as you did in Step 3, allowing the print to make contact with the mount board.

Step 10. Press the print to the mount board with a clean cloth, or cover it with a sheet of paper, and use a roller to bond it to the mount board.

5

Advanced Matting Materials, Tools, and Techniques

Once you have mastered matting basics, it will be apparent that the possibilities for variations and creative twists are manifold. You will be limited only by your imagination and your tastes.

As I have recommended before, spend some time at galleries, examining what others are doing with mats. No doubt, some techniques will intrigue you and pique your interest, while others will scarcely catch your eye.

Although I am fairly liberal in my use of colors in matting jobs, I'm conservative with the techniques, mainly because I feel mats should complement the art, not overwhelm it or in any way distract the viewer. It would be unfair (if not downright silly) of me to insist that you follow my conservative example when making mats, or for that matter, my liberal bent in the selection of mat colors.

I can't dictate tastes and preferences to you. What I can do, though, is offer suggestions, tell you why I do things a certain way, and why I don't do other things. But only you can make the ultimate decisions in any matting job – unless, of course, you're doing it for someone else who has specific requests.

Although the majority of mats I cut are simple rectangles, I do occasionally make mats with notches, cutouts, or special corner treatments. I also make oval mats, and I sometimes cover mats with various materials. So these are the topics I will cover in this chapter. They will serve you well. Master these techniques, learn from my mistakes, and you will be able to apply this knowledge to any mats you want to make, with the possible exception of intricately carved and free-hand-cut mats, which no amount of instruction will help you make. For those, you will simply have to create your own designs and practice until you achieve the effect you're after.

I don't make odd-shaped mats or mat windows because, at best, they're distracting. Some are just too ugly for words. I generally avoid square and round mats, because these formats are visually dull and almost always unnecessary. For similar reasons, I don't like mats, mat windows, or frames in the shape of equilateral hexagons and octagons.

I suppose the best advice I can offer is to think about every matting job and what you hope to accomplish with it. Consider how best you might display each work and how the mat or mats will serve those ends. And if you're occasionally overcome by whim or whimsy, ride it out. If you have a notion to do something unusual or unconventional, try it. If it doesn't work, all you will have lost is a little time and perhaps a few square feet of mat board. In the process, you might have learned some important lessons.

Multiple Mats

I'm a great fan of multiple mats, because they usually do the best possible job of setting off artworks or even something so personally mundane as a diploma or certificate. A single mat can serve to confine or open an image, whichever your intention might be, and it can amplify a color or shade. Multiple mats can also provide a confining border or subtle openness, and they can combine two or more colors or shades that serve to prepare the viewer's eye for the work they contain. Or they can perform

such a simple task as displaying school colors when matting a diploma, school-related certificate, or even school pictures.

Because I like what I can do with the border provided by the inner mat, I almost always use at least two mats these days, sometimes three. I rarely use more than three, and then only for special effects.

A general rule for determining exposed border width when using multiple mats is to vary the widths to avoid the visually boring stairstep effect. So if the exposed border of the innermost of three mats will be ¼ inch, make sure the exposed border of the middle mat is wider or narrower: ⅛, ½, or ¾ inch. Of course, the outer or third mat should be the widest of the three.

As with any rule, though, there are notable exceptions. Few things in art or nature are symmetrical, but when you do discover symmetry, you might wish to emphasize it by using interior mats with equal-sized borders. I have seen this done with symmetrical designs, and the effect works.

Whether the borders of the outermost mat should be equal on all sides or wider at the bottom is mainly a matter of choice. Sometimes the only way to find out is to cut the mats and see how you like the effect.

Most of the time, you will be able to pick the right colors or shades of mat board by checking the work with mat corners. And if you plan carefully and sketch the more complicated jobs, you will rarely go wrong. But when you do come onto that difficult work and don't like the results, all you have to do is try something else until you find the combination that suits you and the artwork.

I earlier warned against using more than one heavily textured mat in any job. Sometimes, because of availability or color, you might have to use a lightly textured mat with one more heavily textured. In such cases, or when I'm using a textured mat with smooth-surfaced mats, I try to put the textured mat or the most highly textured mat on the outside. Not only is the outer mat most visible and therefore the most suitable position to show off texture, but textured mats hide overcuts better than smooth mats do.

Arrangement of color in multiple mats is also important. The darkest and most saturated colors can overwhelm works if they're used as outer mats. On the other hand, they can be the perfect arresting touch as narrow-bordered inner mats. Conversely, lighter colors and pastel shades usually work best as outer mats.

Notched and Cutout Mats

Notches and cutouts are two of the simplest and most frequently employed variations on conventional matting. A notched mat has a cutaway section, usually centered along the bottom edge of the mat window for the purpose of highlighting a work's title. A cutout is simply an extra, smaller window cut into the mat border for displaying something related to the artwork.

Notched mats are most often used with limited-edition, titled prints. Generally, such prints have portions of the print margins exposed to show the artist's signature and the print number. A notch is then cut into the bottom edge of the window, slightly larger than the print's title.

Cutouts are most often used to display the artwork and another item within the same mat and frame. Wildlife-art prints and stamps are usually displayed this way, for example the federal duck stamp issued each year in the United States and prints made of the painting the stamp is based on. Some wildlife conservation associations have copied the U.S. government and issued stamps and limited-edition prints as a way of raising funds.

Another use for cutout mats is for displaying documents and related three-dimensional items. I have seen citations and medals displayed in separate windows in the same mat, and the effect is pleasing. A diploma matted with a small window cut into the mat's bottom border for a Phi Beta Kappa key or similar item is a nice touch.

There seems to be no end to the variety of uses for notches and cutouts. I recently visited a gallery and saw notched mats I didn't like and then attended an exhibit where I saw an unusual cutout mat I liked very much.

At the gallery were some remarqued, limited-edition prints by my favorite marine artist. The matting and framing

The three mats used with this limited-edition print are notched to show the print's title.

jobs were flawless, but notches were cut into the lower left edges of the mat windows to display the remarques. Normally, the framer simply exposes enough print-border area to show off the remarque in a conventional rectangular mat window. I did not care for the effect of the off-center notch.

A friend of mine felt just the opposite. He said the remarque notch was striking, that it immediately drew his attention to the remarque. I disliked it for precisely the same reason. To my way of thinking, the viewer's attention should be drawn first to the subject, not to some subordinate detail, such as a signature, number, or remarque. But, as I have said before, that's just one person's opinion.

The unusual cutout mat that caught my eye had a large, horizontal, rectangular window displaying a fine print of a pair of ringnecked pheasants flushing in the foreground, while a stagecoach rumbled by in the background. On each side of the main mat window was a narrow vertical window cut the same height as the main window. Displayed in each was a slender cock-pheasant tail feather. Rather than distract me, the feathers seemed to draw me to the focal point of interest in the print.

When making cutout mats, you must consider the thickness of the item you will fit into the cutout. In the case of stamps or other similarly thin items, you can use single mats if you wish. But for other items, such as medals, you will probably have to build the depth by using multiple mats.

There are several materials suitable for mounting the various items in mat cutouts. Stamps should be mounted with stamp hinges, available at hobby shops. Other paper items can be similarly mounted or attached with any suitable adhesive.

The material you use to mount three-dimensional items will depend on the size and weight of the item and whether or not you want the process to be reversible. Epoxy cement will stick just about anything to anything else — permanently. I like the five-minute epoxy kits that consist of a tube each of resin and hardener. It works fast and holds well. When I want something reversible, I use either silicone sealer or double-sided foam mounting tape.

Cutting Octagonal Mats

The simplest and easiest of the special corner treatments is the octagonal mat. By cutting off each corner diagonally, you end up with an eight-sided mat window instead of the conventional four-sided rectangle. Those extra sides can be as long or as short as you want them, provided that they don't obscure or crowd the work being matted.

You can make small (¼ inch to ½ inch) diagonal cuts in about any mat for an attractive variation on the traditional squared corners. This is particularly pleasing when done with multiple mats.

For practice, cut a piece of mat board to 8 x 10 inches; then follow these simple steps to cut an octagonal window.

Step 1. Lay the mat board face down on the mat-cutting guide, set the guide bar at 1¾ inches, and scribe guidelines 1¾ inches from each edge.

Step 2. Reset the guide bar at 2¾ inches, and scribe short marks across the top and bottom of each line scribed in Step 1.

Octagonal mat window, Step 2.

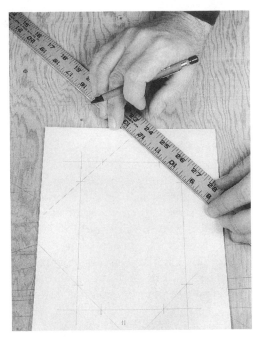

Octagonal mat window, Step 3.

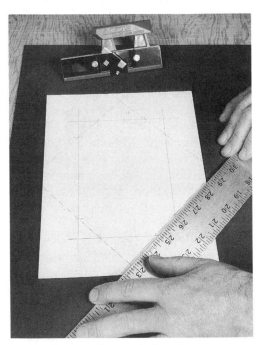

Octagonal mat window, Step 4.

Finished octagonal-windowed mats.

Step 3. Align the guide bar or a straight edge with the marks scribed in Step 2, and scribe a line across each corner of the mat board, from one edge to another.

Step 4. Align the guide bar or straight edge ⅛ inch outside each line scribed in Step 3, and use the mat cutter to cut along the line.

Step 5. Now set the guide bar for cutting at 1¾ inches, and cut along the lines scribed in Step 1, between the diagonal corner lines, to complete your octagonal mat.

Use identical techniques to cut octagonal mat windows to any size you desire. For an attractive variation, make curved diagonal cuts in the corners instead of straight ones. Simply follow the first two steps above, but position an upside-down coffee mug (or other round object) just outside the guide marks at the corners, and make curved corner cuts with the mat cutter. Use a scrap piece of mat or

Finished curved-corner mat.

poster board under the mat, and press down firmly on the mug during the cut. Then complete the mat window as in Step 5 above.

The only tricky part of cutting these curved lines is applying sufficient pressure in the right directions to keep the mat cutter in contact with the cup rim. Start the cutter as you would when cutting a straight line; then simultaneously press the cutter down, forward, and toward the cup as you make the semicircular cut. Concentrate as you cut, and you should have no problems.

Cutting Zag-Corner Mats

A zag corner is a smaller and simpler version of the indented corner (see be-

Cutting a curved-corner mat.

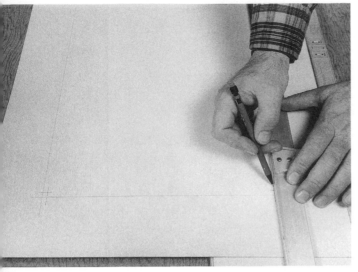

Zag-corner mats, Step 2.

low) and can be used with most items suitable for matting. Vary dimensions and measurements to fit your needs, and use zag-corner mats wherever they seem to fit.

For purposes of demonstration, I picked a lithograph of a Bill O'Neill pen-and-ink drawing for its standard sizes. The image size is 12 x 18 inches, and the outside dimensions of the mount board and mats are 18 x 24 inches. I decided on three mats: black, white, and Bar Harbor Gray. Here's how to duplicate the steps I took to mat this work:

Step 1. Set the guide bar at 3⅛ inches, and scribe guidelines on the back of the inner mat 3⅛ inches from each edge.

Zag-corner mats, Step 4.

Zag-corner mats, Step 7.

Step 2. Move the guide bar to 3⅜ inches, and scribe lines about 1 inch long across the top and bottom of and perpendicular to each line scribed in Step 1. These lines form the zag corners of the mat.

Step 3. With the guide bar set to cut at 3⅜ inches, use the mat cutter to make the ¼-inch cuts along the lines scribed in Step 2.

Step 4. Reset the guide bar to cut at 3⅛ inches, and make the four cuts to complete the zag-corner window in the inner mat.

Step 5. Reposition the guide bar at 2⅞ inches, and scribe guidelines on the back of the middle mat at 2⅞ inches from each edge.

Step 6. Move the guide bar to 3⅛ inches, and scribe zag-corner lines, as in Step 2.

Step 7. Now use the mat cutter and guide to cut the zag corners and complete the mat window as with the inner mat in Steps 3 and 4.

Step 8. Set the guide bar at 2⅜ inches, and scribe guidelines on the back of the outer mat.

Step 9. Move the guide bar to 2⅝ inches, and scribe zag-corner lines as you did with the first two mats.

Step 10. Then cut the zag-cornered mat window out of the outer mat, as you did with the other mats.

Finished zag-corner mats.

Indented-corner mats, Step 2.

Indented-corner mats, Step 3.

Indented-corner mats, Step 6.

Cutting Indented-Corner Mats

Of the various special corner treatments, the indented corner is my favorite and perhaps the most useful. Although it is a bit more complicated than the zag corner, it is easier than the notched corner.

To illustrate the techniques, I chose a limited-edition Don McMichael print of a square-rigged sailing vessel with an image size of roughly 11 x 15 inches, which allowed me to cut mount and mat boards to standard 16 x 20 inches. Here's how to cut indented-corner mats for items of like size.

Step 1. Set the guide bar at 2⅝ inches, and scribe guidelines on the back of the inner mat 2⅝ inches from each edge.

Step 2. Move the guide bar to 3¾ inches, and scribe lines about 1 inch long across the top and bottom of and perpendicular to each line scribed in Step 1.

Step 3. Reset the guide bar at 2¾ inches, and scribe lines top and bottom about two inches long, inside and parallel to the lines scribed in Step 1. These lines will form the indented corners.

Step 4. Set the guide bar for cuts at 3¾ inches, and use the mat cutter to make the ⅛-inch cuts along the lines scribed in Step 2.

Step 5. Reset the guide bar for cuts at 2¾ inches, and cut along the indented-corner lines scribed in Step 3.

Step 6. Then with the guide bar set for cuts at 2⅝ inches, make the final cuts to complete the indented-corner inner mat.

Finished indented-corner mats.

Step 7. Set the guide bar at 2⅜ inches, and scribe guidelines on the back of the outer mat 2⅜ inches from each edge.

Step 8. Move the guide bar to 3½ inches, and scribe lines about an inch long across the top and bottom of and perpendicular to each line scribed in Step 7.

Step 9. With the guide bar set at 2½ inches, scribe indented-corner lines, as in Step 3.

Step 10. Now use the mat cutter and guide to cut out the mat window as you did with the inner mat in Steps 4, 5, and 6.

Cutting Notched-Corner Mats

Notched corners are less confining and more open than indented corners and are most suitable for active subjects. They're a little trickier than other corner treatments, but the techniques are worth knowing.

I picked another McMichael limited-edition print to illustrate this matting job, one with an image size of roughly 11 x 14 inches, making it ideal for outside dimensions of 16 x 20 inches. Here's how to cut double mats for any similarly sized picture.

Step 1. Set the guide bar at 3 inches, and scribe guidelines on the back of the inner mat 3 inches from each edge.

Notched-corner mats, Step 2.

Notched-corner mats, Step 3.

Notched-corner mats, Step 4.

Notched-corner mats, Step 5.

Notched-corner mats, Step 6.

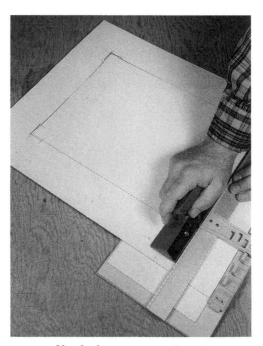

Notched-corner mats, Step 7.

Step 2. Reset the guide bar at 4 inches, and scribe lines about 1 inch long across the top and bottom of and perpendicular to each line scribed in Step 1.

Step 3. With the guide bar set at 2⅞ inches, scribe lines top and bottom about 1½ inches long, parallel to the lines scribed in Step 1. These lines will form the corner notches you will cut out.

Step 4. Move the guide bar to 4⅛ inches, and make small marks at the top and bottom edges of the mat board on all four sides.

Step 5. The short cuts along the lines scribed in Step 2 should not be made with the guide bar on the cutting base, as this will create reversed bevels. Instead, lay a scrap strip of mat board on your bench and the mat board on top of it. Align the guide bar with the marks scribed in Step 4, and use the mat cutter to make the ⅛-inch cuts along the lines scribed in Step 2.

Step 6. Set the guide bar on the base for cuts at 2⅞ inches, and use the mat cutter to cut along the outside-corner lines scribed in Step 3.

Step 7. Position the guide bar for cuts at 3 inches, and make the final cuts to complete the corner-notched inner mat.

Step 8. Set the guide bar at 2¾ inches, and scribe guidelines on the back of the outer mat 2¾ inches from each edge.

Step 9. Reset the guide bar at 4¼ inches, and scribe lines about 1 inch long across the top and bottom of and perpendicular to each line scribed in Step 8.

Finished notched-corner mats.

Step 10. With the guide bar set at 2⅝ inches, scribe lines top and bottom about 2 inches long, parallel to the lines scribed in Step 8.

Step 11. Move the guide bar to 4¾ inches, and make small marks at the top and bottom edges of the mat board, on all four sides.

Step 12. Now cut out the corner-notched windows from the outer mat the same as you did with the inner mat in Steps 5, 6, and 7.

Cutting Oval-Windowed Mats

The oval is second only to the rectangle as a suitable format for matting. It is particularly useful with portraits and can be worked into multi-windowed mats with other oval and rectangular windows.

For high-speed production, there are expensive, pin-registered mat cutters ranging in price from about $800 to well over $1,000, but a person would have to need a tremendous quantity of oval mats to justify such an outlay.

Alto's Oval Template Kit.

Among the oval mat cutters more appropriate for use in the home or small framing shop, the best buy is, again, a product produced by Alto Albright. Alto's oval templates come in a kit that sells for the same price as his EZ/Mat System. The kit includes four oval templates and four spacers that enable you to cut twenty different sizes of ovals. The kit also comes with a standard mat cutter and a template for drawing decorative lines and making French mats.

The No. 1 oval template produces a 3 x 4½-inch window in a 5 x 7-inch mat board and is for use with 3½ x 5-inch prints. The No. 2 template is for 5 x 7-inch prints and makes a 4½ x 6½-inch window in an 8 x 10-inch mat board. With the No. 3 template, you can display

an 8 x 10-inch print in a 7½ x 9½-inch window cut in an 11 x 14-inch mat board. And the largest template, No. 4, is for use with 11 x 14-inch prints; it produces a 10½ x 13½-inch window in a 16 x 20-inch mat board.

Spacers, which attach instantly to the mat cutter, are $1/16$, $1/8$, $1/4$, and $3/8$ inch. With any of the spacers and any of the ovals, you can cut larger oval windows, either to accommodate larger images or to use with multiple mats.

When using these templates, you will work with the mat face up, and you will need a scrap piece of mat board or poster board beneath any mat you are cutting.

Templates No. 1 and No. 2 are solid and should be centered on the mat board by eye or with the use of a steel tape or other rule. The two larger templates can be centered the same way or by use of layout lines. To prepare a mat for the No. 3 or No. 4 template, lay a straight edge or yardstick diagonally across the face of the mat, from one corner to another, and scribe a line about 3 inches long near the center. Reposition the rule at the oppo-

Use a steel tape rule to center the small templates.

Scribe intersecting diagonal lines near the center of the mat for positioning the large templates.

Cutting oval-windowed mats, Step 1.

Cutting oval-windowed mats, Step 4.

site corners, and scribe an intersecting line to form an *X*.

Then, to cut an oval mat window, follow these easy steps.

Step 1. Lay the mat board face up on a scrap of mat or poster board, and center the oval template on it. Push one of the template tacks into each hole in the template, and tap it into the mat board with the end of the mat cutter handle.

Step 2. Put the mat cutter against the template with the two contact points touching the template's outside edge. Make sure the bottom of the cutter is parallel to the face of the mat board when the blade point touches the board.

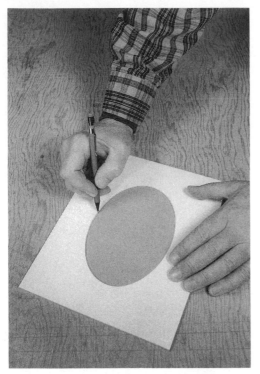

When cutting double oval mats, cut the inner mat first, and use it to make guidelines on the outer mat for positioning the template.

Step 3. Keeping the contact points touching the template's edge, simultaneously push the cutter forward, downward, and against the template.

Step 4. Move the cutter counterclockwise along the template, making sure the rear of the cutter doesn't drift off the template edge. Cut in several sections. As you round the template, stop and turn the mat for the next section. You should be able to cut the oval out completely in three or four sections.

The most important advice I can offer is to concentrate completely. If your mind drifts, so will the cutter, and you'll botch the job. The first time I tried cutting an oval mat window with one of Alto's templates, I did a near-perfect job. Then I got cocky about it and ruined my second attempt.

If you make a bad cut, don't discard the mat, as it is salvageable. Simply attach one of the spacers to the cutter, and make another, larger cut around the template. You'll end up with a mat you can use on another work with a slightly larger image area or one that will be part of a multiple-mat arrangement.

In addition to cutting oval mats, you can use these same templates to add curved accents to rectangular mats. You can give a rectangular mat an arched top or arched top and bottom. And you can also use sections of the templates to guide you in freehand cuts, if you're so inclined.

Decorating Mats

Mat decoration is a personal endeavor that depends more on individual tastes than on any particular rules. There are various materials and methods for decorating mats, and the decorations range from simple lines or corner brackets to elaborate carvings and cutouts.

The French mat is perhaps the most commonly used decorated mat. In such a mat, lines are used to provide extra borders to set off the matted image. The simplest French mat will have a single line running parallel to the edges of the mat window. More elaborate French mats will display several lines of various widths, and areas between one set of lines might be colored, shaded, or gilded.

Colored or shaded areas are often filled in with watercolor or ink washes. Felt markers can be used, as long as their colors are permanent. Whether you apply color with a brush or marker, there is a chance of running over the guidelines, so apply the color or shading before laying down final lines that will conceal any minor errors.

The French mat is not as popular as it once was, perhaps because of all the easier alternatives, such as using colored or black-cored mats, for achieving similar effects. In its simplest form, however, the French mat is still an attractive way to display some photographs and artworks, particularly black-and-white works.

India ink or drawing ink is best for scribing narrow lines on a mat. You can use drafting pens or ballpoint India-ink pens that come with points of different diameters or gauges. For wider lines, graphic tape is best.

Once you have decided how many lines you want and where you want to place them, use a mat-cutter guide or straight edge to scribe light pencil lines on the mat face. If you're using a straight edge, the Boyne Mat Corner Marker can speed things up.

Use an art-gum eraser, kneaded eraser, or draftsman's film eraser to remove pencil lines extending beyond the corners. Then lay down ink lines with pens and an inking ruler to avoid smearing.

Graphic tape, also called graphic-art tape or border tape, comes in a variety of widths and configurations and several colors. Although you might occasionally

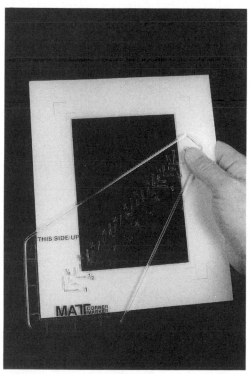

Using the Boyne Mat Corner Marker to scribe guidelines.

Scribing French lines with India-ink ballpoint pen and inking ruler.

Scribing guidelines with Alto's EZ/Mat guide.

Use the blade point to lift the end of the tape after cutting it.

Use an X-Acto knife to miter cut graphic tape at the corners.

find uses for the green, yellow, blue, or red tapes, matte black will prove the most useful for white and gray mats. White tape can add a striking touch to a black or gray mat.

Of the various widths the tape comes in, I find $1/32$, $1/16$, $1/8$, and $1/4$ inch the most useful for decorating mats.

To use graphic tape, prepare the mat with pencil guidelines, as you would if you were inking the lines. Start the tape an inch or so beyond one corner, and lay it along the guideline just past the opposite corner. With an X-Acto knife angled at 45 degrees, miter cut the leading end of the tape; then do likewise at the other corner. Lay down subsequent tape lines the same way with miters at the corners.

Using Alto's line guide and template to scribe a French line on an oval mat.

Decorating an oval mat with transfer-type brackets.

It you cut oval mats with Alto's templates, you can use the special line guide to scribe lines around the oval mat. Either scribe the lines before you cut the mat window or after the cut but before you remove the cutout portion. Holes in the guide are spaced at $1/32$-inch increments. The small holes are for pens and pencils, and larger holes for markers. To use, simply put the guide against the outer edge of the oval template, insert the pen or marker into the appropriate hole, and push the guide around the template while applying pressure toward the template. The guide works in either direction.

Companies that make transfer type that you apply to paper with a plastic

Inking the mat bevel with a permanent felt marker.

burnishing tool also make transfer symbols, some of which are useful in decorating mats. You'll find this material at office-supply stores and wherever engineering and drafting supplies are sold. In department stores, check the hobby aisle or department where calligraphy pens and supplies are displayed.

Some framers decorate mats by coloring the mat bevels. Again, be sure to use permanent colors, such as watercolors, India ink, or permanent markers. Always test a scrap piece of mat board to make sure it will take ink or watercolors along the edges without feathering into the surface paper. If you want a black bevel, you can also use black-cored mat board.

Use a small camel-hair brush to apply watercolor or ink to the bevel, or carefully run a felt marker along the bevel. With felt markers, you will have to use a fine-pointed pen to fill in at the corners.

Covering Mats

There are two primary reasons for covering mats. One is to achieve an effect that is impossible with currently available mat boards. The other is to salvage mats damaged in cutting, coloring, or inking. Don't discard mats with minor damage or surface blemishes; keep them and cover them with any of a number of suitable materials.

Among the many possible materials for covering mats, fabrics — such as burlap and linen — and leather-imitating vinyl are probably the most popular. Con-Tact brand self-adhesive plastic also works well, as it is repositionable, easy to keep clean, and available in a variety of patterns and colors. With most materials, you can use aerosol adhesive, adhesive mounting sheets, or self-adhesive mounting boards.

Mats covered with burlap, vinyl, and Con-Tact.

Step 1: Cut the covering material oversize.

Step 2: Apply adhesive to mat face.

Step 3: Use a roller to bond mat to covering material.

Step 4: Make diagonal cuts from the mat-window corners.

To cover a mat using an aerosol adhesive, such as 3M Super 77, first cover part of your work surface with freezer paper and masking tape; then follow these steps.

Step 1. Use scissors to cut the covering material about an inch larger on all sides than the mat.

Step 2. Lay the mat face up on the freezer paper, and apply a coat of adhesive to it. Let it "tack up" according to the manufacturer's directions.

Step 3. Lay the covering material face down on the bench and the mat face down on it. Press the mat to the covering material, and make a complete bond with the use of a roller.

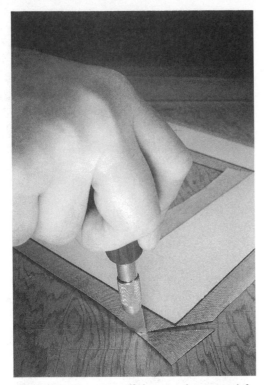

Step 5: Cut corners off the covering material.

Step 7: Press the covering material to the mat back.

Step 4. With a utility knife, make a short diagonal cut from each inside corner of the mat window toward the center. Then cut the center of the material away to within ½ inch or so of the edges of the mat window.

Step 5. Use the utility knife to make a diagonal cut across each outside corner of the covering material to remove excess material down to the mat corner.

Step 6. Lay the mat and material face down on clean freezer paper, apply a coat of adhesive to the back of the mat, and let stand until tacky.

Step 7. Pull the inner strips of covering material up and over the edges of the mat window, and press them to the mat back. Pull the outer strips up and over the outer edges of the mat, and press them to the mat back. Make sure all material is firmly pressed in place; then let stand until the adhesive cures.

Basically, you follow similar procedures to cover mats using adhesive mounting sheets or mounting boards. To cover a self-adhesive board, for example, first lay it face down, and mark guidelines on the release paper with a permanent-ink pen. Then use a mat cutter and guide to cut out the mat window, turning the self-adhesive board into a mat.

Run a strip of double-sided tape or adhesive transfer tape across the top and bottom and along each side of the board face. Trim the covering material as required, and lay the mat face down on it. Press the mat to the material to make the bond. Then cut the material as in Steps 4 and 5 above.

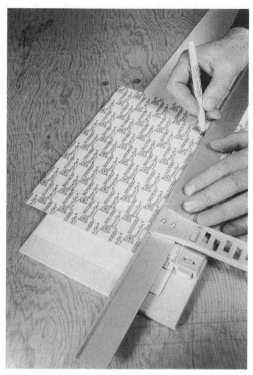

Mark guidelines on self-adhesive board with a permanent pen.

Cut covering material slightly larger than the mat.

Apply transfer adhesive to the mat face.

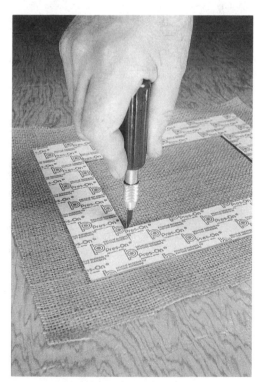

Make diagonal cuts from the mat-window corners toward the center.

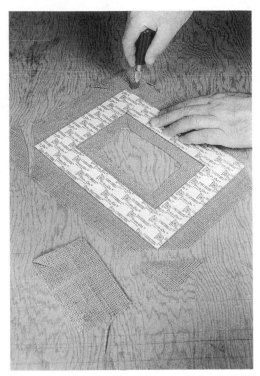

Cut away center and cut off the corners of the covering material.

Press the inner edges of the covering material to the adhesive back of the mat.

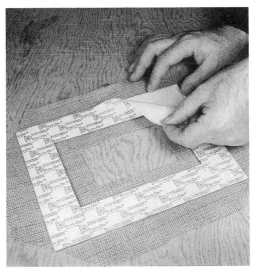

Peel the release paper from the back of the mat.

Press the outer edges of the covering material to the mat.

Peel the release paper from the back of the mat. Then pull the covering material up and over the mat and window edges, and press in place, as in Step 7 above.

The technique is a little different for covering a mat with Con-Tact sheeting. First, use a straight edge and utility knife to trim the edge of the sheeting to square it, so that at least two edges will square up with two edges of the mat. Unroll enough of the material to cover the mat with about an inch excess, and cut the sheeting with the straight edge and knife.

Peel the release paper from the back of the sheeting, and carefully lay the adhesive plastic onto the mat, starting at one corner. Align the two squared edges and, working toward the opposite corners, press the material to the mat, repositioning as necessary.

When the Con-Tact is pressed to the mat with no wrinkles or bubbles, lay the mat face down, and trim the excess along the mat edges with the straight edge and utility knife.

Make cuts in the center of the material,

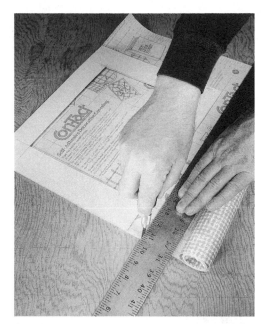

Cut the Con-Tact about an inch larger than the mat.

Square the cut edge of the Con-Tact with a straight edge and X-Acto knife.

Peel the release paper away and press the Con-Tact to the mat face.

Trim away excess.

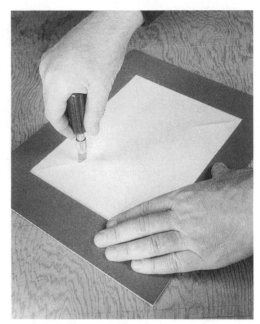

Make diagonal cuts from the corners of the mat windows.

Then cut away the center portion.

And press inner edges to the back of the mat.

as in Step 4 above, and pull the excess sheeting up and over the edges of the mat window and press them to the mat back.

With Con-Tact it is also possible to cover the face of a piece of mat board before doing any cutting. Then simply mark for and cut out the mat window as you normally would. The result is a covered mat with a bevel-cut window.

Covered mats can be used alone or in conjunction with other mats. Those covered with heavily textured materials or distinctly patterned Con-Tact usually look best with smooth-faced inner mats.

As I write, C.E.I., Inc., is introducing a product that promises to make mat covering even simpler and neater. CustoMat is a mat board faced with pressure-sensitive adhesive and release paper and is available in standard sizes from 8 x 10 to 25 x 30 inches. To use CustoMat, select any covering material you wish—fabric, wallpaper, vinyl, gift wrap, or whatever. Peel the release paper from the board, and press the covering material to it. Trim away any excess material, and cut out the mat window with a mat cutter. CustoMat's white core then provides an attractive beveled window edge.

6

Framing Materials and Tools

Although a great variety of materials are suitable and useful in building picture frames, the essential materials are few. Some are common and ordinary; others are specialized and peculiar to framing.

Likewise the tools of the trade. Some are so common as to be found in every workshop; others have been designed specifically for framing and won't likely be found outside the framer's shop. All of them, even the specialized tools, are easy to master.

Essential Materials

Picture-frame moldings come in an endless variety of widths, thicknesses, styles, and finishes. Although most are made of wood, metal moldings are also popular for a variety of applications, and acrylic or plastic moldings are finding favor in some quarters.

Both finished and unfinished moldings are available at frame shops and at many artist-supply outlets and department stores. Most home-improvement centers and wood specialty shops also stock wooden moldings.

In addition to moldings made specifically for picture framing, there are construction and decorative moldings that are useful to framers, and these are commonly stocked at lumber yards and home-improvement centers. There, also, you will find the hardwood and softwood boards and strips from which you can make your own moldings.

Unless there are certain cost or other advantages, or you're doing a lot of framing on a regular basis, there's no need to keep a large supply of frame molding on hand. Buying or making it as you need it allows you to pick the right molding for every job.

Of course, you will always have odds and ends of molding and other materials left from various projects, as I do. I also turn many of the wood scraps left from other building projects into usable molding. And when I find good buys on moldings or woods I can make moldings from, I lay in a supply.

The fasteners I use most often in framing are brads, and I keep them on hand at all times. I stock them in ¾, 1, 1¼, and 1½-inch lengths.

For assembling frames and attaching dust seals, among other jobs, you will need white glue or a good wood glue. I use Elmer's Professional Carpenter's Wood Glue. This is an aliphatic resin glue that bonds fast, dries clear, and cleans up with water. I watch for sales and buy this glue in quart sizes or larger and then refill an 8-ounce applicator bottle.

The screw styles used most often in framing projects are flathead, roundhead, and ovalhead.

Brads and finish nails are the most common fasteners used in framing. (Other styles are shown for comparison.)

Sanding is time-consuming and tedious, so I try to avoid it. But there is always some sanding to do, so I keep 120-grit (medium) and 220-grit (fine) garnet paper on hand to see to most of my sanding needs. For special purposes, I sometimes use coarser and finer abrasives.

An abrasive sponge is good for getting into areas where sandpaper won't reach. I keep a fresh one handy that has a medium abrasive on one side and fine on the other.

I buy stains as I need them, and I always have plenty of leftovers on hand. If you purchase stains only for frames, you will probably want to get them in half-pint cans, unless you're doing a good bit of framing. A little stain goes a long way. What's more, buying in small quantities allows you to experiment with a variety of stains without having to lay out much money.

There are a number of acrylic sanding

Abrasive sponge gets into frame contours.

sealers on the market, but I don't like any of them for frames. Such sealers require light sanding before the application of any final finish. As I said, I try to avoid this boring task whenever I can. Moreover, even simple frames can be difficult to sand.

I seal most of my wooden frames with shellac, which seals very well, dries quickly, and requires no sanding. I usually follow that with a spray coat of satin-sheen polyurethane. When I want a semigloss finish, I use Deft Clear Wood Finish, which is a lacquer that seals and finishes simultaneously. It dries quickly, and two coats are enough for most jobs.

Although I always have shellac on hand, I don't buy it in large amounts,

because it doesn't store as well as other products. I do watch for sales on aerosol polyurethane and Deft lacquer and stock up on them whenever I can.

Most of the glass I have on hand at any given time is for projects I'm working on or is left over from earlier jobs. I normally buy glass as I need it and often have it cut to size at the glass shop. If you plan to do any production work in standard sizes, you can save money buying standard-sized glass by the carton.

Kraft paper is the material to use for dust seals. It is commonly available at frame shops and department stores in 30-inch-wide rolls. This is the width I use most, so I usually have a roll or two in my shop. When I need something wider, I buy it at a local frame shop.

Picture hangers regularly go on sale at department stores, so I stock up then and keep a good supply on hand. I buy picture wire by the spool, and I stock screw eyes in several sizes.

Those are the materials required for the craft of frame building. There are a good many others that are useful, either generally or specifically, and I will cover them in later chapters. For now, though, these are the ones you need to know about.

Essential Tools

The most useful and essential tool in any framer's shop is a miter box. Used with a backsaw, this is the tool that enables you to make those frame-corner cuts at a 45-degree angle. With it, you can also make perfect right-angle cuts. A fully adjustable miter box allows you to cut any other angle in between.

Miter boxes come in a variety of sizes and designs and offer several options you should know about. The simplest are no more than three-sided wooden boxes with saw slits for making crosscuts and left and right miter cuts. This is the cheapest miter box available and is adequate for those who don't wish to invest much in framing tools or have only a little framing to do.

I would urge you, however, to buy the best miter box and backsaw you can afford. Examine what's available and determine which features are most important to you. In addition to wooden miter boxes, there are plastic models, metal ones, and those made of wood and metal.

Some boxes are adjustable, and the ones offering locking stops at the most-used settings are best. My first adjustable box could be set for cuts at any angle between zero (crosscut) and 45 degrees, but it had no positive stops. Consequently, it was not only common for me to be just slightly off on a cut, but the tool was also impossible to fine tune.

The Sears Craftsman box I use now and have for years is a large-capacity metal box, fully adjustable, with locking stops. Perhaps most important, the design offers me the ability to adjust and fine tune the tool for perfect cuts every time. When, from extensive use, the tool starts making inaccurate cuts, I spend a few minutes with a screwdriver and a square making the necessary adjustments, and soon it's operating like a new miter box.

This particular box will accept 9-inch-wide material for crosscutting and will miter cut material up to 6 inches wide,

Adjustable miter box with locking stops and 26-inch backsaw.

which means it will easily handle all frame moldings with room to spare.

I use a fine-tooth, 26-inch backsaw with this miter box, which enables me to make quick, clean cuts in all wooden moldings. The saw rides in ball-bearing guides for smooth operation.

About a year ago, I decided to replace my miter box with a costly model that was advertised to provide all the features I was used to, plus the ability to cut compound miters. This thing turned out to be a poorly designed, expensive piece of junk that would not make an accurate cut and could not be fine tuned. I returned it, and went back to using my old miter box, which I will probably use for years to come.

Author's most used measuring and marking tools: combination square, thin-lead pencil, yardstick, and steel tape rule.

The simplest miter boxes are available for under $10, and you can pay well over $100 for larger models with more features. Miter boxes comparable to the one I own are available for under $100, which includes the price of the backsaw.

If I were in the market for a good miter box today, I would probably buy one of the well-made Swedish-style boxes with a specially designed saw that features a thin blade for making fine cuts and narrow kerfs. The blades are also interchangeable with ones that cut metal, a feature worth considering. Such tools are carried by a number of mail-order suppliers for under $100.

Measuring and marking instruments are important. I know that some framers like a folding rule as an all-purpose tool, but I prefer a steel tape rule. I also frequently use a yardstick, and mine is aluminum, which is easy to keep clean.

I also use a combination square for a variety of jobs. Most often, I use it to check other tools—miter box, miter saw, table saw, and bench sander—for accuracy. It's useful for measuring right-angle and 45-degree accuracy. It also does various other jobs in the framer's shop, such as serving as a depth gauge for checking cuts when making moldings.

Forget about carpenter's pencils in the frame shop; their lead is too thick for the kind of accuracy you will require. For most of my work, I use a mechanical pencil with thin, soft lead.

Hammers are basic tools, which perhaps explains why they're so often taken for granted and misused. To many, a hammer is a hammer is a hammer, and any one will do. Consequently, we find every kind of hammer imaginable pressed into service in the making of picture frames. The cover of one framing book shows a ball-peen hammer lying next to some brads. Another has illustrations of frame making with a cross-peen hammer. Yet another shows a frame maker driving brads with a riveting hammer. None of these is a nail-driving hammer. Although the ball-peen is considered a general-duty hammer, it is a machinist's hammer and should not be used for driving nails, as its face does not have the proper toe-in for nail driving.

Although the bill-poster's or magnetic tack hammer is meant for driving tacks and small nails, it's not necessarily the best frame maker's hammer, even though it is widely used in this capacity. This is a light hammer, with a head weight of about 5 ounces, which is simply too light for many jobs. What's more, the head is narrow and tapered and will leave quite a dent in frame molding if you miss your mark. You can get into tight places with it, and for that reason some framers like the tack hammer for driving brads into the rear of frames to hold mounted artwork and backing in place. But there are better ways to do this, especially in hardwood frames, which I will cover later.

The ideal nail-driving hammer is the claw hammer, and you will find them with head weights ranging from 7 to 28 ounces. A 16-ounce claw hammer is usually recommended as an all-purpose woodworker's hammer, but you will probably want something lighter for building picture frames.

For years, I owned a 5-ounce tack hammer and 16-ounce claw hammer and usually reached for the latter when I was building picture frames. The tack hammer was always too light for my likes, and never felt quite right. While the claw hammer felt better, it was a bit unwieldy

Author's favorite 10-ounce claw hammer, center punch, and nail set.

at times. So I went hammer shopping one day and tried a number of small claw hammers. One that felt perfect was a 10-ounce model, and it has proved ideal for me. So my advice to you is to do what I did: try a bunch of them, and buy the one that feels best. It will probably turn out to be the best for you.

Not only has the 10-ounce claw hammer proved an excellent choice for driving brads into both softwood and hardwood frame moldings, but it also has enough heft to drive a nail set, which is one of two punches I use in frame building. This is the tool to use for countersinking brad heads and for making pilot holes for screw eyes in softwood moldings. When I occasionally need to make drill-starter holes, I use a center punch.

You'll need an electric drill to make pilot holes in hardwood frames.

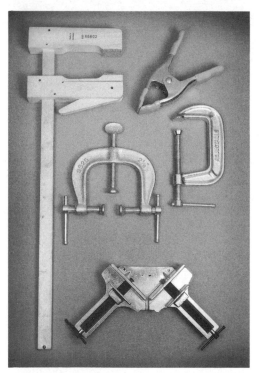

The most useful clamps for framing projects: bar clamp, spring clamp, edge clamp, C-clamp, and corner clamp.

You should have a pair of slip-joint pliers for general duty. With one jaw padded, this tool is also useful for driving brads and for mounting sawtooth hangers on frames.

Long-nose pliers are good for holding tiny brads in places where your fingers won't fit. Most also have wire cutters in their jaws, which you will need for cutting picture wire.

If you will be making frames with hardwood moldings, you will also need an electric drill and bits ranging in size from 1/16 to 1/8 inch for drilling pilot holes for brads and screw eyes.

You will need at least one pair of C-clamps for general duty. They are handy for a variety of chores and come in sizes from about 1 to 6 inches or more. Three-inchers are probably about the best size for most jobs.

Corner clamps are essential, and you will want a set of four. These clamps, also known as miter clamps or picture-frame clamps, hold strips of miter-cut or crosscut molding at right angles for gluing and nailing. You will find them indispensable, and if you do much framing, you might want to invest in a second set.

You will want to keep a damp sponge handy when you're doing any gluing. Damp sponges can damage whatever they rest on, so I installed a metal soap dish on the wall above my workbench, and that's where I keep mine.

Helpful but Optional Tools

So far, we have covered the tools that are essential to frame building. You *must* have those tools for making frames from manufactured moldings. There are other tools you might find useful in a variety of applications, and some that are essential for making your own moldings. Others simply make framing easier, faster, cheaper, or all three.

Some unfinished manufactured frame moldings and some you can make yourself require sanding. A pad sander will speed up that process. If you own a stationary or bench-type belt and disc sander, you might find that another useful tool, but there's no need to rush out and buy one. Some framers deliberately overcut their frame pieces by $1/16$ inch at each end, then sand them down to finished length on a sanding disc while holding the molding in place with a miter gauge. This makes for clean, precise joints.

If you plan to produce frames in quantity, you might want to invest in an electric brad nailer. There's nothing faster for driving brads, which come in various sizes and colors to match many frame

Ryobi quarter-sheet palm or pad sander.

Black & Decker quarter-sheet palm or pad sander.

Black & Decker half-sheet pad sander.

The Finishing Machine by Black & Decker is good for finish-sanding the miter-cut ends of frame molding.

Black & Decker 10-inch table saw.

The Black & Decker Electric Brad Nailer drives and countersinks a 1- or 1½-inch brad at the touch of the trigger.

finishes. The one I own drives and countersinks a 1-inch or 1½-inch brad at the touch of the trigger.

Some style of stationary or bench-type saw is a valuable asset in any workshop and is worth considering as a frame-making tool. There's an age-old argument over which is the best to buy – a table saw or radial-arm saw. If you already own one or the other, then that's the best one. If you're shopping for one, you must consider how you will use it.

I wrestled with this same problem several years ago and ultimately decided that my first stationary saw should be a table saw, because I was finishing a house we had just built and doing a lot of work with paneling and other sheet stock. I was also going to work on a book of plywood projects, so I needed the wide ripping ability offered by the table saw. I never regretted my decision, and the table saw turned out to be valuable on many other projects, including making frame moldings.

If I were making the same decision today, however, and wanted a stationary saw mainly for the frame-making craft, I think my vote would have to go for the radial-arm saw. Although this saw will not rip stock as wide as the table saw can handle, the materials moldings are made from aren't that wide. What's more, the

MITER GAUGE
LOCK KNOB

MITER GAUGE
HEAD

MITER GAUGE

BLADE GUARD

SAW BLADE

ANTIKICKBACK
PAWLS

SPREADER

RIP FENCE

TABLE INSERT

HOLES FOR
ATTACHING
FACING

TILT HANDWHEEL

ELEVATION HANDWHEEL

RESET BUTTON

ON-OFF SWITCH

RIP FENCE
LOCK KNOB

Sears Craftsman 10-inch table saw.

DeWalt 10-inch radial-arm saw.

Black & Decker 10-inch radial-arm saw.

radial-arm saw is a much better choice for crosscutting and, more important, miter cutting. With various attachments this saw can also do all sorts of decorative cuts. There are even heads available that convert a radial-arm saw into a shaper.

A shaper, itself, is another tool any serious frame maker might consider. It will allow you to turn strips of wood into frame molding about as fast as you can feed them into the machine. Shapers are expensive, though, and you have to be planning to build a lot of frames or make a bunch of molding to justify the purchase.

A good interim tool, though, is a router, which, when attached to a router table, becomes a light-duty shaper. Although few models will hold up to the rigors of high-volume production work, a good-quality router will see to the needs of most frame makers, even professionals. You can put a router and router table in your shop for considerably less than what a shaper would cost you, and router bits are much cheaper than shaper cutters.

Mine is a Swiss-made Elu plunge router with a variable-speed, ramp-start motor that has easily handled every piece of wood I've shoved through it. I keep it attached to an Elu table, which is the Cadillac of router tables. I have the whole outfit affixed to a plywood base that quickly clamps to the top of my Workmate. Black & Decker has purchased the Swiss company that makes Elu woodworking tools, so they should be available throughout the United States and from mail-order tool suppliers.

One optional tool so useful that I consider it essential in my own shop is the Black & Decker Workmate, which the manufacturer bills as a portable work center and vise. When this item was first introduced, I lived in an apartment and decided this would be an ideal accessory on many jobs, especially since it could be folded for storage. Since then, I have

The Swiss-made Elu plunge router by Black & Decker.

The Cadillac of router tables is the Swiss-made Elu. Matched with the Elu electronic plunge router, it's the perfect combination for making frame moldings.

Black & Decker Workmate.

DUST SPOUT
UPPER PIVOT BOLT
LOCK PIN
FENCE
TABLE TOP
TRIGGER SWITCH
UPPER GUARD
MITER SCALE
MITER CLAMP KNOB
MITER ARM
MITER LATCH

LOWER GUARD WING SCREW
BLADE
MOTOR
LOWER GUARD
KERF
MITER POINTER

Black & Decker 9-inch power miter saw.

lived in two different houses, each with a large shop and big workbench, but I still use my Workmate on nearly every job. In fact, I own two of them and wonder how I ever got by without them.

I use the Workmate by itself or in conjunction with other tools and accessories. My miter box, for example, is mounted to a plywood base made to fit the Workmate jaws. Whenever I need it, I clamp the base into the jaws of the Workmate and in seconds it's ready to use. In this way, my miter box is as stable as if it were mounted permanently to a bench, but it can be moved anywhere and can handle stock of any length because of this portability.

A power miter saw is another tool that can make short work of any framing job. It's probably not a tool you would want to consider if you already own or are planning to buy a radial-arm saw, because the latter will do everything the former will do and more. But a power miter saw will crosscut and miter cut frame molding every bit as well as a radial-arm saw and better than a table saw, as it will handle long stock with ease. What's more, power miter saws are considerably cheaper than table or radial-arm saws.

If you own or plan to own any of the power saws I've discussed, you should know that not all blades are the same. Some are meant for fast cutting where smoothness of the cut is of little or no consequence. Others are designed for slower, finer cutting. There are blades specifically for ripping, others for cross-cutting, and combination blades that perform marginally at either task.

There are so many different makes and designs of blades available now that trying to find the right one or ones can be mind-boggling. Several years ago, I was

Center piece of oak plywood was cut with a top-brand carbide-tipped saw blade (notice the splintered edge). Left and right pieces show entry and exit surfaces cut with a Matsushita 10-inch 80-tooth blade. There is no better power-saw blade for cutting frame molding.

introduced to a then-new line of blades made by the Japanese, who are sticklers for clean, splinter-free cuts and tight joints. I was so impressed with the performance and price of Matsushita blades that I began gradually replacing all my blades with these far superior blades.

Matsushita offers blades ranging in size from 5½ to 14 inches to fit any saw requiring a circular blade, and prices range from about $20 to just under $100.

The extra-thin blade plates and the way the teeth are beveled and ground are what make these blades perform the way they do. I haven't found any blades that cut as smoothly and cleanly as these, and I recommend you try one for yourself. I have one on my 7¼-inch circular saw, another on my 9-inch miter saw, and two for my 10-inch table saw.

7

Framing with Commercial Frames and Moldings

Some very competent framers have never built a frame in their lives. Others build frames, but for one reason or another use only commercially made moldings. With either approach, a person can still save money and do a good job of protecting, preserving, and displaying framable items.

Among the reasons for using ready-made frames is a lack of frame-making tools. Although frame making requires relatively few tools, if you're just starting out you needn't wait until you have a fully equipped framing shop to get to work. In fact, it's probably best to start by buying matting and mounting tools and learning how to use them first; then buy ready-made frames until the proper framing tools are on hand.

Similarly, if you have no interest in making your own moldings or are simply waiting until you can buy the necessary tools, you can easily begin making frames with commercial moldings and a minimal tool investment. Most of us probably start out making frames with commercial frame moldings, and even after we own the tools for making our own moldings, we continue to use ready-made frames and store-bought moldings whenever it makes sense.

Ready-made frames are commonly available in standard sizes – from 4 x 5 to 24 x 36 inches – at department stores, discount stores, drugstores, some lumber yards and home-improvement centers, artist-supply shops, photography-supply stores, and frame shops. Some frame shops even stock frames in odd sizes – such as 5 x 9, 9 x 13, and 10 x 14 inches – and in some fractional sizes.

Frames often go on sale at various outlets, sometimes even below cost. Keep an eye out for such sales, and stock up on the sizes you use most.

Likewise with commercially made moldings. Recently, a lumber yard where I deal began phasing out most of the picture-frame moldings in stock and marked them down to about a third of their original prices. It doesn't take a rocket scientist to figure out what to do in such a situation; I bought nearly every piece of molding they had. One of my favorite commercial moldings had been costing me $8.80 for an 8-foot strip, or $1.10 a foot. The close-out price was $3.20 for each 8-footer, or 40¢ a foot.

Nielsen and Intercraft metal section frames.

Framing with Metal and Acrylic

Metal section frames, usually made of aluminum, are popular for framing photographs, posters, and all sorts of artwork. Their lean, clean lines lend them to numerous applications and assure users that they will never overwhelm the works they frame. They come in all standard sizes, ready made or in kit form, or can be cut to any desired size.

These frames offer excellent protection to the works they contain, yet they are easily dismantled and reassembled with no more than a screwdriver. (Some don't even require that.) Consequently, these frames are often favored by photographers and artists who exhibit their works at museums and galleries and must frequently change their show items about. For similar reasons, they're popular in the home wherever changeability is desired.

The most readily identifiable metal frames are those with highly polished or brushed metallic finishes—namely, silver, brass, and bronze. But anodized

frames are now available in dozens of colors and shades. In fact, an attractive way to use the colored metal frames is to match frame color to inner-mat color in a multiple matting.

These frames also now come in a number of different depths and shapes, from shallow to deep, from flat to curved. Hanging hardware is available in several configurations, from snap-in eyes for use with picture wire, to sawtooth hangers that require no wire.

Intercraft offers metal-section frames in standard sizes that are available through many retail outlets. This is an extremely easy frame to use, as it requires no tools to install photographs or artworks. Each frame is equipped with four spring clips that span the corners and hold mats, work, and backing securely in place against the glass. Two hanger clips are also provided, one on a long section and one on a short section, for vertical or horizontal use. These clips are also removable.

Most typical of the metal and acrylic

Intercraft frame comes with four spring clips and two hanger clips that install by hand.

section frames are those made by Nielsen and distributed mainly through frame shops and mail-order suppliers. The frames come assembled or in kit form, or cut to any length.

Molding sections are held together at the corners with two-part corner braces with integral setscrews. The setscrews are tightened to hold the sections together and loosened to dismantle the frame or change the contents. Contents are held in place with spring-tension clips.

To install artwork in and assemble one of these metal-section or similar acrylic frames, just follow these easy steps.

Step 1. Insert a two-part corner brace into one end of one of the mitered frame sections and the other end of the brace into the adjacent frame section. Tighten the setscrews until the two pieces are secure. Attach another frame section the same way to the opposite end of the section you started with.

Step 2. Carefully slide the clean glass, mounted photograph or artwork, and

Assembling the Nielsen frame, Step 1.

Assembling the Nielsen frame, Step 3.

Assembling the Nielsen frame, Step 4.

You can, of course, cut your own metal moldings to fit your needs, if you have the right tools. For metal, you will need a metal-cutting blade for a power-miter saw or one of the special backsaws with interchangeable blades for wood and metal. But there's really little need to invest in such equipment. You can usually get these frames cut to size at frame shops, and at many shops the charge is nominal or nothing at all.

Framing with Commercial Wood Moldings

You will find commercially made wood moldings in dozens of sizes and shapes at lumber yards, home-improvement centers, some discount and department stores, and frame shops. They come

backing into the partially assembled frame, and attach the remaining two corner braces and frame section with the setscrews.

Step 3. With the frame face down, position two spring-tension clamps on the backing near each frame section—eight in all. Press each clamp down with your thumb, and slide it under the rear lip of the frame.

Step 4. Attach snap-in or screw-type eyes and picture wire, or snap a sawtooth hanger into the rear of the top frame section, and your frame is ready for hanging.

Profiles of a few of the many commercial wood frame moldings available.

finished or unfinished; the latter is always cheaper and often the better choice.

Prices vary widely from source to source, sometimes for no apparent reason. So it's wise to shop around. In fact, it's a good idea to locate all the molding sources in your immediate vicinity and spend some time comparison shopping.

Usually, the larger and more intricate the molding, the more expensive it will be. Prices for unfinished moldings generally range from about 50¢ to $1.50 or so a lineal foot. The simplest finished moldings usually run at least $1 a lineal foot, and prices increase dramatically with the size and complexity of the molding. At some shops, it's not uncommon to find finished moldings costing $4 to $6 or more per foot, which is one of the best reasons I can think of for making and finishing your own.

Most unfinished and many finished moldings are sold in 6- and 8-foot lengths and sometimes 4-foot strips. If you have reason to buy any of the most expensive finished moldings, though, insist on buying it by the foot to avoid expensive leftovers.

Making frames from any of these moldings is easy, but there are a few tips and tricks that will help make it even easier for you. The steps that follow demonstrate how to cut frame sections with mitered ends and how to join these sections to make a frame. If you have never done any framing, this is the most important method you will learn, because these are the same techniques you will use to make all miter-joined wood frames and liners. What's more, you can apply what you know about picture framing to many other projects.

The size of the work to be framed determines the inside dimensions of the frame, and molding width determines outside dimensions. Because of humidity and temperature fluctuations, framed works expand and contract. To keep them from buckling, allow extra room inside your frames by making them ⅛ inch larger than what you're framing. For example, if your mats, mount board, and glass are 11 x 14 inches, the inside dimensions of your frame should be 11⅛ x 14⅛ inches. That means your molding should have a rabbet at least ⅜ inch deep (or a lip ⅜ inch wide).

When you buy molding, you will need more than might be apparent at first. You will be cutting miters at each end of each frame section, which means there will be some waste. The general rule is to take the width of the molding and multiply it by two for each frame section, or by eight for any conventional four-sided frame, and add that to the section lengths. The saw kerf doesn't amount to much—about ⅛ inch with most blades—but that too must be considered. So for the eight cuts necessary, you'll need to add another inch.

To frame your 11 x 14-inch work with a 2-inch-wide frame molding, then, you would need two sections at 11⅛ inches and two at 14⅛ inches, or 50½ inches. To that, you will add eight times the molding width, then tack on an inch for the saw kerfs, for a total of 67½ inches. It's smart to add a little for good measure, so you might as well buy a 6-foot strip.

The more expensive the molding, the more careful you have to be about these measurements. If you do much framing at all, you'll find eventually that you will keep certain favorite moldings on hand all the time, and if you make your own moldings, you will accumulate plenty of stock, as well as the raw materials for making more as you need it.

Once you've found the right molding for your picture and have bought as much as you will need, it's time to make the frame. For purposes of illustration, we'll use the 11 x 14-inch dimensions we've been discussing, but the same techniques apply to any size frame. Here's how it all goes together.

Step 1. Lay the frame molding face up or face down in your miter box with the rabbeted (lipped) edge toward you. Clamp the molding to the miter-box table or fence with a pair of cushioned spring clamps. Then cut one end off the molding at a 45-degree angle.

Step 2. Align one end of a yardstick with the inside edge of the miter cut, along the rabbet, and mark for the next cut at 14⅛ inches, and make that cut at a 45-degree angle opposite the first cut, to form one frame section.

Step 3. Cut the end off the molding strip as you did to begin with in Step 1. Now lay the strip back to back with the frame section you cut in Step 2, and align the mitered ends. Using the frame section as a guide, mark the molding strip for another cut, and cut a second section to 14⅛ inches.

Step 4. Following the same procedures as in Steps 1, 2, and 3, cut two more frame

Building a wood frame, Step 2.

Building a wood frame, Step 3.

Building a wood frame, Step 5.

Building a wood frame, Step 7.

Building a wood frame, Step 6.

sections to 11⅛ inches each. Lightly sand any rough edges at the miter cuts, and you're ready to assemble the frame.

Step 5. Apply a thin but even coat of wood glue or white glue to one end of a long frame section, and clamp a short section to it with a corner clamp.

Step 6. Apply glue to the other end of the long strip, and clamp the other short strip to it. Then glue and clamp the remaining long strip to the ends of the short strips.

Step 7. At one corner of the frame, drive a small brad through a long section into the end of a short section. Nail the remaining corners identically, countersink the brads with a nail set, and let the frame stand with clamps in place for an hour or overnight.

In large moldings, drive two brads at each corner – one near the rear edge, and the next from the opposite direction and near the front edge.

Finished frame.

and other works that are customarily framed without glass and mats. Liners serve much the same visual purpose as a mat, separating the work from its frame. Filets serve a similar but subtler purpose.

You will find liner moldings stocked with frame moldings at most outlets. You can also make your own. You can paint or texture your own liners, but if you want to use a covered one, you would probably do best to buy finished liner molding at a frame shop.

Cut and assemble liners the same way as frames. When using a liner, cut it ⅛ inch larger than the work you're framing, but then make the frame only ¹/₁₆ inch larger.

Build the liner first; then make the frame to fit the liner. To install the liner, lay the frame face down and the liner inside it. Then toenail brads through the liner into the back of the frame molding. With most frames, two brads per section should suffice.

That's all there is to cutting and assembling a wood frame. When the glue has set, the frame is ready for finishing. If you're using finished molding, you're ready to frame your picture.

Making and Installing Liners and Filets

A liner is a narrow strip-frame that fits inside a larger frame, and a filet is narrower yet. Liners are usually painted, covered, or textured, and filets are often gilded or painted silver or gold. Some filets are even made of metal and are left natural.

Both liners and filets are used primarily with oil paintings, acrylics, batiks,

Fabric-covered liner separates the image from the frame, much the way a mat does.

Gold-colored filet provides a subtle, narrow border for this large oil painting in a massive frame.

If you want to use a filet and make it yourself, cut it ⅛ inch larger than the artwork. Then make the liner ¹/₁₆ inch larger than the filet and the frame ¹/₁₆ inch larger than the liner.

Ten Tips for Building Better Wood Frames

1. When cutting molding with a miter box and backsaw, move the saw in smooth, even strokes, being careful to keep the blade teeth running parallel to the miter-box table. A rocking saw motion results in uneven miters.

2. Although it's possible to measure and mark frame sections individually, it's best to use one section to mark the cut

for its opposite section. A measurement that's only slightly off will create gaps in the miter joints, but if opposite pieces are identical—even if the first one cut was slightly over or under the desired length—the joints will be tight.

3. Don't horse the backsaw when cutting molding. Use only enough pressure to cut through the molding in a reasonable time. Usually the weight of the saw provides sufficient pressure. If it takes too long to cut most moldings, your saw probably needs sharpening.

4. Use a thin-lead pencil when marking moldings for cutting. Thick lead, such as in a carpenter's pencil, can cause your cut to be as much as ¹/₁₆ inch off.

5. Saw teeth are staggered, left and right of the blade. Always align the teeth slanting toward the pencil mark along the edge of the mark and you won't have problems with inaccurate cuts.

6. When assembling wood frames, dry clamp them before gluing and nailing. That is, carefully align the pieces and clamp them together with corner clamps. Then loosen one screw in one clamp, remove the piece, apply the glue, and reclamp it. This way, the clamps serve as guides to ensure accurate clamping.

7. Don't overnail; use only as many brads as necessary. In some small moldings, one brad in each corner is sufficient. In some thin liner or filet moldings, there's no room for brads. So just glue and clamp. All the brads do anyway is hold the frame pieces together as the glue cures. So if you wish, you needn't use brads at all. If you have only one

frame to build and you have four corner clamps, just glue and clamp, and don't worry about joints coming loose. Glue dries stronger than wood.

8. Wipe seeping glue away from frame joints immediately and completely. Any glue left on the face of an unfinished frame will show up when the frame is stained, as the glue will not take the stain.

9. When assembling frames with hardwood moldings, you should mark the corners where the brads will go, punch drill-starter holes with a small center punch, and drill pilot holes slightly smaller in diameter than the brads. This will make the brads much easier to drive and will prevent the wood from splitting.

10. When using small brads with narrow moldings, use long-nose pliers to hold the brads if you can't grip them adequately with your fingers. You can also wedge a brad between the teeth of a comb and hold the comb instead of the brad.

8

Making Frame Moldings

As I said in the introduction to the last chapter, a good many competent framers, for one reason or another, use only commercially made moldings for making frames. I certainly have no quarrel with them, and in fact recommend the use of commercial moldings to anyone new to picture framing and their continued use when they meet your needs or can be had at the right price. But for several reasons, I strongly urge all readers to seriously consider making their own frame moldings.

First, making moldings is a great learning experience. Once you find the various materials at your disposal and begin turning them into useful moldings, you will gain new insights into the craft. Ideas will breed more ideas. And you will rarely, if ever, face a framing problem you can't solve.

You will also save tremendously in many ways. You will discover that some of the cheapest wood products can be turned into the finest picture frames. By staying alert for good buys on raw materials, you will be able to lay in supplies when prices are their lowest.

If you're a woodworker, you will be able to use many of the scraps from other projects to make picture-frame moldings. With these random lengths of molding on hand, you can put a frame together when you have an extra twenty or thirty minutes you might otherwise waste.

Some moldings are simply made of strips of material glued together to form the necessary rabbet or lip characteristic of all picture-frame moldings. Others require power tools. If you are already a woodworker, there's a good chance you currently own or plan to buy the necessary tools. So making frame molding is just one more use you can put them to.

Best Woods for Framing

Many woods are good for making frame moldings. Among the most popular softwoods are pine, fir, hemlock, cedar, and redwood. Favorite hardwoods include oak, walnut, birch, cherry, mahogany, and maple. No doubt you will soon begin to favor certain woods for their beauty, suitability, availability, and cost. Depending on where you live, you will probably find other species that are locally popular, such as ash, yew, hickory, myrtle, and alder, to mention only a few.

So-called exotic woods from all over the world are usually only available at wood specialty shops. Although most are too expensive for use in frame making, you might want to experiment with some from time to time or buy small quantities that you can use for inlays to decorate moldings made of cheaper domestic woods.

You will find an amazing variety of colors, patterns, and degrees of hardness in the woods of the world. Between the extremes of white and black are woods that are blood red, purple, yellow, green, blue, and every shade of brown imaginable. Some are coarsely grained and heavily textured; others are smooth, almost waxy, and as finely grained as marble. There are woods that are extremely light and so soft they can be gouged with a thumbnail, others so dense, heavy, and hard as to seem petrified.

You really don't have to possess a wealth of knowledge about woods to buy them wisely and make frame moldings from them. If you're new to woodworking, you should learn a bit about sizes and grades and how the mills treat the wood before it reaches your retail outlet. The salesperson at your local lumber yard or home-improvement center should be able to answer all your questions and lead you to the right products. So don't be afraid to ask. Most of these folks are experts, and there's nothing experts like more than showing off their expertise.

Even when you have gained some knowledge of woods and their characteristics, there is still no substitute for close physical examination of the wood products you are considering buying. Also, nosing around a lumber yard will often lead you to other materials and good buys. So spend some time at local lumber yards and home-improvement centers just prospecting. Keep a notebook handy to jot down dimensions, prices, and other pertinent information.

Lumber comes in such well-known sizes as 1 x 2, 1 x 6, 1 x 10, 2 x 2, and 2 x 4, to mention a few. These are *nominal* rather than actual sizes, and most of the lumber you use will be nominal 1-inch and 2-inch stock. Although 1-inch and 2-inch lumber start out at those thicknesses, they're reduced to ¾-inch and 1½-inch thicknesses, respectively, during the drying process and when their broad surfaces are milled. As the remaining two sides are finished, they are similarly reduced, so a 1 x 2 is actually ¾ x 1½ inches. A 1 x 3 is 2½ inches wide; a 1 x 4 is 3½ inches; a 2 x 2 is 1½ inches by 1½ inches. In other words, from rough board to finished product, 1-inch-thick stock is reduced by ¼ inch,

2-inch stock by ¾ inch. Widths are re-duced by ½ inch through 7 inches (actually 6½ inches). Beyond that, they are reduced by ¾ inch. So a 1 x 8 is 7¼ inches wide; a 1 x 10 is 9¼ inches wide; and a 1 x 12 is actually 11¼ inches wide.

Hardwoods are sometimes sold the same way, or might be labeled according to actual widths and thicknesses expressed in quarters. The designation ⁴/₄ is expressed as "four quarters," and ⁸/₄ is "eight quarters." These are 1-inch and 2-inch thicknesses, respectively. This is the language generally used in the mills, and it often finds its way into retail outlets as well.

Most lumber and moldings are sold in lengths of 6, 8, 10, 12, 14, and 20 feet, with 8-footers the most common. Hardwoods are sometimes available in standard lengths and are also available in a variety of random lengths.

I have read a number of books on lumber, wood products, and woodworking and have been told by the authors that our system of lumber grading is meant to help us in our selection of woods for various purposes. It is not meant to confuse us—they keep telling me. But grading and grading language might differ according to manufacturing association designations or U.S. Department of Commerce standards. There are certainly differences among the various wood products and how they are graded, among the regions of the country, and even from one mill to another or one inspector to another. What's more, when a load of wood arrives at a retail outlet, the owner's opinion of it might differ from how the grader saw it. It's not easy to sort all this out, but I will try.

First, grades might be expressed numerically, alphabetically, or literally. Nu-merical gradings, best to poorest, are 1 to 4. Alphabetically, they are A to D, and literally they go from clear to common.

Clear lumber is the most nearly flaw-less and most expensive. *Select* grades have more and larger knots than clear lumber, but often possess more character as a result of the knots and attractive grain and are therefore often better for natural finishes. What's more, they're cheaper. *Common* is the cheapest. Depending on its numerical grading, it might range from lumber with numerous small knots and other minor blemishes to wood that is full of loose knots, knotholes, and pitch pockets.

Construction, standard, utility, and *economy* are all grades of common lumber and coincide with No. 1, No. 2, No. 3, and No. 4 grades. No doubt, you will come across other designations, such as *stud grade, shop grade,* and more other variations than you care to know, such as the vague designation *standard-and-better*. If it's something you're not familiar with, ask for a translation. And always examine the product closely before you buy.

Another term you'll come across is *K.D.,* which stands for kiln dried and is the way most lumber is dried these days. Some is air dried, but this is a more time-consuming, less efficient process. What's more important to know is that some lumber is sold "green," which means it has not been dried.

Here's one rule in picture framing you should never break: buy only dried, preferably kiln-dried, wood for making frames. Green or wet wood shrinks as it dries and might also warp, crack, and split. Such woods can also be dangerous to work with, as they can bind up power saws and cause kickback.

Green lumber is cheaper than dried

lumber, but the savings aren't worth the potential problems and hazards. Furthermore, you're going to be able to make frame moldings so cheaply from kiln-dried stock that you won't need wood that's any cheaper.

The two woods I use more than any others for making frame moldings are oak and pine. Oak is my favorite hardwood, not only because of its inherent beauty, but also because it is easy to work with. In fact, in many ways it's like a softwood. It is easy to rip, drill, rout, and sand. Yet it also exhibits the strength and durability of hardwood. I also like walnut and mahogany for similar reasons.

The pine I use is kiln-dried No. 4 common that I buy in fairly large batches. What I look for are the boards that others don't want – those with the character that others view as flaws. Most of what I buy is 1 x 4 stock, although I sometimes find wider boards that fit my needs. Then I rip most of this stock into 1 x 2s that I sort and store for later use.

In any batch of pine, I will end up with greatly varied material for moldings. Strips of clear or nearly clear wood I keep mainly for making router moldings. Some of the pine will be deeply colored brown or even red, and I sort those for striking frames that will be finished naturally. But the bulk of it – the so-called blue pine, the material honeycombed with borer holes, and the pieces full of knots and pitch pockets – I use for making rustic frames in various sizes and configurations. And all these pine 1 x 2s that I end up making so much molding from costs me a mere nickel a foot.

And that's not a sale price. I pay 10¢ a foot for each pine 1 x 4 that I turn into two 1 x 2s at 5¢ a foot. Believe it or not, I

have made frame molding for half that.

Several years ago, the folks at a local lumber yard had a big stack of 1 x 12 incense cedar they wanted to get rid of to make room for other products that would move faster. They put it on sale for 15¢ a foot, and I hauled off a pickup-truck load. I used much of it for shelving and various building projects, and I still have a good bit on hand. Recently, I started ripping 1 x 2s from it and making picture-frame molding. I can get six 1 x 2s from each board, which means the cedar I'm making frame molding with cost me 2½¢ a foot.

Using Construction Moldings

The most abundant and widely available moldings are construction moldings, used mainly in house building but also in woodworking projects. It's usually construction moldings that give the finishing touch to carpentry. And some of these are also useful to the frame builder for making frame moldings.

For several reasons, I won't attempt to cover all the construction moldings or even all the ones suitable for picture framing. First, there are just too many to deal with. More important, though, is that many of them differ considerably from East to West, so I will cover only some of those that are common throughout the country.

In the East, most construction moldings are made of clear pine. In the West, they are generally clear hemlock or white fir. There are hardwood construction moldings available – mainly oak, mahogany, and birch – but they are expensive. Nevertheless, some are ideal for certain framing jobs.

A major difference between eastern

Common stock and construction moldings used in making frames: *(left)* **1 x 4, 1 x 3, 1 x 2, ¾-square, parting bead, and two sizes of lattice;** *(center)* **two sizes of bullnose stop, base shoe, ogee stop, shingle molding, and drip cap;** *(right)* **ceiling cove, two sizes of cove molding, and three sizes of outside corner molding.**

and western construction moldings is style. The older styles of the East are more ornamental and decorative, exhibiting their colonial heritage. In the West, styles are simpler and relatively unadorned. Of course, there is some crossover and some moldings that are used universally.

The simplest of all are not really moldings at all, but strips of various configurations smaller than 1 x 2; they are usually found stocked with the moldings. Parting bead, ¾-square, and lattice are three that are useful in framing.

Parting bead is no more than a strip of wood with dimensions of ½ by ¾ inch. Similar is the ¾-square, which, as the nomenclature suggests, is a strip of wood

with dimensions of ¾ x ¾ inch. Both parting bead and ¾-square can be turned into simple, narrow frame moldings by merely routing a rabbet along one edge with a straight router bit. Such moldings are useful for framing certificates and other items that are often displayed in simple, narrow frame moldings.

Parting bead and ¾-square are also used in conjunction with other moldings and with common stock to create frame moldings. Often the different strips are simply glued together to form frame molding.

Lattice is ¼-inch-thick stock that comes in widths of 1, $1^{1}/_{8}$, $1^{5}/_{16}$, and $1^{5}/_{8}$ inches and can be ripped to narrower widths to suit your purposes. Lattice can be used in various glued moldings and to make simple slat-style frames. It is also good for making floater frames for photographs.

Base shoe is a ½ x ¾-inch molding with one corner rounded over. It can be turned into an attractive certificate-frame molding by simply routing a rabbet along one edge. It is useful in glued moldings and functions well as a liner molding.

Bullnose stop is similar to lattice, but is larger and has one corner slightly rounded over. It's 7/16 inch thick and comes in widths from ¾ to 1⅝ inches. Use this molding with other moldings and common stock, or use it by itself for slat and floater frames that are a bit more decorative than those made with lattice.

The smallest ogee stop is 3/8 x 3/4 inch. Other sizes are 7/16 inch thick and range in width from 1⅛ to 1⅝ inches. With an ogee molded along one edge, this molding is good for use with other moldings and for making liners.

Shingle molding is 5/8 inch thick and 1½ inches wide. It is a decorative molding and one of the most useful for the picture framer. It can be used with other material in the construction of complex frames. You can also slap together a good-looking molding by ripping a 1 x 2 or other inch-thick stock to a 1¼-inch width, then gluing that to a strip of shingle molding. Rout a rabbet into the thick end of shingle molding, and it can be used by itself as a frame molding.

Drip cap is another useful molding that comes in several sizes; 3/4 x 15/8 inches is the most common. This one, too, works with other moldings and common stock, or can be used by itself as a deep or shallow molding, depending on how the rabbet is routed into it.

Cove moldings come in a variety of configurations and sizes. The most useful are ½ x ½-inch cove, ¾ x ¾-inch cove, and 5/8-inch-thick ceiling cove that's 1⅝ inches wide. The smaller cove moldings make attractive liners and are useful for decorating larger frames. Both cove and ceiling cove work well in glued moldings and in some shadow-box frames.

Outside corner molding comes in three sizes: ¾ x ¾, 1 x 1, and 1¼ x 1¼ inches. It's among the most useful of the construction moldings in making a variety of frames and related items, such as bulletin boards, pegboard organizers, and calendar frames.

One of the easiest construction moldings to convert to frame molding is brick molding. This is large molding, 1⁵/16 inches thick and 2 inches wide. To make

With a router or table saw you can turn brick molding into frame molding.

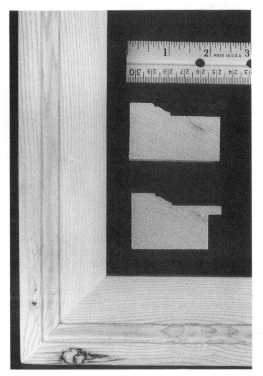

Brick-molding frame.

be used with construction moldings. You can also tilt the saw table and fully bevel one of the narrow edges of 1 x 2 stock. Then rip other 1 x 2 strips (or any nominal inch-thick stock) to strips 1¼ inches wide. Glue these to the beveled strips with the beveled edge creating the lip of the rabbet. This simple molding can be used alone or in conjunction with other material. Attach corner molding to the outside edge for an attractive frame molding.

Far more useful than the bandsaw, though, are radial-arm and table saws, with the latter shaking out a little ahead for its ease of setup for various ripping jobs. The following moldings can be made with either a radial-arm or table saw, although directions are for the table saw. If you already own a radial-arm saw, you know how to use it and will have no trouble making these moldings.

an attractive frame molding, you need only rout a rabbet into its narrowest edge.

There's no substitute for experience, so as I have recommended before, visit your local lumber yards and home-improvement centers, and spend some time in their molding departments. Find out what is available in your locale, and imagine how these moldings might be used to make frames. Try various combinations to find out what works.

Saw Moldings

If you own a bandsaw and no other stationary or bench-type power saw, you can use it to make a few simple frame moldings. Of course, you can rip stock to

Box Molding

After ripping your favorite inch-thick wood into 1 x 2s, remove the blade guard to perform the following steps. Exercise extreme caution when operating the saw without the blade guard. Follow all the manufacturer's safety precautions, and be sure to use push blocks to move material along the fence and over the blade.

Step 1. Set the table-saw fence ¼ inch from the *far* teeth of the blade, and set the blade for a 1¼-inch depth.

Step 2. Stand a 1 x 2 on its narrow edge on the saw table, with a broad side against the fence. Then use push blocks to run it over the blade.

You can rip 1 x 2 from wider stock with a table saw.

Box molding, Step 2.

Step 3. Reset the fence ¼ inch from the *near* teeth of the blade, and reset the blade for a ¼-inch depth.

Step 4. Lay the 1 x 2 on a broad side, with the ungrooved narrow edge against the fence, and use push blocks to run it over the blade.

Step 5. Lightly sand the strip to remove any slivers or smooth out any rough spots, and your box molding is ready for framing.

Flat Molding

The flat molding is just as simple as the box molding, except that it is rabbeted on

Box molding, Step 4.

Box-molding frame.

a narrow edge instead of a broad edge to make a shallow molding. Again, exercise extreme caution with the saw, follow the manufacturer's safety precautions, and use push blocks to move the material.

Step 1. Set the table-saw fence ¼ inch from the blade's *near* teeth, and set the blade for a ¼-inch depth.

Step 2. Stand a 1 x 2 on its narrow edge on the saw table, with a broad side against the fence. Then use push blocks to run it over the blade.

Step 3. Reset the fence ¼ inch from the *far* teeth of the blade, and reset the blade for a ½-inch depth.

Step 4. Lay the 1 x 2 broad side down on the saw table, with the grooved edge

Flat molding, Step 2.

Flat molding, Step 4.

against the fence, and use push blocks to run it over the blade.

Step 5. Sand the strip, as required, to smooth any rough edges and remove slivers, and your flat molding is ready for use.

Grooved Molding

To make a single-grooved molding, start with 1 x 2 stock and set up the table saw as in Step 1 of the flat-molding directions. But before making the first cut for the rabbet, run the face side of the 1 x 2 over the blade to cut a groove ⅛ inch wide and ¼ inch deep. Now turn the 1 x 2 over, with the face surface up, and follow Steps 2 through 5 to complete the molding.

To make a double-grooved molding, set

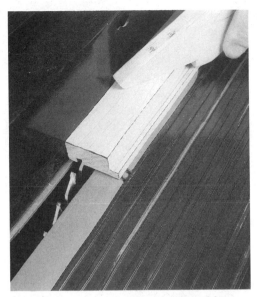

Cutting a groove in molding with a table saw.

Flat-molding frame.

Grooved-molding frame.

the saw up the same way as above. Make one pass to cut the first groove ¼ inch from one edge. Then turn the 1 x 2 so the opposite narrow edge is against the fence, and with the face down on the table, run the piece through again, creating a second groove ¼ inch from the other edge. Now turn the 1 x 2 over, and complete the molding, as above.

You can cut grooves wider than ⅛ inch by simply moving the fence to different distances from the blade and passing the 1 x 2 over the blade to remove more material. Of course, you can also adjust the blade to cut shallower grooves. I don't recommend cutting any deeper than ¼ inch, though, for structural reasons.

Beveled Molding

You can tilt your saw table to bevel the outside edge of either box or flat molding. You can also bevel the inside edges if you wish. You might want to combine techniques by putting a slight bevel on one or both face edges of the flat molding after you have grooved the face.

Router Moldings

If I had to decide on which power tool to recommend first — a table saw or a router and router table — I would be hard pressed to make up my mind. I would hate to be without my table saw; I use it for most of my moldings. But it's possible to make a great assortment of moldings with a router and router table, and the combination is cheaper than a table-saw setup.

You need some way to rip boards into 1 x 2s, which are the most useful strips for making frames. But you can also buy 1 x 2s, in which case you could get by without a power saw, or you could get wider stock ripped at the yard or by a friend who owns a table or radial-arm saw.

I guess you're the only one who can decide. Meanwhile, I'll tell you about what you can accomplish with a router set up for making picture-frame moldings.

If you already own a router, you will find router tables from several manufacturers available through tool and hardware outlets, discount stores, and mail-order suppliers. Simply make sure that the table you are buying will fit your router.

If you plan to buy a router specifically for making frame moldings, then look for a router and table combination. Sears offers routers and tables, as do Black & Decker and several other manufacturers. Black & Decker also offers the Elu line of woodworking tools, which includes a superb plunge router and perhaps the finest router table on the market.

Although you can use various sizes of stock to make frame moldings with your router, you will probably find the 1 x 2 the most useful size. If you need a smaller or narrower molding, either rip 1 x 2 or inch-thick stock to any desirable width under 1½ inches, or use parting bead or ¾-square for the narrowest moldings. If you want something wider, use 1 x 3 or 1 x 4. I doubt that you will want anything wider than molding made with 1 x 4.

To avoid putting undue stress on your router motor, overheating bits, and damaging the wood you're working with, make all but the shallowest cuts in several passes. For example, instead of trying to rout out a ⅜-inch cove or groove in one step, set the bit for a ³/₁₆-inch depth and make the first pass. Reset the depth at ⅜ inch, and make a second pass to remove the rest of the material.

All router moldings shown in this section, incidentally, were made with 1 x 2 stock.

Box Molding

Tighten a ½-inch or ⅝-inch straight bit into your router's collet, and adjust for a ¼-inch-wide, ¼-inch-deep cut. With a 1 x 2 broad side down on the router table, run it over the bit to rout a ¼ x ¼-inch rabbet. Move the router ¼ inch out from the fence, and make another pass. Continue moving the router in ¼-inch increments until you have made five passes, resulting in a ¼ x 1¼-inch rabbet. The molding will be *L*-shaped, with a ¼-inch lip. It can be used by itself as a box molding, or in conjunction with other moldings for more complex frames.

J-Molding

To make a J-molding, start by routing a box molding from 1 x 2. Replace the straight bit with a ⅜-inch-radius corner-round bit, adjusted for about a half-cut.

Stand the box molding on its unrouted narrow (face) edge, with its broad surface against the fence. Run the strip over the bit. Rotate the strip, and round over the lip edge.

Set the bit for its full ⅜-inch depth, and repeat the process to fully round over both face corners. Then clamp the molding in a Workmate or woodworker's vise, and use a pad sander to finish rounding the molding face with 120-grit sandpaper.

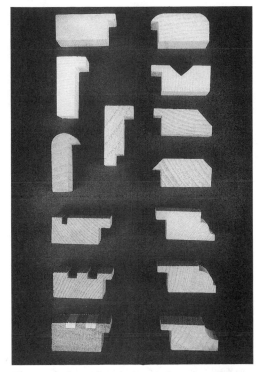

The author used a router and router table to make all these moldings from 1 x 2 stock.

Making J-molding with a router and table.

Finishing J-molding with a pad sander.

Flat Molding

Use a ½-inch or ⅝-inch straight bit to make the flat molding. Set the bit for a ¼-inch-wide, ¼-inch-deep cut. Lay a 1 x 2 broad side down on the table, and run it over the bit to create a ¼ x ¼-inch rabbet. Move the bit up ¼ inch and make another pass, leaving a ¼ x ½-inch rabbet and ¼-inch lip.

This molding is used as is for making a simple, shallow frame, or it can be used in conjunction with other moldings. This is also the basic configuration to begin with when making the router moldings that follow.

Grooved Moldings

You can use several different bits for making grooved moldings. The straight

J-molding frame.

Making flat molding with a router and table.

Straight bit.

V-groove bits.

Round-nose bits.

bit you used to make the rabbet will make a broad groove on the molding face. A narrower straight bit will make smaller single and multiple grooves. A V-groove bit will make V-shaped grooves at various depths.

To make a centered groove on the molding face, start by setting a combination square at ¾ inch and making a centered pencil mark on one end of a strip of

Align the bit with the mark on the end of the molding.

Making double-grooved molding.

Making V-grooved molding.

Double-grooved frame.

V-grooved frame.

flat molding. Lay the molding on the router table, and move the router until the bit is aligned with the guide mark on the end of the molding.

Always start shallow. Not only will this make the routing easier, but a shallow groove might turn out to be all you want. You can always make it deeper, but you can't correct a groove that's too deep.

To make a double-grooved molding, use a combination square to mark one end of a piece of molding ¼ inch from one narrow edge. Put that edge against the router-table fence, and align a ¼-inch straight bit with the guide mark. With the bit set for a ⅛-inch depth, lay the molding face down and pass it over the bit to create a ¼-inch-wide, ⅛-inch-deep groove. Rotate the molding so the opposite edge is against the fence, and make another pass to create a second groove.

A ⅜-inch V-groove bit is the ideal size for 1 x 2 flat molding. With it, you can make ⅛-inch to ¼-inch single and double grooves and ⅜-inch centered grooves.

Cove bits.

Coved Molding

This is not a cove molding, as discussed in the earlier section on construction moldings. Rather, this is a picture-frame molding with a cove routed into it.

To make the molding, start with the flat molding, face down on the router table. With a ⅜-inch-radius cove bit set for about ³/₁₆ inch, run the molding over the bit to rout a cove into the edge opposite

Making coved molding.

Coved-molding frame.

the rabbet. If you want a deeper cove, set the bit for full depth, and run the molding through one more time.

Beaded Molding

You will see in the profile of this molding that when fully beaded the routed edge has two sharp corners. As you produce this molding in steps, though, you will end up with a different molding on each pass over the bit. Note the different effects you can accomplish at different depth settings, and choose the one you prefer.

Use a ⅜-inch-radius beading bit, set for about a ⅛-inch depth. Lay the flat molding face down on the router table, and run it over the bit. Reset the router for a ¼-inch depth, and make another pass. Finally, set the router for full depth and make one last pass. You can even make

Beading bits.

subsequent deeper passes for different effects entirely. Experiment.

Roman Ogee Molding

Start with a ⁵/₃₂-inch-radius Roman ogee bit, and use it as you would the beading bit on flat molding. Set the

Making beaded molding.

Beaded frame.

Making Roman ogee molding.

router for a ⅛-inch depth, lay the molding face down on the table, with the routed edge against the fence, and run it over the bit. Then continue resetting the depth in ⅛-inch increments and noting the effect of each pass. Pick the one you like.

Rounded Molding

Corner-round bits come in various sizes and can be used at different depths, much the way beading and ogee bits are used. To simply round over one or both front corners of a molding, though, you

Roman ogee frame.

Roman ogee bits.

Making rounded molding.

Corner-round bits.

face corner of flat molding to a depth of ⅜ inch. You can round over both face corners, but you should not go the full depth on the molding lip, as you will lose material if you do.

As with the other bits, round over the corners in at least two steps. With a ¼-inch corner-round bit, though, you can set it for full depth and make one pass on each face corner for a fully rounded molding. The molding shown was rounded this way with a ¼-inch bit.

must limit the depth of cut to the radius of the bit.

Earlier, I used a ⅜-inch corner-round bit to make the J-molding. You can use the same bit to round over the unrouted

Beveled Moldings

You can do shallow beveling with the ⅜-inch V-groove bit used for making V-grooved moldings. But if you want to

Rounded frame.

Making beveled molding.

Making double-beveled molding.

Beveled frame.

bevel the face edges deeper, use a ½-inch chamfering bit.

As with other bits, take off about ⅛ inch with each pass, until you achieve the effect you desire. You can bevel one or both face edges. If you bevel the molding lip, be careful not to go so deep as to change the width of the molding lip.

Other bits are useful in making frame

Chamfering bits.

Double-beveled frame.

Rabbeting bits.

Classical bit.

TWO FILLET   ONE FILLET

Ogee bits with filets.

Raised-panel bit.

moldings, as are various sizes of the bits covered here. The ones demonstrated, though, are probably the most generally useful and are certainly good ones to start with.

Be sure to browse at your local tool and hardware outlets to find out what is available. And when you own a few bits, do some experimenting with them to find out what they will do. Combine some of the techniques covered here. For example, try a centered *V*-groove on the face of a double-beveled molding. Add a straight groove to a beaded or Roman ogee molding. Work with some wider stock. Glue up thicker, more complex moldings.

There's no end to what you can accomplish, once you turn your imagination loose.

Decorative Frame Moldings

The more framing you do, and the more you think about framing and study the work of other framers, the more ideas you will come up with for making your frames distinctive. You will find various materials—vinyl, leather, cloth, cork, acrylics, Formica, twine, rope, and others—that you can use for decorating frame moldings. Keep in mind, though, that decorating frames is like cooking with garlic: a little goes a long way, and you can overdo it.

I don't think it's a good idea to just decorate frames willy-nilly. Try to match the frame to the subject, if not entirely, at least partially. You won't always be able to do so, but some frames can be suggestive. A frame can even blend with a room's decor, though it needn't and probably shouldn't match the drapes or carpet.

Be subtle in your approach to decorative frame moldings, and if you might err, do so on the side of conservatism and you'll stay out of trouble. Most important, think about what you are doing and what you hope to accomplish. Remember that the art is the object of interest, not the frame. The frame should complement the art, prepare the viewer for the subject, and keep the viewer interested. It should never distract the viewer or detract from the work.

There is really no end to the materials you can use to decorate frames or to the methods and materials you can use to add flair to some frames. I have seen beaded frames that I really didn't care much for, but I'm sure others liked them, or no one would have spent all that time gluing beads. I remember seeing several shells in a frame that was covered with hundreds of tiny shells. Too much of a good thing, I thought at the time.

On the other hand, I once saw a small frame made from a flat molding that was covered with hundreds of tiny seashells all glued into a fascinating mosaic. All that was in the frame was a mirror. I liked the effect and wished I had the patience to sit long enough to glue all those shells in place.

Of course, much of this is a matter of taste, but I do think that there is a limit to

the use of highly decorative frames and some rather loose guidelines you can use. The more decorative the frame is, the simpler the subject should be. And what could be simpler than a mirror? In that case, the shell-covered frame *was* the subject.

Many decorative materials at your disposal are fairly subtle and unobtrusive. Formica and other similar acrylics, for example, are often effective when cut in strips and glued to frame moldings. White, off-white, charcoal, and black are the best colors for general use.

Leather and leather-imitating vinyls are also noncommittal, but can be used evocatively. While wood-and-leather moldings work well with many different subjects, I think they are particularly striking in use with western art, a genre enjoying great popularity today.

Frames decorated with rope are also fairly universal in their adaptability, but these, too, suggest certain subjects or motifs to me—marine art in particular. Rope-and-wood moldings also work well with western art and pastoral scenes.

Rope also changes any molding or frame dramatically without being overwhelming, because it mainly changes the texture and pattern of a molding, rather than color or bulk. Rope is also easy to use in framing. And for these reasons, it is one of the most useful of all decorative items.

Sisal and Manila hemp ropes are the best for use in making picture frames. Both are coarse, natural-fiber ropes that stain well and are easy to work with. You will find these ropes at variety and hardware stores, where they are available in several diameters and are sold by the foot. Some sizes are also available in small spools you might want to keep on hand. I buy ¼-inch and ⅜-inch sisal rope in 50-foot spools. When I need a larger diameter, I buy it by the foot for a specific project.

With rope, it's best to decorate the frame rather than the uncut molding. You can stain the frame first, then attach the rope, or attach the rope and stain frame and rope together. If you stain the frame and not the rope, the two will contrast, and the rope will be more noticeable. If both rope and molding are stained, the effect is subtler. The choice is yours.

Rope can be used with some commercially made moldings or moldings you make. Use ¼-inch rope with moldings that have ¼-inch grooves, such as the double-grooved molding shown earlier. The molding deeply grooved with a ⅜-inch V-groove bit is ideal for use with ⅜-inch rope. You can also rout a ¼-inch or ⅜-inch cove into the edge of a frame molding, and attach ¼-inch or ⅜-inch rope along that edge.

To attach rope to a frame, first cut one end of it at a 45-degree angle with an X-Acto knife. Lay it along the groove of one section of the frame, mark it for the second miter cut, and cut it. Cut the rope for the remaining three frame sections the same way.

Use wood glue or five-minute epoxy to attach the rope to the frame. If you have

Sisal rope in ¼-inch and ⅜-inch diameters comes in 50-foot spools.

Use a utility knife or razor-blade scraper to cut ¼-inch rope at a 45-degree angle, run a bead of glue along ¼-inch grooves, and press rope into grooves.

With a V-grooved frame, run a bead of glue
along the groove, clamp the rope in the groove,
and tack the rope with wire nails.

When glue sets, pry nail heads up with a screwdriver, and pull nails out with pliers.

enough spring clamps, use them to hold
the rope in place until the glue sets. Or
you can temporarily tack the rope to the
frame with brads or small wire nails.
When the glue has set, pull out the nails
with pliers.

In the molding department of your favorite home-improvement center and at
some department stores, you will find
carved or pressed moldings that are used
for decorative purposes in various woodworking and finish-carpentry projects.
Some are also useful in making frame
moldings.

These decorative moldings are usually
¼ inch thick and come in various widths,
from about ¾ to 1½ inches, and lengths

Finished rope frames, ready for staining.

Three styles of decorative molding.

of 6 or 8 feet. Most can be glued to the face of nominal 1-inch-thick stock cut to the same length. The ¾-inch molding can also be used on the ¾-inch edge of nominal 1-inch-thick wood.

If you prefer, you can inlay the molding. Use a straight bit on a router attached to a router table to rout a groove in the face of the frame molding, making as many passes as necessary to accommodate the width of the molding to be inlaid. For a flush inlay, simply match the depth of the groove to the thickness of the decorative molding. For a different effect, make the groove slightly deeper. You can also cut grooves with a table or radial-arm saw.

To attach the decorative molding, ap-

ply wood glue to the groove, and clamp the decorative molding in place. If you don't have enough clamps, lay a strip of parting bead or ¾-square on top of the inlaid decorative molding, and tightly wrap masking tape or rubber bands around everything about every 12 to 15 inches. Let stand until glue sets, and the molding is ready for cutting.

Contrasting woods also make attractive inlays. Rather than make long strips of such moldings, though, I prefer to use scraps leftover from various projects. The Micro Wood I use for many of my laminating jobs is hardwood that comes in ⅛-inch and ¼-inch thicknesses and 3 x 24-inch strips, and I always have a lot of odds and ends of this material on hand in such species as oak, walnut, cherry, and maple. I use various species of hardwood in nominal inch-thick stock and always have random lengths in the scrap bin.

There are certain woods that work well in combination. I like oak with walnut inlays, walnut with oak inlays, maple with cherry inlays, and mahogany with maple inlays.

To make the molding in the accompanying photographs, I made a double-grooved molding from scraps of mahogany 1 x 2. I used a ¼-inch straight bit to rout ⅛-inch-deep grooves. I then used a bandsaw to rip some scraps of ¼-inch maple Micro Wood to a width of ³/₁₆ inch. Then I cut them to match the length of the mahogany scraps.

Next, I ran a bead of glue along each groove in the mahogany, tapped a strip of maple into it with a soft-faced mallet, and let the molding stand until the glue dried.

I sanded the face smooth with a belt sander and medium-grit belt. When I

Applying glue to double-grooved molding.

Sanding molding smooth with a belt sander.

Tapping maple strips into grooves with soft-faced mallet.

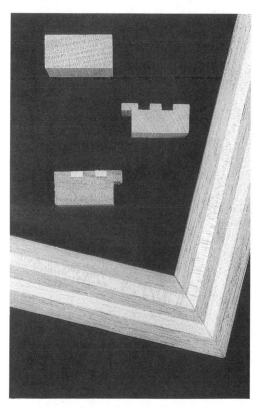

Maple and mahogany inlaid frame.

later made the frame, I sanded it with a pad sander and 120-grit and 220-grit sandpaper.

Always a Frame in the Making

I enjoy making frames, especially from my own moldings. Perhaps what I like most is that the gratification is almost instant and comes in several phases of the framing process. I get a kick out of turning a strip of 1 x 2 into an attractive frame molding and another out of turning that molding into a handsome and useful frame.

After a hard day at the typewriter or in the studio or darkroom, I welcome the opportunity to relax for a few minutes or a half hour in my workshop. But I'm certainly not going to build a cabinet or refinish a table in that length of time. I can in that half hour, though, turn out up to 100 feet of frame molding, or cut the sections for several frames, or build an entire frame, or build two if I use sections cut earlier.

I keep a list of items needing framing, and I often have framing to do for others. And I make frames in standard sizes that I'm always able to use or sell. When I just feel like cutting some frame sections, I do so, bind each set of four with rubber bands, and store them on shelves in the shop. When I feel like building frames for therapy, I usually work with these "kits" I keep on hand. Or sometimes I just go through the scrap bin, looking for lengths of leftovers that I can turn into moldings and frames.

I'm sure once you begin making your own moldings and building frames from them, you'll be doing the same kinds of things. In your shop, as in mine, there will always be a frame in the making.

9

Finishing Wood Frames

Considering all the woods suitable for picture framing and all the ways there are to finish these frames, I could fill a book with a discussion of the various finishing methods and materials. Consequently, to allow but a chapter on the subject means I must leave out some information and include only what I deem to be most important.

I know I'm asking for trouble – or at least an argument – but mainly what I am leaving out of this discussion is what some professional framers and authors of framing books consider to be most important: all their gessos, patinas, and gilds and how to use them.

I'm a woodworker, not an artist. So I finish my frames with woodworkers' techniques and materials. I am also a busy person who values his time, spare and otherwise. So what I look for in the finishing of any frame is the quickest way to get the job done right. And frankly, many of the methods covered in other books and used by some professional framers seem terribly time-consuming and a bit old-fashioned.

That these methods are covered adequately elsewhere is good enough reason to exclude them here. Nevertheless, I recognize that there will be a few readers who either do not entirely agree with me or simply wish to know about the other ways to finish frames. So I will direct them to the book, *How To Make Your Own Picture Frames,* third edition, by Hal Rogers and Ed Reinhardt (Watson-Guptill Publications, 1981). This book was first published in 1958 and includes the materials and techniques that were widely used then. The book will tell you how to mix gessos and patinas, how to cut in and build up texture, and how to tone and gild.

Just as many new mounting and matting products and techniques, developed in recent years, have provided us with many more options, so have some of the wood-finishing products and methods. What's more, there are a few old stand-bys worthy of rediscovery, and some that are particularly suitable for finishing picture frames.

Filling and Patching Wood Frames

The kind of wood patch or filler to use on any frame depends on the type of finish you plan. If you will be painting the frame, use spackling paste. If you plan to stain the frame, use a stainable wood filler, such as Zar Wood Patch, Dap Wood Dough, or Plastic Wood. For natural finishes, hot-melt shellac sticks are best.

With most frames, the only patching you will need to do is to fill brad holes at the corners. On some frames, even those

If you plan to paint a frame, fill and patch with spackling paste.

can be left unfilled. If you have a miter joint that refused to come together completely (and all of us face that problem from time to time), you can fill that too.

You can use spackling compound that mixes with water for patching frames that will be painted, but the latex paste that comes in a can is much quicker and neater to use, and it's always ready. You can use a putty knife to fill brad holes with spackling paste, or you can work it in with a finger. Either way, build it up slightly above the molding surface, as it will shrink as it dries.

With simple, unadorned frames, you can patch gaps in miter joints with spackling paste and the putty knife. Where contours of the molding pose problems, work the paste in with your finger, and wipe away all excess. In areas that will be difficult or impossible to sand, use your finger to completely smooth the paste and remove as much as possible.

Not long ago, my day's mail included a sample tube of Zar Wood Patch, which I put on my bench as a reminder to give it a test next time I had any filling to do. Since then I have come to prefer this filler for many jobs on items that will be stained and varnished or lacquered. The paste is the consistency of peanut butter and doesn't seem to dry out, as other fillers do. It goes on as easily as spackling paste, but takes a stain as readily as the plastic wood fillers do. What's more, I have found no need to thin it, and it doesn't seem to shrink as other fillers do. It dries fast, and is as easy to sand as spackling paste. Apply it with putty knife or fingers, as you would spackling paste.

The bad news about the plastic wood fillers, such as Dap Wood Dough, is that they aren't quite so easy to apply as spackling paste or Zar Wood Patch, they

Zar Wood Patch is a neutral-colored latex filler that dries fast, is easy to sand, and takes a stain.

ing maple frames that I don't plan to stain. Likewise with Mahogany and Red Cedar Wood Dough, both of which also work well with the various shades of redwood.

With most rustic or roughly finished frames, you needn't worry about patching, but if the frame is to be finely finished, then all flaws should be removed or hidden. Small pitch pockets, cracks in and near knots, tiny borer holes, and the like must be filled. For frames that will be naturally finished, the best material to use for these blemishes is hot-melt shellac sticks.

The sticks are available in a wide array of colors and hues to match most woods perfectly. You can apply the material with a heated putty-knife blade, or you can buy one of the electric burn-in knives designed for such purposes, which are available by mail for about $20 or so.

To patch any hole, crack, or other imperfection, touch the heated blade of the applicator to the end of a color-matched shellac stick, and transfer the melted material to the flaw in the frame. Smooth

will shrink some as they cure, and in time they will dry out in the container. The good news is that you can easily get around the shortcomings. Dap is relatively cheap, it cures hard, stains easily, and comes in wood-tone colors as well as natural. This is a good filler to use on frames you plan to finish naturally without staining.

Dap Wood Dough in "natural" will darken somewhat with the application of oil, shellac, polyurethane, or lacquer, so it fairly well disappears when you use these finishing materials. The "natural" product will also take stains. The colored wood-tone products are the best to use on specific species that will be finished without stains. I keep Dap Maple Wood Dough on hand, for example, for patch-

Dap Wood Dough is available in natural and various wood tones. Keep it thinned and workable with solvent.

Shellac sticks are melted and applied with an electric burn-in tool or a heated putty knife.

the shellac with the hot blade, and remove any excess. Let the shellac harden for a minute and it is immediately ready for sanding.

Sanding and Preparing Frames for Finishing

The best way to save time and enjoy sanding is to avoid it entirely. For most of us, sanding is a tedious chore, but with some moldings and frames it is necessary. It is the way to achieve the finest finish, and it's a way to correct mistakes.

There is a little sanding to do on just about every wood frame, but rustic frames and those made with prefinished

moldings require the least. After you cut frame sections, the miter cuts often have tiny splinters on the saw-exit surfaces. Gently sand these edges with 120-grit sandpaper to remove the splinters.

Moldings are not always consistent in width and thickness. Moldings you make yourself and those that are manufactured commercially can be slightly off, keeping your miter joints from matching perfectly. When the width of two adjoining sections differs slightly, always match the inside corners and allow the resulting overhang at the outside corners. Then when the frame is assembled, simply sand down the overhang.

Similarly, when molding thicknesses vary slightly, the face or rear surface of one section will be higher than that of the adjoining section. During assembly, align either the face or rear surface, depending on the intricacy of the molding, and sand the other surface smooth when the frame has been assembled.

Only rarely should any frame require coarse sanding, unless you wish to use coarse abrasives to create texture. When you do need to remove a good bit of material quickly, though, as in the case of inlaid moldings where the inlays might be 1/16 inch or more above the molding surface, use a belt sander and 80-grit belt to sand the surface smooth and flat. If you don't own a belt sander, use a pad sander and 80-grit sandpaper.

Next, sand the surface with a pad sander and 120-grit sandpaper until all scratches left by the belt sander are gone. Follow that with a sanding with pad sander and 220-grit sandpaper. You will rarely need to go to any finer abrasive than this.

When you want the finest finish—perhaps to simulate the superb hand-rubbed oil finish used on some furniture and gunstocks, or the rubbed lacquer look—continue sanding with the pad sander and 320-grit waterproof sandpaper. Then hand sand with 400-grit waterproof sandpaper, and polish with #0000 steel wool.

On some frames you will want sharp corners and edges; on others rounded corners and edges are better. Round over the corners and edges as you sand, beginning with the 120-grit step. A ¼-sheet palm sander is handy for this operation, as it is easy to handle and to rock back and forth along a sharp edge to round it over.

To sand corners and other confined areas in any frame, fold a sheet of sandpaper and sand with the creased edge. Another handy item for sanding tight spots and contours is an abrasive sponge. Buy one with a medium-grit abrasive on two sides and fine-grit on the other two sides. Some flap-sanding attachments that fit grinders and electric drills are good for sanding intricate moldings, but I don't recommend them for use on softwood moldings, as they will remove too much material and ruin the molding.

During the sanding operation, you must clean frame surfaces frequently to check your progress. I carry a 3-inch, pure bristle paintbrush in a back pocket when I'm in the shop. This is my dusting brush, and I don't use it for any other purpose. With it, I dust the surfaces I'm sanding and inspect them closely. In this way, I know when I have removed scratches and have achieved a consistent smoothness with any particular grit, which is my signal to change to a finer abrasive or stop sanding altogether. With such open-grained woods as oak, walnut, and mahogany, a brush is the only

efficient tool for cleaning sanding dust from the grain.

When I have finished sanding any frame, I use the dusting brush and a vacuum cleaner to thoroughly clean the frame. Then, just before applying any stain, oil, paint, polyurethane, or lacquer, I wipe down all surfaces of the frame with a tack cloth.

You can extend the life of any tack cloth by "snapping" the dust out of it frequently and storing the cloth in an airtight container to keep it from drying out and losing its sticky characteristics. I keep mine in a Ziploc plastic sandwich bag.

A 3-inch, pure bristle paintbrush makes a good dusting brush.

Staining Frames

Most natural-wood frames that won't be painted should be stained before the final finish is applied. Of course, some woods and inlaid frames require no stain. Black walnut, teak, redwood, and a number of other dark woods look best without staining. And some rustic frames should be finished sans stains. With many woods, however, stains bring out the beauty of the wood and enhance the character of the frame.

Stains come in a great variety of colors and shades, and their colors will vary further depending on the kinds of woods they are applied to. For example, a Medium Walnut stain looks one way on oak, quite another way on pine, and different yet on cedar. Paint stores, department stores, and home-improvement centers where stains are sold display charts or boards with actual samples of woods treated with various makes and colors of stains. These can help you make decisions about what kinds of stains to buy. But even with such assistance, you should always test every stain on a sample of wood that matches the wood of the frame you plan to stain.

Eventually, you will settle on a few favorite woods and a few favorite stains, and you'll know without experimenting and testing what the right combination is. As I said earlier, I use pine and oak more than any other woods for my framing jobs. Similarly, I have a few favorite stains and other finishes that I use on most frames. Occasionally, though, I will try out a new stain or finish, or one that's new to me. Or I will work with different woods. And then I always test the stain and wood.

Most of the stains you use will be transparent oil-base stains that require no thinning. Different colors of these stains can be mixed for even greater diversity and variety.

You can also use different colors of oil-base stains in consecutive steps to achieve different effects. For example, apply one of the wood-tone stains—such as medium walnut, cherry, golden oak, or fruitwood—to an open-grained wood, such as oak. After sufficient penetration, wipe it dry with paper towels, and let it dry overnight. The next day, apply a coat of Fuller O'Brien Pen-Chrome #640-13 Platinum stain, being sure to work it into the grain with a brush. Wipe the frame dry, and let it stand overnight. The result will be a lightly frosted finish that is quite attractive in picture frames. You can slightly tone down the effects to suit your

Apply stains to frames with a brush.

tastes by polishing the frame with #0000 steel wool.

Such oil-base stains can be applied with a brush or rag, but for picture frames, I suggest using a brush to get into all the corners and crevices. After frames are stained, clean brushes with paint thinner, turpentine, or mineral spirits.

Most manufacturers recommend applying the stain and letting it penetrate and dry overnight, but this might darken a frame too much. So I suggest you apply the stain, let it penetrate for about ten to fifteen minutes, and wipe the frame dry with paper towels. Let the frame stand overnight, and determine then if additional staining is required. You can always apply more stain if it's needed; it's quite a chore to lighten a frame that's too darkly stained.

Don't assume that because two or more manufacturers offer stains in identical tones or shades that they are identical in their effects on any particular wood. For example, several companies offer stains they call English Oak, and each is at least slightly different from the others. For me, the one that comes closest to what I think English oak ought to look like is Fuller O'Brien Pen-Chrome #640-11 English Oak.

When I apply this stain to frames made of red oak and wipe it off in ten or fifteen minutes, it darkens the oak to a color that can best be described as an aged brown with hints of charcoal gray residing in the open grain and pores. This is precisely my interpretation of English oak — what I expect it to look like.

This is not to say that other English oak stains are inferior. Rather, they produce different results that don't meet my expectations. Only by experimenting with different brands and colors of stains can

you discover those that meet your needs and expectations. For that reason, I always recommend buying stains in small containers until you find the ones that work best for you.

Once a frame has been stained and allowed to dry, it is ready for sealing and final finishing. Although you can store the stained frames until you're ready to finish them, it's best to finish them immediately, or at least seal them before storing them.

The Danish Oil Treatment

There are a number of oil-and-resin finishes on the market today, and all will work well on picture frames. I suggest you start with Watco Danish Oil Finish. It's easy to use, is available in the widest variety of colors, and produces a superb finish. And for many frames, this is the final finishing step.

Watco finishes include natural, medium walnut, dark walnut, black walnut, cherry, fruitwood, golden oak, English oak, and iced oak. You can also mix colors for a broader range of effects. For example, I use a half-and-half mixture of natural and medium walnut on inlaid frames of oak and walnut.

Although the various Watco finishes share common characteristics, they should be treated like other stains as regards the different colors and their effects on various woods. Experiment and always test any Watco and wood combination you haven't tried before.

I mentioned English oak earlier as one of my favorite stains for use on oak frames, and I discussed the differences among the various brands. Watco English Oak produces a finish that is much darker and grayer than the Fuller O'Brien product I prefer when I want to achieve the English oak effect. But it's this same overall charcoal tone that makes me reach for the Watco product when I want to make a pine frame look like driftwood.

Use a brush to apply a liberal amount of Watco Danish Oil Finish to a picture frame. Let the oil penetrate for thirty minutes, applying more to spots that absorb the oil and dry faster. Then apply another liberal coat, and let stand for fifteen minutes. Wipe the frame dry, and let stand for twenty-four hours.

Such open-grained woods as oak and walnut will bleed excess oil from their pores after being finished with Watco Danish Oil Finish, producing sticky, often discolored spots on the frame surface. Don't rub these spots with rags or paper towels; the friction will only compound the problem. Instead, let the frame stand until the spots dry completely; then take them off with #0000 steel wool.

If you plan to use the frame with an oil painting, acrylic, batik, or anything else where archival or conservation methods aren't required, the final step is wet polishing with wax. Brush on Watco Satin Wax, and lightly wet sand the frame's exterior surfaces with 600-grit waterproof sandpaper or polish with #0000 steel wool. Let stand ten minutes, and buff with a soft cloth.

For conservation framing, the frame must be sealed. But before applying any sealer, lacquer, varnish, or polyurethane over Watco Danish Oil Finish, let the frame stand for seventy-two hours, and do not apply the Watco Satin Wax.

Clean brushes with paint thinner or mineral spirits. Rags used during the Danish Oil treatment should be thoroughly soaked with water and discarded to prevent spontaneous combustion.

As great as the Watco products are, their container caps leave a lot to be desired. They're the kind of childproof caps that only children can open. We adults must use pliers and the appropriate language, and then when the container is opened, it's impossible to pour the stuff without making a mess. So be sure to lay newspapers on the floor of your work area, and wear old clothes or a shop apron. As my neighbor, a professional wood carver, says, "You have to love Watco; why else would you put up with their containers?"

Sealing Wood Frames

Sealing a wood picture frame provides a barrier between the frame's contents and the acid in the wood—a necessity in conservation framing. Sealing also prevents the leaching of natural resins and moisture in the frame. Even properly cured or kiln-dried wood has a moisture content of 15 to 19 percent, and temperature fluctuations can cause this moisture to percolate to the frame surface and discolor the finish.

Although some finishing materials, such as Deft Clear Wood Finish, seal and finish in one step, others either don't adequately seal the wood, or work better when a sealer is applied first. Even paints applied over raw wood can be stained by leaching resins and moisture. So it's a good idea to seal before painting as well.

Although most varnishes and polyurethanes will seal the wood, sealers dry much faster. So you will save time by applying a sealer and then a finish coat, instead of two finish coats.

Acrylic sanding sealer is popular as a base coat for polyurethane, as it will be dry and ready for sanding in two or three hours. The problem is it must be sanded before the finish coat is applied, which can be difficult with the more intricate frame moldings.

Shellac is an excellent sealer, and nothing dries faster. What's more, it need not be sanded before the finish coat is applied. For those reasons, I use shellac almost exclusively for sealing frames.

You can brush on shellac or spray it on, and either method works well with picture frames. Apply a thin base coat, let it dry, and you're ready to apply the final finish. You can thin shellac and clean paint brushes with denatured alcohol.

Painting Frames and Liners

Today's modern paints are a joy to work with. The odorless latex flat and semigloss paints can be mixed to match nearly any hue. They dry without leaving brush marks, and clean up with water.

These are the paints to use for many frames and most liners. When you are trying to match the liner to a color in a painting, stop by a paint store or home-improvement center and check the paint chips that show the various color mixtures available. When you find the right one, have the paint mixed at the store, and it's ready to use. Apply two coats to the sealed liner.

High-gloss enamels and lacquers make fine finishes on some frames. If this is the sort of finish you're interested in, prepare the frame by sanding it to the finest finish described earlier in the chapter. Then seal it with shellac, and lightly burnish

Shellac can be brushed on or sprayed on. It thins and cleans up with denatured alcohol.

the shellac with #0000 steel wool. Then apply high-gloss enamel or lacquer and let it dry. Burnish again with steel wool, and apply another coat.

Although these glossy finishes can be applied with a brush or can be sprayed on, brush-on lacquers are sometimes hard to find. What's more, both glossy enamels and lacquers are available in aerosol cans that are ideal for finishing frames.

Some of the rust-inhibiting enamels for metal are also useful for painting wood frames. Some dry to a flat finish, while others dry to a high gloss.

Modern metallic-finish paints—gold, silver, bronze, copper, and the like—are a vast improvement over their predeces-

Use paint-sample chips to find the precise colors, and have them custom mixed.

sors. Use these for simulating metal or for painting liners, filets, and molding edges in lieu of gilding.

Clear Finishes

Although I have worked with many different kinds of varnish, polyurethane, and lacquer over the years, I have settled on a few that have served me well. I like those that dry fast to a keen, uniform finish without showing every tiny bubble or speck of dust.

Most of the clear finishes I use are available in brush-on form, but I mainly use aerosol cans now for their convenience and the ease of even application. Clear finishes dry to dull matte, satin sheen, semigloss, or glossy finish, depending on the type of material you use.

I don't care for glossy finishes on frames, so the finishes on most of mine are either satin sheen or semigloss, or occasionally dull matte.

When I want a semigloss clear finish, I skip the sealing step and apply three coats of Deft Clear Wood Finish, which seals and finishes simultaneously. For

those who like a glossy finish, Deft is available in glossy.

For other clear finishes, I start with shellac to seal. Over that I apply an even coat of dull matte or satin sheen polyurethane, depending on the finish I want.

Removing Finishes from Frames

For some frames—namely those you have found at garage sales, flea markets, and second-hand stores—finishing is mainly a matter of refinishing. Part of the refinishing process is the removal of the original finish.

Although some finishes can be re-

Two of the author's favorite finishes are Deft Semi-Gloss Clear Wood Finish and satin-sheen polyurethane. A plastic gun handle that snaps to the can makes application easier.

moved with abrasives, chemical finish removers are better for picture frames, as they will get into hard-to-reach places and take off the finish without removing wood.

With some chemical finish removers, the old finish is softened, then scraped off with a putty knife. Another type allows you to hose off the old finish with a garden hose, and this is the better choice for picture frames.

You will find such finish removers stocked with the paints and other finishing materials at hardware, department, and paint stores and most home-improvement centers. Read the labels to find the one that best suits your needs.

Keep It Simple

The simpler you keep the finishing process, the more time you will save and the more you will enjoy it. And you don't need to spend tedious hours, days, or weeks trying to achieve the ultimate finish on any frame.

You needn't be an expert on every kind of finishing material available or every technique known. In fact, if there is a secret to success, it has to be simplicity. Experiment and test as a way of finding the best products for your purposes, and when you find a few that work well, stay with them and learn all their characteristics.

10

Glazing, Installing, and Hanging

Essentially, there are two types of framable works: those that get framed behind glass, and those that are framed without glass. Ordinarily, we frame mounted and matted originals and reproductions behind glass, as well as some three-dimensional objects, and delicate items that require glass to protect them from dust and other damaging elements. Conservation framing calls for the use of glass. We also use glass with some artworks on paper that we frame without mats. Oil paintings, acrylics, batiks, and similar works should be framed without glass. With photographs, glass is optional.

Most of the framable items found in the average household should be glazed, so it's important for any framer to learn how to work with the various glazing tools and materials and how to pick the right type of glass or acrylic (Plexiglas is a brand of acrylic) for any particular job.

For most framing, you will probably want to use either standard picture glass or nonglare glass, both of which are $1/16$ inch thick. For very large works, you might need the added strength of window glass, but use this material only if you must. It is thicker, thus heavier, and is not manufactured to the same exacting standards as picture glass and nonglare glass. Consequently, it might exhibit bubbles and other flaws.

Acrylic or plastic glazing material offers some advantages and disadvantages. Some framers prefer it for glazing large works because it is lighter than glass. But the product isn't always as flat as glass, especially if it has not been handled and stored properly. It is not so susceptible to breakage as glass, but it scratches easily, so you must exercise more care in handling and cleaning it. Acrylic also builds up static electricity so that dust and lint cling to it.

Perhaps acrylic is most useful in framing color photographic prints, which are prone to damage from ultraviolet (UV) radiation. Ultraviolet is present everywhere in natural and artificial light and causes photographic dyes to fade. By using a specially formulated ultraviolet-filtering acrylic in front of a print, you can greatly prolong the print's life. This product filters more than 90 percent of the harmful rays.

Acrylic is usually more expensive than glass. It is cheaper in large sheets that you cut yourself, but is also available at some outlets in standard sizes. Sometimes the precut material ends up being cheaper in the long run, because you can save time using it.

An alternative is to use a sheet of ultraviolet-filtering polystyrene behind picture glass. This material is only .040 of an inch thick, filters about 75 percent of the harmful radiation, and comes in standard sizes, from 8 x 10 to 16 x 20 inches.

There is now a special process for coating color photographic prints with a special UV-inhibiting lacquer. The process is complicated, however, so is not something you can do at home or in your shop. The service is now available from many commercial photo labs. Check with a local lab or photography dealer, or write to Meisel Photochrome, the lab I use (see directory).

The advantages of using this process are several. First, it's a time saver, as someone else does the work. Although the cost works out to be more than that of the polystyrene filter sheets, it's much

PRE-CUT GLASS STANDARD SIZES

8" x 10"
9" x 12"
11" x 14"
12" x 16"
14" x 18"
16" x 20"
18" x 22"
18" x 24"
20" x 24"
22" x 28"
24" x 30"
24" x 36"
26" x 32"
30" x 40"
36" x 48"

less of a nuisance. It also provides the only practical way I know of to frame prints without glass while protecting them from UV rays.

The biggest decision you'll have to make in glazing most works, though, is whether to use picture glass or nonglare glass, and here only you can be the judge. For some reason that continues to baffle me, many professional framers adamantly oppose the use of nonglare glass in *any* framing job. The reasons they give are that the nonglare glass diffuses light and thereby gives the illusion of softening the image or reducing clarity. They further argue that mats only compound the problem, because the farther the glass is from the image, the greater the reduction of clarity. Moreover, they warn that works viewed obliquely or from askance are obscured by nonglare glass. Finally, they point out that picture glass seems to improve clarity and color saturation.

Of course, all these arguments dissolve like sugar in water when the surface of ordinary picture glass reflects so much light as to obscure the work behind it. The common-sense approach to glass selection is to examine each framing job individually and pick the glass most suitable for the medium, the matting, and the area where the work will be displayed.

Nonglare glass does, indeed, slightly diffuse light, which will cause an apparent loss of clarity in some works and some media. It seems to be more of a problem with some watercolors (but not all) and intricately detailed pen-and-ink works. It also seems to work admirably with lithographs, serigraphs, and other reproductions. It's an excellent choice for glazing diplomas, certificates, and other documents. And it is ideal for many land-

Print on left is under nonglare glass, and print on right under standard picture glass. Notice the distracting reflections on the latter.

scapes, scenics, and portraits, regardless of whether or not reflections would pose problems with standard glass.

I routinely use nonglare glass with single and double mats and have used it with triple mats on large works. I would not recommend using it with more than two mats on small works that are normally viewed at close range or more than three mats for larger works. But then, I double mat most works I frame and rarely ever use more than three mats, so I simply don't have a problem with extreme reduction of clarity.

No work is meant to be viewed at a sharp angle, so that argument is specious. If you look at a work head-on, you will have no problem with distortion, regardless of the type of glass used.

With some works, such as certain watercolors, drawings, and black-and-white photographs, standard picture glass does seem to offer more clarity. I have trouble accepting the notion that it provides better color saturation, because display techniques and ambient light play major roles there and can affect any work.

In short, determine what sort of glass best fits the work. If you're framing a color photograph that you want to last, you might need UV-filtering acrylic. If you're planning to hang a collection of prints in a bright area where reflections obscure them, you will probably want to use nonglare glass. Where reflections are not as severe, you might still want to use nonglare glass, and that's your prerogative. If you prefer standard glass, that's fine too. And standard might prove best for some works. Just don't let someone else's unfounded prejudices influence you.

I keep at least one sheet of each type of glass on hand all the time. Then, if I'm not sure what kind of glass will be best for any work, I try it with each type. I also check the room where the work will hang if I'm not sure how reflections will affect it. If you do the same, you needn't worry about picking the wrong glass.

Glazing Tools and Techniques

There is really no need to ever cut a piece of glass yourself, but I recommend learning how to do it, for several reasons. First, it's an easy enough skill to learn and requires little in the way of tools. It can prove to be worthwhile, and you can usually save money over the long run. What's more, if you know how to cut glass, you can salvage usable pieces from larger ones that have been chipped, cracked, or broken.

Picture glass and nonglare glass are available in standard sizes, from 8 x 10 to 36 x 48 inches. Where precut acrylic is available, it usually comes in standard sizes from 8 x 10 to 20 x 24 inches. You'll save time and money using this precut material, so when you can, try to make your framable items conform to standard sizes. Some odd-sized works can be made standard by cutting mats to standard outside dimensions.

With certain popular sizes, you can save by buying a large sheet of standard-size glass and cutting it into several smaller sizes. For example, if you need a number of 8 x 10-inch pieces of glass, keep in mind that you can easily cut four from a single 16 x 20-inch piece.

Whenever you need a piece of glass or acrylic that is not standard size, you must either buy a larger sheet and cut it yourself, or have it cut at the glass shop. Sometimes the cutting charge is so small

Stanley glass cutter for under $2.

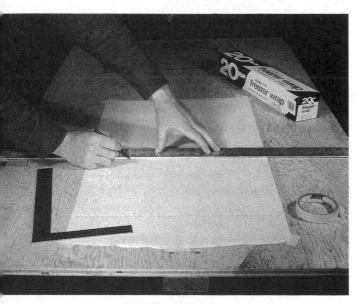

Scribe guidelines on freezer paper.

that it's hard to justify cutting your own. So you'll just have to use your own judgment.

Glass size in any framing job is determined by the outside dimensions of the mounted work. So you simply cut the glass the same size as the mount board and mats.

To cut your own glass, you will need a good glass cutter. They range in price from about $2 to $15, and they all work the same way. You will also need a solid working surface, a straight edge, and a few other items you probably already have around the house or shop.

One of the easiest ways I have found to cut glass is to mark a sheet of paper with guidelines instead of the glass. Start by taping a sheet of freezer paper to your bench or table top. Scribe a line across it, near one end. This is your edge-alignment guide. After determining where your cut should be made on the glass, scribe a second line parallel to the first at that distance. Scribe a third line 1/8 inch beyond the second, or whatever distance is dictated by the width of your cutter head.

Pour a little kerosene or turpentine into a small container, and keep it nearby for lubricating the cutter head. (Make sure you have a strip of masking tape running the length of the underside of your straight edge to keep it from slipping on the glass.) Align one edge of the glass along the first line you scribed on the freezer paper. Align your straight edge on the third line. Dip the cutter head in kerosene, and scratch a line in the glass along the second line scribed on the paper. Keep your elbow stiff, and move the cutter by moving your upper body backward in one fluid motion.

There are several ways to part the glass

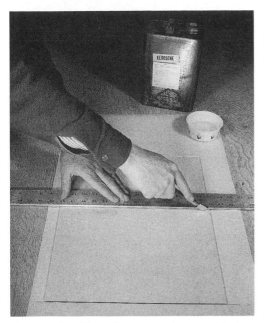

Cutter should make a continuous hissing sound as you scratch a line into the glass.

You can use glazier's pliers to snap glass in two.

along the scratched line. Some simply tap the underside of the glass at one end of the line, then grasp the glass with thumbs and forefingers near the edge, and snap it in two. You can also align the scratched line with the guide mark on the upper jaw of a pair of glazier's pliers, squeeze the plier handles, and thereby part the glass along the line. A third way is to lay a pencil on your work surface, position the glass atop it, and align the pencil with the scratched line. With your hands on the glass, a few inches left and right of the scratched line, press downward quickly but gently, and the glass will part along the line.

Glass edges are quite sharp, so handle them carefully. Run the glass under warm water to flush away tiny glass particles. Then mix a cup of detergent ammonia in two quarts of warm water,

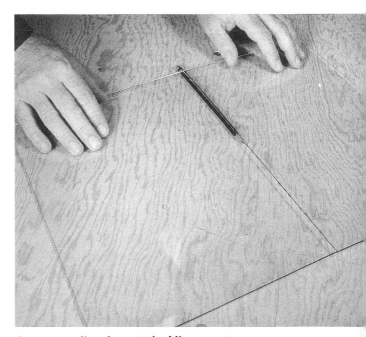

Or you can align the scratched line over a pencil and press down on the glass to snap it in two.

Folding acrylic knife.

and use this to wash away kerosene and fingerprints. Rinse with warm water, and dry with paper towels.

Cutting acrylic is no more difficult. For this job, substitute an acrylic-cutting knife for the glass cutter, and don't bother with freezer paper, because you can scribe cutting marks or lines onto the protective paper or plastic covering the acrylic.

When you have scribed your cutting marks or lines, align a straight edge along the first one, and draw the point of the knife along the line. Repeat the process as many times as necessary to cut nearly all the way through the acrylic—usually three or four passes for picture-frame acrylic.

Lay a length of dowel ¾ inch in diameter (or larger) on your bench. Lay the acrylic on top of it, and align the cut with the dowel. Put your hands on top of the acrylic on each side of the cut, and press down quickly to snap the piece in two. Then make subsequent cuts the same way.

Before removing the protective paper or plastic from the acrylic, inspect the edges for burrs. If you find any, remove them with 120-grit sandpaper. Then

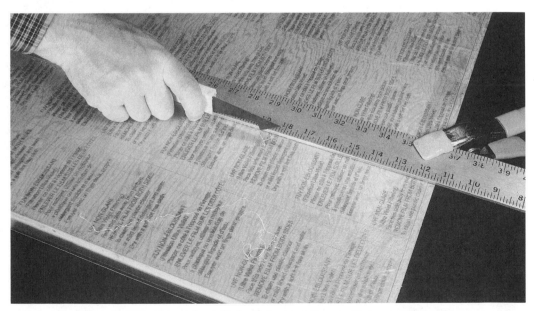

Use a straight edge and acrylic knife to score the acrylic in several passes.

wipe the edges clean with a damp sponge or rag. Remove the protective paper when you're ready to install the acrylic in the frame.

Installing Mounted Works

Most of the works you frame behind glass will probably be matted. Remember that one of the functions of a mat is to provide the necessary air space between the glass and the surface of the work. So if you're framing something without a mat, you must take other measures to provide that important air space.

I'm amazed by the number of unmatted works I see framed right against the glass, and I have seen such shoddy work in some pretty highfalutin galleries. One in central Oregon springs to mind, because it was a spendy spot meant to tempt the well-to-do tourists who frequent the area. I was looking at a collection of color photographs that were only a small cut above okay. The frames were mediocre, and the prints were sandwiched against the glass without mats. The only thing outstanding about any of the prints was the price.

I would have been perfectly contented to mosey on, but some silver-tongued dandy cornered me and began expounding on the many virtues of the photographs and the photographer. For all I know, it was the photographer himself. After his tediously long-winded spiel, I said, "Well, that's all fine and wonderful news for someone who doesn't know a photograph from an epitaph, but I'm afraid the ignoramus who framed this collection has rendered it worthless."

He sputtered and choked and asked, "Why would you say such a thing?"

"Simple," I said, "look here." I brought

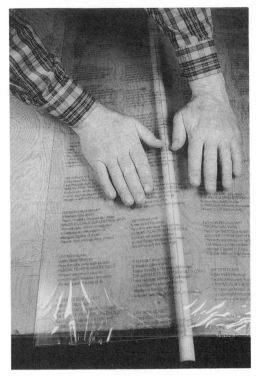

Then align the scored line on a dowel rod, and snap the acrylic in two.

him up for a close inspection and pointed to one of the prints that was exhibiting damage obviously caused by condensation on the inside of the glass. It had laminated the print surface to the glass, and I was sure the rest of the prints were already suffering similar damage or soon would be. "These photos don't have a plug-nickel's worth of collector's value," I told him, and all he could do was agree with me.

Photographers or people who frame their photographs are some of the worst offenders when it comes to this damaging practice. Perhaps the reason is that photographs are often mounted and displayed without mats. Sometimes photographs are simply mounted to mount boards, either flush or with borders, and are displayed without glass or frames. Fine. Sometimes, photographs are framed and displayed without glass. Fine. But if they're framed behind glass without mats or spacers, not so fine.

As a general rule, don't let any work you're framing touch the glass. There are, however, some notable exceptions to the rule. Some framing techniques call for contact, but in such cases I can only recommend using works that have no potential collector's value.

For example, sometimes photographs and posters are displayed with so-called frameless frames: hardware that's used to sandwich glass, work, and backing material without the use of a conventional frame. If the work is of little or no commercial or sentimental value, then by all means display it against the glass if

When framing behind glass without mats, use Framespace to provide the necessary separation between glass and the work.

you wish. But if you want to preserve and protect it, mat it first.

For works displayed in conventional frames without mats, a simple product is available that's easy to use and provides the necessary air space between glass and artwork. Framespace is an archivally safe plastic material that can be cut with scissors to fit on the edges of picture glass or acrylic. It comes in white, black, or clear. If you're framing without mats, this is the material I recommend for providing that important air space and protecting the work from condensation and other damage.

By the time you're ready to install any work in a frame, the frame should be finished. To protect the finish, spread a piece of felt, carpeting, or other protective material on your work surface. Clean the frame to remove any dust and lint, and lay it face down on the protective material.

Then everything simply gets stacked inside the frame: glass (with Framespace, if necessary), mounted and matted work, and backing if required. Backing material should be cut the same size as glass, mats, and mount boards, and you should use backing with any large works that might require the added support the backing can offer.

Once everything is stacked in the frame, hold it in place by hand, and gently lift the frame for inspection. Carefully examine the glass to make sure there are no pieces of dust or lint on the inside surface. If there are, there's nothing to do but take everything out and clean the glass again.

When you're satisfied that all is clean and ready for the finishing touches, it's time to secure everything inside the frame. For this, you can use either brads

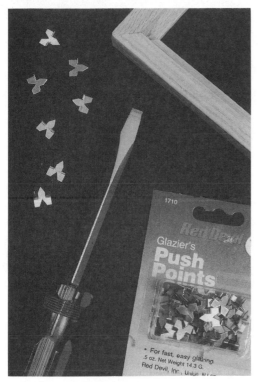

One style of glazier's points can be pushed in with a screwdriver or a putty knife.

a nail set. Grasp the nail set in your hand, and press its flat side against the head of a brad. Loop your thumb over the molding, and press toward the brad to squeeze it in. This method works best with softwood moldings.

For hardwood or softwood moldings, you can use a tool specifically designed to seat brads. Known as a brad squeezer or brad setter, this tool is adjustable for different sized moldings and brads. One jaw is rubber-covered to prevent marring the finished frame.

You can squeeze brads into molding with the end of a nail set.

or glazier's points. In case of the latter, either buy the kind that you can press in with a screwdriver, or you will need a special tool specifically designed for the task.

You can tap brads into the inside surface of the frame molding with a hammer. If that's the method you will use, you might need a pair of long-nose pliers to hold the brads. You should also C-clamp a strip of wood along one edge of your work surface, atop the protective material. Then brace the face-down frame against this strip as you tap the brads into the molding.

An alternative is to squeeze the brads into the molding by hand with the aid of

A brad squeezer or brad setter in use.

Make a brad squeezer with a pair of slip-joint pliers with one jaw padded.

A glazier's tool drives glazier's points quickly and efficiently.

For narrow moldings, you can make your own brad squeezer with a pair of slip-joint pliers. Cover one jaw with self-adhesive foam weather-stripping tape to protect frame finishes, and put the other jaw against the brad head. Then simply squeeze the brads into the molding.

If you will be doing much framing, or if you would rather use glazier's points, invest in a glazier's tool, which is loaded and used much like a staple gun. With the tool positioned on the backing, and against the inside of the frame molding, you drive a diamond-shaped glazier's point every time you squeeze the handle.

Whether you use brads or glazier's points, you must drive enough to hold the work securely in place. For the smallest works, that means at least two per side, or eight in all. The larger the work, the more you will need spaced along each side of the molding—a half-dozen or more per side in the largest works.

Attaching Dust Seals

There are several ways to attach dust seals. My favorite way calls for a piece of kraft paper cut slightly larger than the frame and attached with white glue or carpenter's wood glue.

With the frame face down, I run a narrow bead of glue along the rear edge of the frame, and spread it evenly with a folded paper towel (you can use your finger if you prefer). I let that stand while I completely dampen the kraft paper with a sponge. Then I lay the frame, glued side down, onto the damp paper, press it firmly in place, and carefully turn it over. I examine the entire rear edge to make sure the frame is completely sealed, and I press the paper in place wherever necessary.

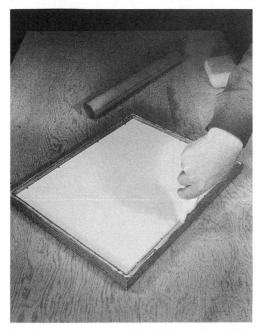

Apply an uninterrupted bead of wood or white glue to the rear edge of the frame.

On wide moldings, spread glue with a finger or paper towel. Then dampen kraft paper with a sponge.

I then let the frame stand until the paper dries completely. As it dries, it shrinks and tightens. Properly attached, a dust seal will become taut as a tom-tom.

Large dust seals can buckle as they dry, so I cut slits into the excess that extends beyond the frame edges. This relieves pressure and allows the seal to cure perfectly.

There are several ways to trim the seal. One way is to lay the frame face up on a mat-cutting board or bench, and use an X-Acto knife at a 45-degree angle to cut away the excess along the frame's edge. This is perhaps the fastest way, but it is also the riskiest way, as one little slip of the knife, and you could shave wood away from your frame.

A much safer way is to lay the frame

Make sure kraft paper completely seals rear of frame.

Cut slits in the excess of large dust seals to keep them from buckling.

One way to trim a dust seal is with the frame face up, using the molding as a guide.

A better way is to lay the frame face down, and crease the paper along the rear edges of the frame.

face down and crease the seal with your thumb along the outer edge of the frame. Then lay a straight edge along one side of the frame, about 1/16 inch inside the edge, and cut along the straight edge with an X-Acto knife. Repeat the process along each edge until all excess paper has been trimmed away.

The easiest way to trim a dust seal is with a framer's border knife, which you can buy for about $5 or so. If you have much framing to do, I recommend the investment. The knife uses X-Acto and similar blades and makes trimming a dust seal a breeze. After creasing the seal along the edge of the frame, cut the excess away, with no need of a straight edge and no fear of cutting into the frame. The knife keeps the blade running about 1/16 inch from the frame's edge and makes trimming foolproof.

You can also attach dust seals with double-sided tape or adhesive transfer tape and the Scotch applicator. Some who use this method recommend cutting the kraft paper the same size as the frame and laying it on the taped rear edge of the frame, but this is risky. Better to cut the paper oversize, as with the wet method, skip the dampening with a sponge, lay the taped frame on the paper, turn it over, and trim the excess.

Then trim away excess with a straight edge and X-Acto knife.

I have never been completely satisfied with my results using the dry method, but maybe that's just my lack of competence. I suggest you try both methods, and pick the one that works best for you.

Installing Oils, Acrylics, Batiks, and the Like

Although most of the works you frame will probably be installed in the manner we have just discussed, you might have occasion to frame oil paintings, acrylics, and other works that are not displayed behind glass. They require different treatment entirely. You won't find much in print on the techniques, perhaps because any method that securely holds a work in a frame without damaging it is sufficient. There are a few practices used by some framers and discussed in some of the framing literature, however, that I want to caution you against.

Before installing paintings on canvas boards, hardboard, or canvas and stretcher frames, stick a small self-adhesive felt cushion near each inside corner of the liner or frame to prevent any damage to the image area behind the molding lip. If the molding lip is too narrow for precut cushions, cut your own from a sheet of self-adhesive felt.

Works on canvas attached to stretcher frames are usually set inside liners and frames or frames without liners, depending on the framer's preference. Many framers nail the stretcher frame to the liner or frame, a practice I avoid, as it makes any later removal of the canvas and stretcher frame difficult and often leads to damage. What's more, nails will eventually rust and stain canvas edges, which might reduce the value of the work.

A framer's border knife makes trimming dust seals easy.

Some framers also seal the backs of such frames with cardboard or kraft paper, and this, too, is a practice you should avoid. Works on canvas and stretcher frames require free air circulation, which such seals inhibit.

I have heard it argued that these seals help protect canvases from damage when they're laid on sharp objects—presumably knives, swords, spikes, barbed wire, bungee sticks, machetes, saws, chisels, and the like. To my way of thinking, any dolt so careless with a valuable painting as to lay it on a sharp object deserves whatever happens. A painting spends most of its time hanging on a wall, where—barring brawls, gunfights, earthquakes, and tornadoes—it ought to reside in relative safety. If you must attach something protective to the rear of the frame, make it a piece of plastic screen, which will afford a modicum of protection while allowing air to circulate.

Liner and frame moldings come in various depths or thicknesses and accommodate stretcher frames differently. In a deep molding, a stretcher frame will fit with plenty of room for attaching hardware. In a shallow molding, the stretcher frame will protrude beyond the rear of the molding, calling for different installation techniques.

Some framers treat stretcher frames as they would mounted and matted works, and in a deep molding simply secure them with brads. In shallow moldings, they drive brads into the rear edge of the

Turn buttons and mending plates are some of the hardware you can use to secure canvases on stretcher frames inside picture frames.

frame or liner molding, then bend the brads over to secure the stretcher frame.

At some frame shops and hardware stores, you will find brass or brass-plated hardware you can use to secure stretcher frames inside most moldings. Use offset clips with brass screws to secure stretcher frames that protrude beyond the frame or liner molding. You can also use offset clips on stretcher frames set in deep moldings, although there are other methods you might prefer.

If there's sufficient room in a deep molding after the stretched canvas is set in place, you can simply secure it with tacking strips. Cut the strips from parting bead or lattice that you can rip to a ½-inch width. Tack them to the inside surfaces of the molding, just behind the stretcher frame with 1-inch brads or wire nails. Use only enough fasteners to hold the painting in place, and the job will be easily reversible, should you ever need to remove the painting from the frame. This is also the method I prefer to use with works done on canvas boards or on hardboard, both of which are considerably thinner than stretcher frames and allow for easy installation.

Other methods and materials work well too. If the rear of the stretcher frame is flush with the rear of the liner or frame molding, you can attach a small piece of mending plate at each corner to hold the stretcher frame in place. You can also use turn buttons attached with screws and even nylon webbing attached with staples.

As I said, any methods and materials are appropriate, as long as they secure a work in its frame without doing damage. On a trip to the Far East, I bought an original oil painting by Roger San Miguel, an artist hailing from Manila. I

Nylon-filament tape and heavy-duty staples at each corner can secure a stretcher frame inside a picture frame.

later decided that shipping it in a frame might help protect it, so I had a rather massive frame made for the large painting in Okinawa, only to learn later that the two would have to be shipped separately.

When my painting arrived in the States some months later, it was in perfect shape, but the frame was broken. I repaired it and temporarily installed the painting in it with strips of nylon-filament (strapping) tape across each rear corner of the stretcher frame. I reinforced each strip of tape with two more strips, and drove staples through the tape into the frame molding. I hung the painting on a wall—the safest place to store it—until I could get around to building a new frame for it, or at least installing it with the proper hardware. That was nearly twenty years ago, and since then that painting has hung in three apartments, a log cabin, and two houses. Those strips of filament tape are still holding the stretcher frame in place as well as any hardware might. So I now use

this method regularly for similar installations.

Installing Hanging Hardware

The most common way to prepare works for hanging is with screw eyes and picture-hanging wire, which is a lightweight braided cable. Keep an assortment of different-sized screw eyes on hand, and use the longer, heavier-gauge ones with large works and massive moldings.

To install hanging hardware, turn the frame face down, and measure about a third of the way down the rear edges of the left and right sides. Make a small pencil mark on each side in the center of the molding, and use a nail set or scratch awl to punch a screw-starter hole at each spot. Then drive a screw eye into each starter hole. Start the screw eyes by hand, and finish driving them with the nail set or awl for added leverage.

Run several inches of picture-hanging wire through one screw eye, double the

Installing screw eye with nail set.

Attaching picture-hanging wire.

On heavy frames, install four screw eyes as shown.

tag end back on the main length, and wrap it in a tight spiral. Secure the other end to the opposite screw eye the same way, so that when the wire is pulled toward the frame top, it will be from 1 to 6 inches from the frame edge, depending on the size of the work and your own preferences. You'll do yourself a great favor by carefully measuring this wire-to-frame distance with a steel rule or with a picture-wire jig you can make. This is doubly important for any pictures you will hang in groups, as this makes precise hanging much easier.

Large and heavy frames require heavy-duty rigging. Install screw eyes as above, as well as two more on the bottom molding strip, about a third of the way in from each bottom corner. Attach the picture wire to one of the bottom screw eyes, thread it through the nearest side screw eye, across to the opposite eye, and finally to the remaining bottom eye. Secure it by twisting, and use a steel tape rule or picture-wire jig to determine the frame-to-wire distance, as above.

Most professional framers attach small, self-adhesive felt cushions to the bottom corners of the frame to prevent dust from collecting and to allow air to flow freely around the frame back. I use the felt cushions on some small frames and where the screw eyes are attached inside the frame so the frame will hang flat against a wall, but then I use cushions on all four corners.

Normally, instead of the felt cushions, I make tiny rubber pads from ¼ x ½-inch self-adhesive, high-density weather-seal tape. I stick a pad several inches inside each bottom rear corner. This not only allows air to flow around the frame and keeps dust from collecting, but it also makes frames hang parallel to the wall.

Attaching self-adhesive rubber pads.

Velcro has a number of uses in the framing craft. It comes in small kits and large rolls.

Moreover, the rubber material clings to the wall, keeping pictures hanging straight.

On some commercial frames where I can't use my rubber pads, and in areas where heavy foot traffic keeps pictures dancing on walls, I have found that Velcro works well. You can buy it in kits of self-adhesive hook-and-loop pieces, or do as I do and buy it by the roll. On small frames, put one piece bottom center on the rear of the frame, and its mate on the wall. On large frames, use two pieces on each frame, several inches inside the bottom rear corners, and mate them with two more on the wall. It takes a bit of adjusting to get each frame set just right on the wall, but once it's done you won't have to do it again.

Sawtooth hangers are useful with some frames, particularly those that are too narrow to accept even the smallest

Sawtooth hangers come in several sizes and styles and can be installed with cushioned pliers.

screw eyes. Some commercially made certificate frames are this small and require sawtooth hangers. To install them, it's best to position them in the rear center of the top frame section, and squeeze the nails in with pliers. The slip-joint pliers with cushioned jaws I described for driving brads work well for this.

There are gummed hangers available for lightweight frames. Although I can't heartily recommend their use, I must confess that I have used them on some commercially made frames. They work well with metal frames, for example, when attached to the backing board. I have never trusted the adhesive on them,

so I always reinforce them with a strip of package-sealing tape or several strips of nylon-filament tape. Truth be known, they have worked well for me, so my reluctance to recommend them must be viewed as a personal prejudice.

Decorative rings are another alternative. On a small work, you can install one in the center of the top frame section. On larger works, install two in the top of the frame, each just inside a top corner.

Since decorative rings allow nails or hangers to show, I don't care much for them. So I rarely use them. There are some decorative hangers, however, that complement the rings and aren't half

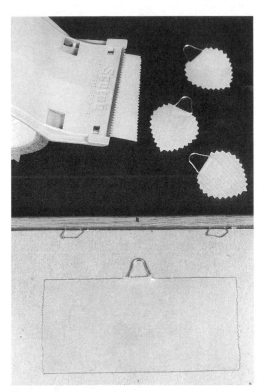

If you use gummed hangers, reinforce them with packaging tape.

Decorative hooks and rings come in several sizes and styles.

bad. I have used them from time to time, and while I haven't been enthralled by them, they haven't made me ill.

How to Make an Adjustable Picture-Wire Jig

With a few scraps, several hardware-store cheapies, and a little time in the shop, you can make an adjustable picture-wire jig that will make picture-hanging jobs foolproof.

Although you can make this jig with softwood scraps, hardwood is better. Even though I made mine from oak, you can use walnut, maple, cherry, mahogany, or whatever you have on hand, and you can make it from two kinds of wood if you wish. And you can use hardwood plywood instead of the ¼-inch Micro Wood.

All you need is a scrap of 1 x 2 at least 12 inches long, a scrap of ¼-inch Micro Wood measuring at least 1 x 8 inches, a ¼ x 1-inch brass flathead machine screw, a ¼-inch brass wing nut, and a ³/₁₆ x ³/₄-inch copper rivet.

If you don't own a table saw, skip Steps 6 and 7, and use a ¼ x 1¼-inch brass screw instead of the 1-inch screw called for. Here's how it all goes together.

Step 1. From a scrap of ¼-inch oak Micro Wood (or plywood) at least 8 inches long, rip a 1-inch-wide strip. Then trim a scrap of oak 1 x 2 to 12 inches.

Step 2. Scribe a line across a broad surface of the 1 x 2 at 6 inches from each end, mark the center of the line, and center punch a drill-starter hole there.

Step 3. Scribe lines across a broad surface of the Micro Wood strip at ½, 2¼, 3¼,

Picture-wire jig, Step 3.

4¼, 5¼, 6¼, and 7¼ inches from one end. Mark the center of each line, and center punch a drill-starter hole at each spot.

Step 4. Drill a ³/₁₆-inch-diameter hole ½ inch from the end of the Micro Wood. Then drill a ⁹/₃₂-inch-diameter hole at each of the remaining spots marked on the Micro wood and through the center of the 1 x 2.

Step 5. Use a conical grinding attachment to countersink the ³/₁₆-inch hole in the Micro Wood to accommodate a ³/₁₆ x ³/₄-inch copper rivet. Then countersink the hole in the 1 x 2 to accept the brass machine screw.

Picture-wire jig, Step 5.

Step 6. Stand the 1 x 2 on a narrow edge, measure along the other narrow edge, and make marks 5½ inches from each end. Then use a combination square to scribe guidelines across the narrow edge at those marks.

Step 7. Remove the blade guard from a table saw, and set the blade for a ¼-inch depth. Lay the 1 x 2 on the saw table with the countersunk hole up. Then use the miter gauge to run the 1 x 2 over the blade repeatedly to remove the material between the guidelines, creating a ¼-inch-deep, 1-inch-wide dado in a broad surface of the 1 x 2.

Step 8. Trim the Micro Wood strip to 8 inches. Then mix a small amount of five-minute epoxy cement, and apply it sparingly to the countersunk surface of the 3/16-inch hole in the Micro Wood. Push

Picture-wire jig, Step 6.

Picture-wire jig, Step 7.

the rivet into the hole, and let stand until the cement sets.

To attach picture-hanging wire with the aid of your picture-wire jig, decide on what distance you want between the picture wire and the top edge of the frame, and set your jig for that distance. The holes in the Micro Wood strip are spaced at 1-inch increments from 1 to 6 inches from the rivet.

With the frame face down and screw eyes installed, attach one end of the picture wire to one screw eye as you normally would. Then scribe a centered vertical line across the top frame section, and align the jig at the top of the frame by centering the guideline in the holes in the Micro Wood stem. Loop the picture wire over the rivet, and run it through the other screw eye. Pull the wire tight, and wrap the tag end around the wire as you normally would. The picture wire will now be a specified distance from the frame top. If you had the jig set at the third hole above the rivet, for example, the wire will be 3 inches from the frame top.

Tips on Hanging and Displaying

Something often said about a clumsy, inept person who has no mechanical aptitude or tool savvy is "He can't even hang a picture straight." The implication is that any dolt with five thumbs on each of his two left hands can hang a picture. Well, it is easy, but there's more to it than pounding a nail into a wall and draping the picture wire over it.

In hanging and displaying pictures, so much depends on tastes, personal preferences, the requirements of the works being displayed, and the characteristics

Attaching picture-hanging wire with the aid of the jig.

of the display environment that it's impossible to lay down laws or rigid rules. But a few general tips and suggestions might help you accomplish what you're setting out to do.

One of the first things to consider in hanging any work or collection of framed items is how high on the wall they should be. Of course, furnishings and fixtures in any room will influence such decisions, but there is a generality that at least provides a starting point. A common suggestion is to hang a picture at eye level. Whose eye level? I daresay, there's a difference between the eye level of the typical NBA star and the average jockey, just as there's a difference between the eye level of a 6′ 2″ man and his 5′ 2″ wife.

And there's possibly a difference between what looks good to me and what looks good to you.

I suspect that there's a tendency among tall folks to hang pictures too high. I know I had that tendency until I started paying close attention to such matters in museums, galleries, and even in others' homes and offices. I soon concluded that the pictures hanging a bit lower than I would have hung them were the ones that looked best. So I began hanging pictures lower.

I wish I could give you a convenient formula for this, but I can't. There is none. What I do now is find the visual point of impact in any framed item, which I try to hold at my eye level as I take my measurements from the floor or ceiling. Then I hang the item 8 inches lower, which is my wife's eye level. When I back off, it looks just right to me. We might surmise, then, that this would be too high for my wife, but I asked her and it seems just right to her.

In a typical room with an 8-foot ceiling, my pictures end up hanging slightly above an imaginary horizontal centerline. And so do groupings, which I consider as single entities, with each picture a part of the whole. But how high they hang depends on a number of variables. In our master bedroom, on a small stretch of otherwise bare wall hangs a large vertical oil painting that's 41 inches high. The bottom of the frame is 30 inches from the floor, and the top is 25 inches from the ceiling. In another room are two vertical prints comparable in size to the oil painting, but they hang 10 inches higher, because beneath them is a stereo cabinet that's 36 inches tall.

In rooms with vaulted ceilings and in open stairways with high ceilings, pictures can be positioned higher. In such areas we can often take advantage of great expanses of wall space to create interesting displays, from low to high. In other areas we can sometimes take advantage of spaces that are confined horizontally or vertically by exploiting them with works that are strongly horizontal or vertical. A strong horizontal, for example, might work well displayed above sliding glass doors, while a strong vertical might fit best next to an entry door or on a wall at the end of a hallway.

Large pictures do well in areas where they can be viewed from a distance, such as at the end of a corridor or on a wall in a large room opposite the entrance. Small works that should be viewed at close range are best displayed where the viewer is forced into closer proximity, such as along a hallway, down a stairway, or in a small bathroom. In our house, a long, narrow hallway that has no furniture in it is where we have our family "rogue's gallery" hanging – portraits and snapshots of friends, relatives, reprobates, pets, kids, and assorted outcasts.

When we hang most items, we intend them to be seen by viewers who are either standing or walking by. Consider, though, that in some rooms occupants will be sitting most of the time. For that reason, in our dining room and in my office, I hung pictures several inches lower than I normally would have.

Some people have difficulty imagining what the visual effect of any picture or group of framed items will be on the viewer in a particular setting. My advice is to sketch out the wall in scale to get an idea of how everything will come together. You don't have to be a skilled artist to do this. I measure any furniture or other fixtures along a particular wall, and sketch their outlines on graph paper with a pencil. I then measure the items I'm planning to hang and sketch them in, erasing and rearranging as necessary until I come up with a pleasing display. Then it's a simple matter to count off the squares on the graph paper and determine where my framed items will hang, relative to floor, ceiling, furnishings, and the like.

Groupings pose the biggest problem for most people. I find my 4-foot aluminum T-square a big help in locating where my nails or picture hangers are to go. And I use a small spirit level to adjust pictures once they're up.

I hang nearly everything with standard picture hangers. Some books on framing and decoration recommend hanging each picture with two hangers to keep them hanging straight, but I have trouble getting two picture hangers nailed into the wall at precisely the same distance from the floor or ceiling. And if one is so much as a mere 1/16 inch off, the picture will hang noticeably crooked. I prefer to use one hanger of appropriate size for each framed item and keep it hanging straight the ways I discussed earlier. One exception is when I'm hanging unusually heavy items, in which case I use two 100-pound-capacity hangers side by side, which is overdoing it, but it makes me feel more confident.

Standard picture hangers do not work on such hard surfaces as brick, stone, concrete, and ceramic tile. For hanging pictures on most brick, concrete, and cinderblock walls, there are special hardwall hangers made of plastic, with three case-hardened steel pins that you

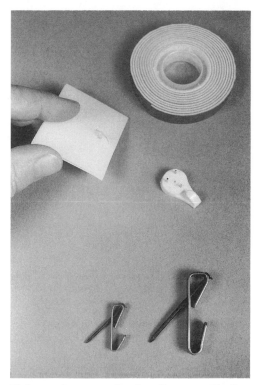

To hang pictures on hard walls, use self-adhesive foam mounting tape, self-adhesive plastic hangers, or plastic hardwall hangers. On other walls, use standard picture hangers (30-pound- and 100-pound-capacity hangers shown).

hammer into the wall. For natural stone, ceramic tile, and other very hard materials, use special self-adhesive plastic hangers made for such purposes, or try the double-sided adhesive mounting tape made by the 3M Company.

Several years ago, I was framing a limited-edition print with which I had received a small sheet of paper telling a bit about the artist and his work. I wanted to keep the paper, but I knew once the print and paper were separated I would never find it again. So I attached it to the dust cover. I now do so routinely with any important papers I wish to keep with the artwork, including brief notes I make on what materials I used in mounting and matting. If I have elected to let the mats cover a signature and number on a limited-edition print, I note that as well. I attach single sheets or envelopes containing several sheets of information and notes with plastic mounting corners I buy from Light Impressions (see directory).

11

Making Rustic Wood Frames

Rustic wood frames are among the most popular and, for many of us, the most attractive of frames. They fit any decor and can be used with the widest array of artworks, photographs, needlework, and three-dimensional items. Their rough finishes stand them in stark contrast to the neat, clean, and orderly contents they house.

If you are a fan of rustic wood frames, you're in luck, because rustic moldings are easy to make from some of the cheapest materials you'll find. Techniques for turning common stock into rustic moldings are easy and fun. What's more, if you remain alert for materials that will work as rustic frame moldings, you'll discover bargains frequently.

Commercially Made Rustic Moldings

The rough-hewn and distressed looks are popular enough for frame-molding manufacturers to offer an assortment of commercial moldings. Some are ordinary moldings that have been artificially distressed, usually by mechanical or chemical means.

Rustic moldings are available at most frame shops and at some lumber yards, home-improvement centers, and department stores. Use any commercial molding that you find attractive or that meets your needs, but exercise some caution when you shop.

Moldings that are simply made of

rough lumber are fine. Those that obviously have been sandblasted or wire-brushed for texture or stained to achieve a weathered look should be safe for any framing job. Those that look like barn siding or driftwood, and others that appear naturally distressed, could pose problems that I will cover momentarily.

Of course, you can ask questions about such moldings and how they were made, and maybe you'll be fortunate enough to find somebody with answers. If your experiences coincide with mine, however, you will find that the people trying to sell you these moldings know little or nothing about them, except the price, which is always too high.

Do you need any more reasons for making your own rustic moldings?

Unsuitable Woods

The rustic look is so popular that there are people who make good money roaming rural areas in search of old barns and other outbuildings they can buy, dismantle, and sell, board by board. And the price a farmer or rancher gets for such a building is usually enough for him to put up a new building and pocket a profit at the same time.

In coastal areas, driftwood is plentiful and free for the taking. Boards, limbs, and whole trees that have done sea duty and then washed up on beaches have that gray, weathered look that is so appealing and useful in many decorating and craft projects.

To be sure, some fine-looking frames have been made of moldings cut from barn siding, fence slats, driftwood, and other salvaged woods. But these are potentially some of the most damaging materials to use in any framing job. I

recommend you steer clear of them entirely.

Most of these woods have been invaded and occupied by any number of wood-boring insects and larvae—critters that can continue to do damage to the wood even after it has been turned into a picture frame. They can also invade the frame's environment (your house) and damage the frame's contents.

Any lumberman might tell you that one sure way to kill these wood borers and prevent any further damage is to run the wood through a kiln. And he's right. During the kiln-drying process, any insects or larvae inhabiting wood are killed, as are various fungi that attack trees. But the average do-it-yourselfer doesn't have access to a kiln. And even if you could put your salvaged wood into a kiln long enough to kill the pests, you would still have to deal with the problems of chemicals, salts, and other contaminants.

All sorts of chemicals, such as various fertilizers and insecticides, are stored in farm and ranch buildings and used near them. Defoliants often get sprayed along rural roadsides, near fence lines and buildings. Driftwood absorbs salt and minerals from the water. So there's no telling what these woods have been subjected to and what sort of damage they might cause.

Best Woods for Rustic Frames

The best woods for rustic frames are often the worst woods for other wood-working projects. Look for the unfinished or partially finished woods, those that are partially or poorly surfaced, the rough-hewn woods, the flawed and blemished boards and strips, the kiln-dried lumber that was once inhabited by wood borers and attacked by fungi.

You can't make frames with rotten wood or any product that is badly warped, cupped, checked, or too damaged to make into a molding. The wood must be flat, kiln-dried, and free of any contaminants. Beyond those, there aren't many strict requirements. In short, you will be looking for woods that others reject. Consequently, you will usually find them at good prices, or you will get them marked down when you point out the imperfections.

Whenever it's possible, I like to use woods that are naturally colored and require no staining. This saves time and money and makes finishing a simple matter. Generally, the darker woods—such as redwood, walnut, and some cedars—are best for such use, although there is at least one exception.

For some time I had kept watch for a suitable substitute for barn siding that would be relatively inexpensive, easy and safe to work with, plentiful, and readily available, but every bit as handsome as barn siding in rustic frames. One day, my search ended as I walked through a warehouse at a local lumber yard. As I passed an area where kiln-dried pine leaned against a wall in lengths from 8 to 20 feet, I noticed a stack of 4-foot 1 x 4s off to one side. They had probably been trimmed from 12-footers and discarded for their shabby appearance.

Rather than the familiar pine blonde, these boards were the dull gray of barn siding, the result of having been invaded by a fungus that attacks pine trees in the forest. Worst of all for most buyers, but perfect for my purposes, the wood was full of borer holes of every imaginable size and shape from having been inhabited by wood-eating larvae. A few tight knots and pitch pockets here and there only added character to the wood. For the average woodworker, handyman, or professional builder, this stuff was junk. For me, it was a treasure.

As I scanned the great stacks of 1 x 4, I could see that beautiful shade of gray showing along the edge of one board every once in a while. I decided I should ask some questions about this wood before I began piling up a load for my pickup truck.

At the sales desk, I learned that it was indeed kiln-dried. It was graded No. 4 common pine, and the price was 10¢ a lineal foot. Eureka!

That day, I loaded 244 feet of usable 1 x 4 into my truck and later turned it into 488 feet of 1 x 2. So I ultimately ended up with 488 feet of rustic molding that cost me $24.40, or about what one

Pine 1 x 4 in the center is what most buyers want, but the gray boards full of borer holes are best for rustic picture frames.

small rustic frame would cost me at a frame shop.

I stop by that lumber yard regularly, and I always check the No. 4 common pine to see if it has been restocked recently. When a new shipment arrives, I sort through it and haul off another supply of framing material. At first, I looked only for the 1 x 4s grayed by long-dead fungi, but I noticed other colors that were striking in their own ways. Some were deep, rich brown; others were redder than Philippine mahogany. And all these were natural colors that penetrated the wood, which meant that moldings made from the material would not have to be stained.

I stay alert for any rough woods that I can easily turn into rustic moldings. I browse in the bargain sections of lumber yards and home-improvement centers where I frequently find small quantities of various species of wood that meet my needs. It's a kind of prospecting that is both profitable and enjoyable. Try it.

In addition to the rough woods and naturally distressed woods, some species are particularly suitable for making moldings that you can distress in the shop. The softwoods are best for this, and my favorites are incense cedar and pine, although I have worked with others to my satisfaction, such as redwood, fir, and hemlock.

I suggest you work with small quantities of inexpensive local softwoods to determine which of these are best. Start with pine and cedar, and try some scraps of local hardwoods too.

Creating Rustic Effects

You needn't have immediate access to a supply of naturally distressed woods, be-cause you can achieve rustic effects in your workshop that are hard to tell from the ravages of nature. In a few minutes, you can create ridges and valleys in the surface of a piece of wood that look identical to those nature took years to create with salt, sand, and sun. You can make holes in fractions of seconds that look like those it took whole populations of wood borers many generations to create. And you can have fun in the process.

You needn't be an artist, skilled technician, or master craftsman to make distressed picture frames. In fact, some of my favorite techniques are those I have discovered through my own klutziness. Perhaps that's one reason I find this sort of work so gratifying; it's as if I'm somehow getting even with those forces that cause a hammer to miss a nail and dent the surface of a fine piece of wood, or that cause the hammer to hit the nail but split the wood in the process, or that make screw threads strip, or that put gaps in miter joints.

Tools required are simple, and most are hand operated. In fact, you won't need power tools except to distress hardwoods. And you need no specific tools. Just look for anything that might work and try it. Chances are, you already have most or all the tools in your shop or somewhere nearby.

Some kind of hammer is good for denting. Any kind of hammer—claw, tack, upholsterer's—will do, but I particularly like the ball-peen for this work. The ball surface is ideal for making circular dents in the wood's surface—the harder the blow, the deeper the dent and larger the circle. With some moldings you might want to strike numerous surface dents of various sizes and depths, creating a sort of randomly textured surface. Then use the other striking surface of the hammer to put dents along the face corners of the frame or molding.

You can also use other objects that you strike with a hammer to create various interesting impressions in the wood. Put a paper clip on the wood, and strike one of the curved ends with a hammer to make a *U*-shaped dent. Bend a piece of wire in various ways, and strike it at random spots on the molding surface. Lay a screw on the molding surface, and strike its shank to make an impression of the threads. Try various sizes and kinds of screws. Use an awl, ice pick, and various sizes of nails to put scratches in the surface; then lightly sand the feathered edges of the scratches.

Use rasps, files, and scrapers to texture surfaces and round over sharp edges. Create texture by scraping the molding surface with a notched paint scraper, the tines of a fork, or the teeth of a coarse rasp.

I use 1 x 2 box and flat moldings for most of my rustic frames. I sometimes distress the moldings before making the frame; other times I distress the assembled frames. Usually, if it is a technique or combination of techniques I can accomplish quickly, I distress the molding. If it's a slower, more tedious process, I work on the assembled frame.

To create the weathered look of driftwood or barn siding with a 1 x 2 flat molding, for example, I start with a coarse wood rasp at one end of the molding, and I scrape the surface with the end teeth of the rasp, following the grain for the length of the molding. This creates a wavy pattern of shallow grooves, running with the grain. Then I use a scratch awl to add deeper grooves—fewer in number and looser in pattern—for the

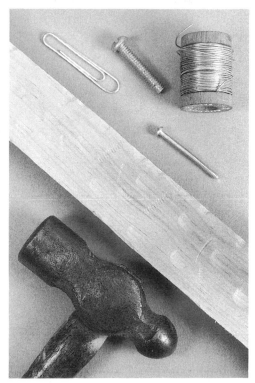

Some of the tools for distressing wood moldings.

length of the molding. I use a rasp to coarsely round over the front corners of the molding and to roughen the outside edge. Finally, I use a scratch awl or ice pick to punch holes of various sizes into the entire surface of the molding to simulate borer holes. I punch some holes straight in and others diagonally, as in nature. And I vary the force of the thrust to change the diameter and depth of the holes.

I get best results using these techniques on incense cedar, with pine running a close second. You can achieve similar effects with hardwoods, but you will probably want to use power tools then. Professional carvers use industrial

Various scrapers, rasps, and awls are good for creating the appearance of naturally distressed wood.

softwood, and use a wood-burning tool to create both texture and color in the frame's surface. Start at one corner miter, and work with the grain toward the center of that frame section. Then work from the miter at the opposite corner toward the center of the frame section. Do all sections the same way, and vary your techniques as you see fit. Start with a loose pattern of fairly deep wavy impressions running with the grain. Then fill in between with lighter and shallower strokes. The effect is stunning.

The Rough-Edge Box Frame

Often, the hardwoods I use in various woodworking projects come in boards that are surfaced (finished to a smooth

grinders, which are high-speed router-type tools, with various round and pointed bits. You can use the same or similar bits in an electric drill or a Dremel Moto-Tool.

You can also use heat to achieve some stunning effects. For example, with a propane torch, you can scorch the surface of pine flat molding until it is uniformly blackened. Then use a wire brush to scrape with the grain to remove the blackened wood, leaving behind a deeply textured surface ready for staining and finishing. With pine already naturally colored, you can skip the stain.

Build a frame of pine, cedar, or another

With a wood-burning tool you can create texture and color in a frame.

surface) only on their broad surfaces, usually referred to as "surfaced two sides" or "S2S." I resaw these boards to the various lengths and widths that I need, and for years I treated the unsurfaced edge strips as scraps for the kindling pile. When it dawned on me, however, that these rough edges would make attractive rustic faces on box-style frames, I started turning those scraps into molding.

I usually rip the strips from the board with my table saw or bandsaw to a width of 1½ inches to make my standard 1 x 2 box molding. I sometimes rip only 1 inch from the rough edges to leave more usable hardwood on the boards for other projects and to create a narrower box molding.

Making molding is a simple matter of cutting a rabbet into the strip with my table saw or routing the rabbet with my router and router table. Often, I accumulate scraps of this rough-edged material in random lengths, and when the mood strikes me, I turn it into frame molding. Then I build the frames at my leisure, or whenever I need one for a specific job.

The Wane Frame

As far as lumber quality and grading go, a wane is a defect that occurs in the edge of a board that has been cut from the outer portion of a log. It is the appearance of bark or the absence of wood along a board's edge. It usually takes the shape of an irregular bevel and is caused by the curvature of the log. Such boards are usually downgraded and sold cheaply. But a few always manage to get by the grader and will be found with the higher grades of lumber.

Keep watch for such boards. When you can buy them cheaply, do so. If you find

Rough-edge box frame and molding.

them with expensive lumber, let a salesman know and ask that they be downgraded and reduced in price. You should know, though, that some hardwoods are sold in slabs with wanes on one or both narrow edges, and these won't be marked down.

Like most people, for years I sorted out and culled such defective boards whenever I shopped for wood. And when I brought home a load of lumber and found a waned board later, I cursed the grader who let it slip by and questioned his ancestry.

On one such occasion, I pulled a badly waned board from a stack of pine and was ready to cut it into kindling when it dawned on me that I could make frame molding from it that might not look half bad. So I ripped the wane from the board and stacked the strip with other 1 x 2 waiting to become molding. I found another piece of pine with a large pitch

Ripping 1 x 2 for wane molding.

Finished wane frame.

Use a wood rasp or scraper to shape pieces at corners.

pocket in it that matched the dark color of the wane in the other board, and later used these pieces in a large frame I made.

My wane frame got favorable comments from many who saw it, and I have since kept a sharp eye out for good buys on such lumber. Most of my wane frames are made of 1 x 2 flat molding. At the outside corners, where adjoining pieces don't usually match because of the uneven bevel of the wanes, I use a small scraper or rasp to form and match the pieces.

If the wanes and pitch pockets in the woods you use are attractively colored, you might not want to stain the frame at all, or you might wish to only lightly stain it. With some wane frames, you might also want to try combining some of the distressing techniques mentioned earlier.

Rustic System Frames

I have developed a system for using my basic box and flat moldings and matching 1 x 2 stock to create a variety of frame configurations. I think you will find the system useful in your own framing. You can also use this same system with finer, smooth-surfaced woods, but my own preference leans toward the rustic appearance.

Consider Frame Style #1 to be the simple box frame, made from 1 x 2 according to directions in Chapter 8. This frame is suitable for framing any work requiring a narrow molding.

Frame Style #1.

Frame Style #1.

Making rustic frame Style #1.

Frame Style #2 is ideal for subjects requiring a wider molding. Start by constructing the basic Style #1 frame. Then clamp a piece of matching 1 x 2 broad side down in a miter box, and cut one end at a 45-degree angle. Use the basic frame as a guide to mark the 1 x 2 for the second cut; the inside edge of the 1 x 2 should match the outside edge of the corresponding piece in the basic frame.

To make a Style #2 frame, start by assembling a Style #1 frame.

Attaching miter-cut 1 x 2s to Style #1 frame to make a Style #2 frame.

After making the second cut, attach the 1 x 2 with glue and 1¼-inch brads, flush with the frame's rear edge. Attach miter-cut 1 x 2s to the remaining three sides of the frame, applying glue to the joints as well as to the inside edges of the 1 x 2s. Finally, drive and countersink a brad at each corner to secure the joints. When the glue sets, your Style #2 frame is ready for final finish.

Although only ½ inch wider than the Style #2 molding, Style #3 molding appears more massive and complex, yet requires only one more strip of molding. It's a good choice for dynamic or dramatic artworks that will be prominently displayed.

Start by building a Style #2 frame. Then miter cut a piece of Style #1 molding to fit one outer edge of the 1 x 2, apply glue to the inside of the molding, and attach it to the 1 x 2 with 1¼-inch brads. Continue attaching molding to the remaining three sides, applying glue to the joints as you proceed. Countersink the brads, and when the glue sets, your Style #3 frame is ready for finishing.

These are the three basic molding styles, but this system allows you to make other combinations as well. Make a flat molding from 1 x 2 stock, for example, and consider that Style #4. Now build a basic Style #4 frame and add the Style #1 molding to its edges for a completely new effect. Call that Style #5.

Attach strips of matching, miter-cut 1 x 2 to the outer edges of the Style #5 frame, and you have a Style #6 frame.

This is a versatile and useful system that should serve you well on many

Frame Style #2.

Making rustic frame Style #3.

Frame Style #3.

framing jobs. In your spare time, play around with some scraps of Style #1 and Style #4 moldings and scraps of matching 1 x 2 and discover some of your own designs.

Finishing Rustic Frames

Rustic frames usually require minimal finishing. You might need to do a little sanding to shape a piece or make two adjoining pieces match. If you're using a wood that has been inhabited by wood borers, use an awl and various sizes of nails and brads to pick clogged dust out of the holes. And clean frames thoroughly before staining or applying final finish.

Most rustic frames can be finished without staining, particularly those that are already naturally colored. But others will need to be stained. As with any other frames, experiment with various stains on scraps of the same wood the frame moldings were made of.

Stains that have black pigment in them work well if you're trying to simulate the weathered look of barn siding or driftwood. Depending on the type of wood you're using, try Watco English Oak Danish Oil Finish straight or diluted with Watco Natural. Try oil-base ebony stains, straight or diluted with mineral spirits or paint thinner.

Seal frames with a coat of shellac; then apply the final coat of your choice. You will probably find a dull-matte or satin-sheen polyurethane works best.

12

Making Floater Fixtures and Frames

Pictures that seem to float off the wall with no visible means of suspension, and those that seem to float as mysteriously inside their frames, are popular illusions. The effects are easy to achieve with simple but deceptive techniques.

Photographs are probably the most popular items to be displayed in such ways, although you might occasionally see paintings on Masonite and some mounted three-dimensional items or carvings floated off a wall or in floater frames. Sometimes whole arrangements are floated at different distances from the wall to form floating collages.

Although commercially made floater or "California floater" frames and floater-frame moldings are on the market, they aren't widely available. So you will either have to do some searching or resort to more reliable and less expensive alterna-

tives: making your own floater fixtures and frames. By now, you should know what my recommendation will be.

How to Make Floater Fixtures

Photographs are often mounted and displayed without mats, glass, or even frames. One attractive way to display flush-mounted or border-mounted prints is with the aid of floater fixtures that are easy to make and install.

If you plan to display pictures this way, you must, of course, mount them first. Although you can use conventional mount boards made of mat board or chipboard, it's best to use something more rigid and durable, such as Gatorfoam, codaFoam, or Masonite.

Mount your photographs to the appropriate material, according to directions in Chapter 4. Depending on the photographs and your intentions, you might wish to coat the edges of the mount board in some way to make them less conspicuous. Most of the prints I display this way are flush-mounted, and I use a permanent felt marker to blacken the edges.

To make floater fixtures, cut scraps of ¾-square stock or 1 x 2 to lengths of 3 inches. (You'll need two for each print.) Sand the ends to remove any splinters left by the saw, and use a combination square set at 1½ inches to scribe a center line across each.

To keep pictures hanging parallel to the wall, you will need to mount two fixtures to the back of each mount board. For pictures 8 x 10 inches or larger, use either ¾-square or 1 x 2 fixtures, and mount onc fixturc 2 inches from the top edge of the mount board and another 2 inches from the bottom edge. For pictures smaller than 8 x 10 inches, use only the ¾-square fixtures, and mount them 1 inch inside top and bottom edges.

To attach fixtures, first scribe a vertical center line on the back of the mount board. Then, depending on the size of the picture, scribe horizontal guidelines across the mount-board back 1 or 2 inches from the top and bottom edges. Mix a small amount of five-minute epoxy cement, apply it to one surface of the fixtures, and press them in place, using the guidelines to center them on the mount-board back, 1 or 2 inches from the top and bottom edges.

There are several ways to hang these pictures. If you are going to hang them on plaster walls or any other wall that might be damaged by adhesives, use a screw eye and nail to hang each one. Before attaching the two fixtures to the

Attaching ¾-square fixtures with epoxy cement.

Top fixture with screw eye attached for hanging.

Velcro on fixtures.

back of any mounted picture, install a small screw eye in the center of the top edge of the top fixture. When fixtures have been attached, use a small wire nail to hang each picture.

On hard walls or wherever you can hang your pictures without concern for any damage adhesives might do, there are two excellent ways to "float" your pictures. After attaching the floater fixtures, apply a strip of double-sided foam mounting tape to each fixture, and mount the pictures directly to the wall. Another way—and the one I prefer—is to attach self-adhesive Velcro tape to the fixtures and to the wall. Pictures mounted with Velcro are easy to adjust, and they can be removed and replaced by other similarly mounted pictures.

You can make fixtures out of other materials, too, and you will want to do so if you wish to display them at different distances from the wall. With fixtures made of screen molding, for example, pictures will hang ¼ inch from the wall (not including the thickness of the mounting medium). Parting-bead fixtures will float them ½ inch from the wall. Fixtures made of 2 x 2 allow 1½ inches distance.

A coat of flat black paint on the fixtures will keep them from being visible in the shadows behind the pictures.

How to Make Floater Frames

What gives the impression of a picture floating inside a frame is the frame's slightly larger dimensions and its black interior. The dark space around the edges of the mounted picture, between the picture and the frame molding, not only creates the illusion, but also functions the way a mat or liner does to separate a work from its frame.

Making floater frames from scratch is easy. For the molding, you can use any wood that is suitable for picture molding, and you can stain and finish it any way you wish.

For the frame illustrated, I used pine 1 x 2 that I ripped from 1 x 10 stock. When the frame was assembled, I stained it with a half-and-half mixture of Fuller O'Brien Pen-Chrome #640-06 Flemish Black and #640-13 Platinum stains to give the frame an overall grayish tint, suggestive of the foggy scene being framed.

You also have a choice of the amount of space you want around the picture, or between the picture edges and the frame molding. You probably won't want this

Floater frame, Step 1.

Floater frame, Step 2.

distance to be more than ½ inch or less than ⅛ inch.

Once you have made decisions on these variables, follow these easy steps to build your floater frame.

Step 1. After mounting your picture to a suitable mount board (Masonite in this case), use a permanent felt marker to carefully blacken the edges. Then measure the height and width of the mounted picture. Double check the measurements, and record these dimensions on a note pad.

Step 2. Set the table-saw fence 1½ inches from the near teeth of the blade, and rip 1 x 2s from available stock.

Step 3. Set the fence 1½ inches from the far teeth of the blade and the blade for a

Floater frame, Step 3.

Rabbeted molding next to a 1 x 2.

¼-inch depth. Lay each 1 x 2 on a broad side, with a narrow edge against the saw fence, and cut a ⅛ x ¼-inch rabbet into the other narrow edge.

Step 4. With a miter box and backsaw set at 45 degrees, cut a vertical frame section 1 inch longer (inside measurement) than the height of the mounted picture, and a

horizontal section 1 inch longer than the width of the picture. (This will result in a ½-inch space around the picture; for a ¼-inch space, cut sections ½ inch longer than picture dimensions.)

Step 5. Cut one end off two pieces of molding at a 45-degree angle. Then use the sections cut in Step 4 to mark the molding strips for second 45-degree cuts.

Step 6. Assemble a basic frame with glue and corner clamps. (If necessary, review frame-building procedures in Chapter 7.)

Step 7. Drive two 1¼-inch brads at each corner, and countersink them.

Step 8. Use a wood filler to fill the brad holes, and let the frame stand with clamps in place until the glue and filler set.

Floater frame, Step 4.

Floater frame, Step 5.

Floater frame, Step 6.

Floater frame, Step 7.

Floater frame, Step 8.

Step 9. Sand the frame with a pad sander and 120-grit and 220-grit sandpaper, rounding over outside corners and edges as you sand. Then clean the frame, apply the stain of your choice, and let it dry.

Step 10. Lay the frame face down, and measure the height and width of the frame inside the rabbets. Then cut a piece of ⅛-inch tempered hardboard ¹/₁₆ inch smaller in height and width.

Step 11. Lay the hardboard smooth side up, and scribe a vertical center line on it. Measure down from the top and make marks at 2⅝ inches and 2⁵/₁₆ inches. Then drill a ¼-inch hole at the topmost spot and a ¾-inch hole at the other spot.

Step 12. Run a narrow bead of glue along the rabbet in the rear of the frame, lay the hardboard in place in the rabbet, and put a can of paint or other heavy object on it until the glue sets.

Floater frame, Step 11.

Step 13. Cut two 1 x 2 glue blocks 4 inches shorter than the inside height of the frame. Mix a small amount of five-minute epoxy cement, and apply it to a broad surface of each piece of 1 x 2. Attach one glue block 2 inches from the top, bottom, and right inside edges of the frame and the other block 2 inches from the top, bottom, and left inside edges.

Step 14. Apply an even coat of shellac to the frame molding, and let it dry completely. Then apply the finish coat of your choice to the face and sides of the molding (satinsheen polyurethane, semi-gloss lacquer, etc.).

Step 15. Attach masking tape to the broad faces of the 1 x 2 glue blocks. Then attach tape to the face of the frame mold-

Floater frame, Step 13.

Floater frame, Step 14.

ing, leaving the inside surface of the molding exposed.

Step 16. Apply two coats of flat black enamel to all interior surfaces of the frame and let dry. Then slowly remove the masking tape.

Step 17. Mix a small amount of five-minute epoxy cement, and coat the broad surfaces of the glue blocks. Lay the mounted picture on the glue blocks, position it carefully with the aid of a steel tape rule, and lay a tissue-paper-covered book on it until the cement cures.

Step 18. Stick a ¼-inch self-adhesive felt protective pad just inside each rear corner of the frame, and your picture is ready to hang with a small wire nail.

Floater frame, Step 16.

Floater frame, Step 15.

Floater frame, Step 17.

Floater frame, Step 18.

Finished floater frame.

You can make floater frames from stock other than 1 x 2 molding, but this is a good size to start with. For a narrower molding, use bullnose stop with the rounded edge as the face of the frame. For an even narrower, slat-type molding,

use lattice. With either of these, follow the same directions as above, except in Step 3. Instead of setting the blade for a ¼-inch depth, set it for a ⅛-inch depth, which will create a ⅛ x ⅛-inch rabbet in this thinner material.

13

Framing without Miters

Although the miter joint is the customary joint to use in building picture frames, there's no law that says all frames must be made the same way. Not long ago, I did some experimenting in an attempt to come up with some simple but attractive alternatives to the miter-joined frame. I ended up with two styles of frames that are not only pleasing to look at but also offer a few other advantages.

I still make the great majority of my frames with miter joints and will continue to do so. But when the mood strikes me to do something a little different, I like knowing I have the option.

Both of my designs for nonmitered frames call for my old standby 1 x 2 stock, and either can be made with softwood or hardwood. Finishes are a matter of the builder's choice, and the frames can be used with any work that

would look good inside a mitered frame made with 1 x 2 flat molding.

So when you're in the mood for a change of pace, build one of my butt-joint or lap-joint frames.

How to Build Butt-Joint Frames

To build a simple butt-joint frame, start by cutting two vertical sections ⅛ inch longer than the vertical measurement of the mounted artwork, mats, and glass. Double the width of the molding material, add that to the horizontal dimension of the work, plus ⅛ inch, and cut two horizontal sections to that length.

To make a 1 x 2 frame for an 11 x 14-inch vertical subject, for example, you would cut two vertical sections of 1 x 2 to 14⅛ inches. The horizontal sections would be 11⅛ inches plus twice the

Butt-joint frame, Step 2.

Butt-joint frame, Step 3.

width of the 1 x 2 (2 x 1½" = 3"), or 14⅛ inches.

Similarly, a 1 x 2 frame for a 16 x 20-inch horizontal subject would require two vertical sections at 16⅛ inches and two horizontal sections at 23⅛ inches (20⅛" + 3" = 23⅛").

For purposes of illustration, let's assemble a 16 x 20-inch butt-joint frame for a vertical subject. Here's how.

Step 1. With a miter box and backsaw set at zero degrees, cut two horizontal pieces of 1 x 2 to 19⅛ inches and two vertical pieces to 20⅛ inches.

Step 2. Stand the two short sections on their narrow edges. Set a combination square at 1 inch, and scribe a line across

the top narrow edge of each piece, 1 inch from each end. Reset the square at ½ inch, and scribe lines across the ends. Set the square at ⅜ inch, and mark the center of each line.

Step 3. Centerpunch a drill-starter hole and drill a pilot hole at each spot marked, using a 7/64-inch bit in an electric drill.

Step 4. Apply glue to the end of a vertical section, butt it to one end of a horizontal section at a right angle, and clamp the two pieces with a corner clamp. Attach another vertical section to the opposite end of the horizontal. Then glue and clamp the other horizontal to the opposite ends of the verticals.

Step 5. Drive a 6d finishing nail through each hole in each vertical, and countersink the nails. Then fill the nail holes and let the frame stand until the glue and filler set.

Step 6. With a miter box and backsaw set at zero degrees, cut two horizontal pieces of parting bead to 17⅛ inches and two vertical pieces to 19⅝ inches.

Step 7. Apply glue to the end of a vertical section, butt it to one end of a horizontal section, and clamp it with a corner clamp. Continue assembling the frame with glue and clamps, as in Step 4.

Step 8. Drive a 1-inch brad near each end of each horizontal into the vertical sections. Countersink the brads, fill the holes, and let the frame stand until the glue and filler set.

Step 9. Sand all surfaces of both frames with a pad sander and 120-grit and 220-grit sandpaper.

Butt-joint frame, Step 5.

Butt-joint frame, Step 4.

Butt-joint frame, Step 7.

Butt-joint frame, Step 10.

Butt-joint frame, Step 11.

Step 10. Lay the large frame face up. Measure in 1 inch from the top and bottom left corners, and make light pencil marks near the top and bottom frame edges. Align a strip of wood with the two marks, and clamp it to the frame with two C-clamps.

Step 11. Run a narrow bead of glue along the front edge of the frame window. Lay the small frame atop the large frame, against the wood strip and 1 inch from the top, bottom, and right edges. Clamp the small frame to the large frame at each

corner and elsewhere as necessary. Then let it stand until the glue sets.

Step 12. When the glue has set, sand the frame, as required, with a pad sander and 220-grit sandpaper, slightly rounding over front edges and corners as you sand.

Step 13. Brush and vacuum the frame to remove all dust. Apply the stain of your choice, and let it stand overnight. Then apply a coat of shellac and the finish coat of your choice.

Of course, there are other ways to finish your butt-joint frames. They can be painted with frame colors matching colors in the work being framed. You might also stain the frame, then paint

Butt-joint frame ready for stain and final finish.

LAP-JOINT FRAME DIMENSIONS

GLASS AND MAT OUTSIDE DIMENSIONS	LAP-JOINT FRAME INSIDE DIMENSIONS	LAP-JOINT FRAME OUTSIDE DIMENSIONS
5 x 7	5-1/8 x 7-1/8	7-3/8 x 9-3/8
8 x 10	8-1/8 x 10-1/8	10-3/8 x 12-3/8
9 x 12	9-1/8 x 12-1/8	11-3/8 x 14-3/8
11 x 14	11-1/8 x 14-1/8	13-3/8 x 16-3/8
12 x 16	12-1/8 x 16-1/8	14-3/8 x 18-3/8
14 x 18	14-1/8 x 18-1/8	16-3/8 x 20-3/8
16 x 20	16-1/8 x 20-1/8	18-3/8 x 22-3/8
18 x 24	18-1/8 x 24-1/8	20-3/8 x 26-3/8
20 x 24	20-1/8 x 24-1/8	22-3/8 x 26-3/8
24 x 30	24-1/8 x 30-1/8	26-3/8 x 32-3/8
24 x 36	24-1/8 x 36-1/8	26-3/8 x 38-3/8

only the smaller frame in a color matching the predominant color in the work. Another option is to build the wide frame with one type of wood (pine, fir, oak, or maple) and the narrow frame with a similar species but contrasting color (redwood, red cedar, walnut, or mahogany).

How to Make a Lap-Joint Frame

The lap-joint frame is a bit more complex than the butt-joint frame. The required cuts can be made with a table saw, even a small benchtop model. Joinery requires simple C-clamps or spring clamps, rather than the usual corner clamps. And the glued lap joints make one of the strongest of frames.

The inside dimensions of your lap-joint frame should be ⅛ inch greater than the outside dimensions of the mounted work, mats, and glass, as with any conventional frame. For standard sizes, refer to the accompanying chart to determine the right length for the 1 x 2 sections of the miterless frame. For odd sizes or frames larger or smaller than those listed, there is a simple formula. After determining the frame's inside dimensions, add 2¼ inches to the length of each frame section.

To turn the 1 x 2 into frame molding, you'll need to cut a ⅜ x ⅜-inch rabbet along one edge of each piece. After removing the table saw's blade guard, set the blade for a ⅜-inch-deep cut, and posi-

Cutting a lengthwise groove in a narrow edge with a table saw.

tion the rip fence ⅜ inch from the far teeth of the blade.

With a frame section resting on a narrow face, and with a broad face against the fence, use push blocks to run it through the saw, creating a lengthwise groove. Lay the piece broadside down, and run it through the saw again, creating the rabbet. Do the same with the other three pieces. (*Caution:* The sliver being removed from each piece will shoot right out of the saw. So stand to one side, as you always should when operating a table saw, and make sure no one else is in the path of the blade.)

Whether you're framing a horizontal or vertical picture, cut the laps into the frame-piece ends the same way. Remove 1½ inches of material to a depth of ⅜ inch at each end of the *face* side of the short pieces, and 1⅛ inches of material from each end of the *back* side of the long pieces.

To accomplish this, remove the saw's rip fence and set the miter gauge at zero.

Making the second cut to create a rabbet.

Making guide marks 1½ inches inside each end of each short piece.

Cutting end laps in short pieces with a table saw.

Four frame sections, ready for assembly.

Mating pieces are shown here face down.

Assembling the frame with glue and clamps.

Closeup of the lap-joint corner.

Finished lap-joint frame.

Measure 1½ inches inside each end of each short piece, and make a guide mark. Lay the piece *face down* on the saw table, against the miter gauge, and position it so the saw will make the first ⅜-inch-deep cut 1½ inches from the end. After making the cut, continue making passes over the blade until the material from the mark to the end has been removed. Do likewise at the opposite end of the piece.

Do the same on the long pieces, except lay them *face up*, and mark for laps 1⅛ inches from the ends. Check joints for fit, and carefully rasp away any excess material.

Apply an ample and even coat of wood glue to the end laps, and join the verticals to the horizontals. Clamp each corner with a C-clamp and clamp cushions or a spring clamp with cushioned jaws.

When the glue has set, sand the frame with a pad sander and 120-grit and 220-grit sandpaper, carefully rounding over corners and edges as you sand. Clean the dust away, and your frame is ready for finishing.

To the red-oak frame shown, I applied a coat of Fuller O'Brien Pen-Chrome #640-11 English Oak Stain, let it penetrate fifteen minutes, wiped the frame dry with paper towels, and let it stand overnight. The next day, I gave it a coat of sanding sealer and a coat of satin-sheen polyurethane and burnished lightly between coats with 400-grit waterproof sandpaper.

Everything else was standard procedure. I stacked the glass, matted work, and backing in the frame, secured everything with glazier's points, and attached a dust seal. I installed hanging hardware, and my framed work—in this case a color photograph of a Labrador retriever—was ready for display.

14

Framing without Frames

It's possible to display some framable items without frames, and should you wish to do so, there are several methods and an assortment of products and materials you ought to know about.

We touched on the idea of frameless display in Chapters 4 and 12 in discussing photographs and posters, which are the items most often displayed without frames. Of course, it is possible to display other items using the techniques that follow, but keep in mind that these are not archivally safe procedures. So I cannot recommend their use on anything of significant value.

Most of the frameless display methods offer easy changeability, which is another reason they appeal to photographers, who often produce more photographs than there is room to display at one time.

Similarly, when children discover the joys of drawing and coloring, they often produce more works than can ever be taped to a refrigerator door. Give them special treatment with some of the quick-change methods and means that follow.

Mainly, this is an idea chapter, something to get your creative juices flowing. Here I will introduce you to some of the various commercial products available and a few of the items you can make yourself. But as I have done before, I'm going to recommend that you browse at the frame shops, photo-supply outlets, and in the frame departments of department stores to see what's available there.

Although there are some products that will be around for a long time to come, this is a changeable area, and the only way to keep abreast of what's in and what's out is to browse.

Passe-Partout's Passé

Some people use vinyl tape or linen tape to sandwich photographs, posters, or inexpensive reproductions between glass or acrylic and backing material. The vinyl tape comes in black, white, and a few bright colors and sometimes can be matched with a color in the work being displayed. This so-called passe-partout method of displaying a work was more popular before the development of quicker and easier alternatives. Those who still favor it argue that it is a better method because the tape keeps dust from collecting behind the glass. Frankly, I would rather use one of the other methods and take my chances with the dust, which I can always remove later if I wish. Remember, we're not talking about displaying valuable artworks here. And the fact is, I have never had a dust problem with any of the alternative methods.

You can use glass or acrylic in this method; each has its advantages and disadvantages. Glass is sharp-edged, so you must be extremely careful when you tape the edges. But glass is more rigid and does not tend to bow as acrylic might. Acrylic is lighter, but it scratches easily and attracts dust and lint.

Both glass and acrylic are difficult to keep clean during the taping process, because you must handle the material so much. Glass will provide sufficient rigidity for any mount-board material, but if you use acrylic, you should make sure

that your mount board or backing is sufficiently rigid. For that reason, such products as Gatorfoam, codaFoam, and hardboard work best with large items sandwiched behind acrylic.

My major objection to this old-fashioned technique is that it is tedious and time-consuming, and the results don't justify the expenditure of energy and time. What's more, there are products on the market now that make displaying without frames quick, easy, and enjoyable.

Frameless Display Aids

I have already mentioned using Velcro hook-and-loop tape for "floating" pictures off walls and for keeping framed works hanging straight. You can also use it for frameless display of any mounted photograph or poster. It's especially valuable for its quick changeability, and for that reason is also good for displaying children's art.

For most mounted works up to 11 x 14 inches, you can usually get by with two 1-inch pieces of Velcro attached to the back of the mount board in the center and an inch from top and bottom edges. With prints and posters 16 x 20 inches or larger, put a 1-inch piece of Velcro about an inch inside each corner of the mounting board. Then attach the mating pieces to the wall, and you will be able to switch like-sized works anytime you wish.

At the hardware store, home-improvement center, or the hardware department of any department store you will find plastic mirror holders that come four to a package, with screws, for under $1. You can use these little clear-plastic brackets to display mounted photos and posters of any size on walls and solid-

Mirror holders.

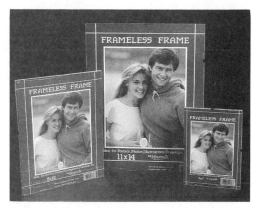

Intercraft Frameless Frames, available in standard sizes.

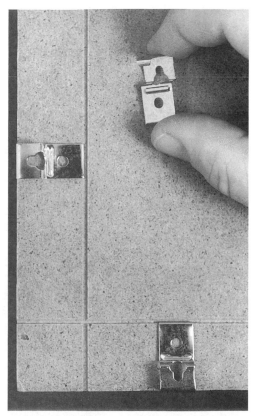

Spring-clip hangers on Intercraft Frameless Frames snap into grooves in hardboard back to sandwich work behind acrylic.

core doors. Always attach the bottom two brackets first. Then use the mounted work as a guide for mounting the top two brackets. Allow ⅛ inch extra room for expansion and to make display changing easy.

Intercraft manufactures a large variety of frames and related items that you will find in the frame departments of department and discount stores. One of their products is called the Frameless Frame, and it comes in all the usual standard sizes. It consists of ⅛-inch hardboard backing material, a matching piece of nonglare acrylic, and four spring clips.

To use one of the Frameless Frames, first disassemble it by pressing each clip inward and lifting it out of the groove in the back of the hardboard. Then separate the acrylic and hardboard, remove the protective film from the acrylic, and clean the acrylic to remove fingerprints and other smudges. Sandwich the framable item between the acrylic and hardboard, attach the four clips, and your work is ready for display.

The clips on the Frameless Frame serve two purposes other than holding everything together. Each also functions as a hanger for vertical or horizontal placement, and all four keep the work hanging parallel to the wall.

Another Intercraft product I like is even simpler to use. It's a clear acrylic box with a white cardboard box that fits snugly inside. These units come in standard sizes. Remove the cardboard box, clean the acrylic as necessary, lay your photograph or other framable item in the

Intercraft acrylic boxes, available in standard sizes.

acrylic box, and press the cardboard box back in place. Punch out the appropriate hole in the back of the cardboard box, and hang your work vertically or horizontally.

The Uni-Frame

There are several products available that provide suitable alternatives to the passe-partout technique. At frame shops and some mail-order suppliers you will find various metal and plastic clips, brackets, and systems designed for sandwiching photographs, posters, and other works between glass and backing.

Eubank Frame, Inc., makes several such products, and my favorite is their Uni-Frame, which comes in two sizes. Uni-Frame 20 is for works with outside dimensions up to 20 x 20 inches and sells for about $4. Uni-Frame 40 will handle prints and posters from 16 x 16 inches to 40 x 40 inches and is the one I use for most of my posters. It costs about $6.

With the Uni-Frame you can sandwich material up to ¼ inch thick, which includes glass, mat, picture or poster, and mount board or backing. I recommend foamboard for mounting or backing, and you can use it in either ⅛-inch or ³/₁₆-inch thicknesses, depending on how thick the rest of the sandwich is. I use the ³/₁₆-inch board, because I don't normally use mats with posters.

Use glass with the Uni-Frame, not acrylic, because glass is rigid and will not bow as acrylic will. The glass edges will be exposed in this arrangement, so you might want to have the edges seamed (beveled) at the glass shop, or you can lightly smooth them over with a fine diamond hone or diamond file, such as the DMT Diamond Whetstone or DMT Crys-

You can lightly smooth over the sharp edges of glass with a diamond file, such as the DMT Crystal Saver.

tal Saver, available at cutlery shops or from Diamond Machining Technology, Inc. (see directory).

It's difficult to make any poster and glass match perfectly in size. Invariably, one will be a tiny fraction of an inch larger than the other. So it's important to check the glass and the poster before assembling a Uni-Frame.

I always lay a poster face down on my matting bench and lay the glass atop it. If the poster is slightly larger, I trim it with an X-Acto knife, using the glass edge as a guide. If the poster is slightly smaller, there's nothing to do but let the backing disguise the fact. If the poster has white

borders, the white of the foamboard conceals the size discrepancy. If the poster has black borders, I don't want white foamboard showing, so I make a black border on the foamboard face with a permanent felt marker. I also blacken the edges of the foamboard.

Foamboard and glass, of course, should be cut to identical dimensions. Whether or not the poster should be mounted depends upon its condition. If it has been carefully stored flat and has no dents or dings, you can simply sandwich it between glass and foam board. If it is curled, wrinkled, or otherwise damaged, mount it or have it mounted.

The Uni-Frame couldn't be simpler. It consists of only four corner clamps, a tension spring, and a length of cord that pulls everything together. Here's how it works.

Step 1. Adjust the four clamps to fit the size and format of the work you're sandwiching, according to the manufacturer's directions.

Step 2. Lay the glass, mat, poster or other work, and foamboard on a work surface

Uni-Frame, Step 2.

Uni-Frame, Step 3.

Uni-Frame, Step 4.

Uni-Frame, Step 5.

in that order. Then position a clamp at each corner.

Step 3. Securely tie one end of the cord to one end of the tension spring with a double knot or clinch knot.

Step 4. Facing the bottom of the foam-board, position the spring between the bottom two clamps, with the cord end on the left, run the cord clockwise around all four cleats, and put it through the remaining ring on the spring.

Step 5. Pull the cord tight enough to slightly tense the spring, loop it around the cleat on the bottom right clamp, and pull it tight to secure it.

By using the four corner pieces in the combinations shown, the Uni-Frame system can be adjusted to support work up to 40″ x 40″

HORIZONTAL RECTANGLE   SMALL SQUARE   VERTICAL RECTANGLE   LARGE SQUARE

Uni-Frame assembly.

That's all there is to it. Use a standard picture hanger, and drape the top horizontal length of cord over the hanger. The plastic corner clamps will then keep the work hanging parallel to the wall.

The whole process takes only minutes and couldn't be easier. What's more, the results are mighty pleasing to look at.

The very day I used a Uni-Frame to sandwich a killer whale poster by popular West Coast artist Don McMichael, I was at a local shopping mall and walked past a gallery displaying that very poster in a Uni-Frame. When I saw the $95 price tag, I walked out laughing.

These posters are on sale at various outlets up and down the coast for $20, unframed. I paid $13.50 for the glass, $6 for the Uni-Frame, and about $3 for the foamboard backing, or $42.50 for everything. The whole job couldn't have taken me more than fifteen minutes, including the time it took to clean the glass and trim one edge of the poster. Yet my labor turned out to be worth $52.50 on this job. That's $210 an hour!

I never cease to be amazed by the amount of money people can save by doing their own framing and related chores.

Make Your Own Frameless Display Brackets

You can make brackets and strips for displaying mounted works without frames that allow for quick and easy changeability. You will find a variety of readily available materials—even scraps—that are suitable for making them, and some require only the simplest of tools. A pair of brackets will display a single item, and two strips will display several.

Don McMichael poster in a Uni-Frame.

All such brackets and strips are similar in that the one designated as the bottom piece has a lip or groove for the mounted work to stand in, and the top piece is identical, but with the lip or groove facing downward to act as a retainer.

The only difference between the brackets and strips is length. Brackets are short; strips are long. You can make the brackets to exactly match the width of the item being displayed, or you can cut them shorter or longer. For example, if you're making a pair to display an 8 x 10-inch horizontal photograph, you can make your brackets as short as 3 inches, exactly 10 inches, or slightly over 10 inches. I prefer them slightly oversized.

No matter whether you're making brackets or strips, and regardless of their size, their lips or grooves should be at least ⅛ inch wide to accommodate mounted works with single mats and to allow easy switching of pictures. If you want to display items with multiple mats, make the grooves or lips wider.

You might make a pair or several pairs of strips to span a few feet or the full length of a long wall. Longer strips should be securely anchored to the wall. Either mount them with screws attached to the studs, or use toggle bolts in hollow sections of the wall.

If you own a table saw, you can make the simplest of brackets and strips by merely cutting a centered groove into the narrow edges of lengths of 1 x 2. Remove the blade guard and splitter, set the blade for a ¼-inch depth and the fence $^5/_{16}$ inch from the near teeth of the blade. Then stand a 1 x 2 on a narrow edge, with a broad face against the fence, and use push blocks to run it over the blade, creating a centered groove ⅛ inch wide and ¼ inch deep for the entire length. Then turn the piece over and groove the opposite edge. Do likewise with the matching bracket or strip.

You can rout the edges of such brackets

Ovalhead screws and finish washers.

and strips, sand them, and apply the finish of your choice. They can be stained and varnished or painted. You can attach the brackets to the wall with adhesive foam mounting tape or screws. Use screws to attach the strips. If the screws will show, use oval-headed screws with finish washers. Or you can counterbore the screw holes and conceal screw heads with button plugs. (See directions below for "Decorative 1 x 2 Brackets.")

If you don't own a table saw, the simplest brackets and strips are those made with lengths of 1 x 2 and ¾ x ¾-inch outside corner molding. You'll need some small scraps of ⅛-inch Micro Wood, hardboard, or foamboard to use as spacers. Cut 1 x 2 to whatever length you deem appropriate for brackets or strips; then cut a piece of corner molding for each to the same length. Prenail one side of each piece of corner molding with 1-inch brads spaced about 6 inches apart. Run a thin bead of glue along the inside surface of the nailed side of the molding. Then press the molding in place on a matching piece of 1 x 2 with the glued edge against a narrow edge of the 1 x 2. Use spacers between the broad surface of the 1 x 2 and the other side of the molding to create a lip ⅛ inch wide, and drive the brads into the 1 x 2. Countersink the brads, and fill the holes with wood filler.

When the filler dries, sand the brackets or strips, as required, with 120-grit and 220-grit sandpaper, and they're ready for finishing and attaching to the wall.

You can make similar brackets and strips by substituting ½ x ½-inch (inside dimension) aluminum corner molding for the outside corner molding. Stain or paint the 1 x 2 before attaching the aluminum molding. Then use a hacksaw to cut the aluminum to the same length as the 1 x 2. Drill screw holes in one side of the aluminum, and attach it to the 1 x 2 with ½ x #4 aluminum roundhead screws.

Micro Wood Brackets

If you own a router and router table and some kind of bench-type or stationary power saw, you can make simple, attractive, and functional brackets from scraps of Micro Wood. Just follow these easy steps.

Step 1. With a table saw, radial-arm saw, or bandsaw, rip ¼-inch Micro Wood into 1-inch-wide strips.

Step 2. Insert a ½-inch straight bit into a router collet. With router attached to a router table, adjust the bit for a ¼-inch-wide, ³/₁₆-inch-deep rabbet, and run each strip through the router and table.

Step 3. Trim each bracket to a length slightly greater than the width of the item to be displayed. Then attach two

Micro Wood brackets, Step 2.

Micro Wood brackets, Step 1.

Micro Wood brackets, Step 3.

or more pieces of double-adhesive foam mounting tape to the rear of each bracket.

Step 4. Peel the release paper from the foam tape on one bracket, and use a spirit level to position it on the wall—with the rabbet up—where you want the bottom of the work to be.

Step 5. Put the mounted work on the attached bracket, and use it as a guide to mark light pencil lines at the top corners of the mount board. Then make marks ⅛ inch above those, and erase the first marks.

Step 6. Peel the release paper from the foam tape on the remaining bracket. Align it with the guide marks made in Step 5, and press it in place with the rabbet facing down.

Your Micro Wood brackets are now ready to display your mounted work. Simply slide the work behind the brackets' retaining lips, and change your display instantly, any time you wish.

A bas-relief print of a caribou stands with vinyl-covered mat in Micro Wood brackets.

Decorative 1 x 2 Brackets

These brackets are a bit fancier than the others we've discussed, but they're still easy to make. What's more, they have one design improvement over the others. Since they have rabbets at the top and bottom, they can be used in multiple displays, and in such use, fewer brackets are required. For example, you can display two mounted prints with only three brackets, or four prints with six brackets, and so on.

The brackets are made of 1 x 2. Use your favorite hardwood—oak, walnut, maple, cherry, birch—and buy some matching ⅜-inch button plugs (you'll need two per bracket). Apply the stain and finish of your choice, and don't forget to finish the button plugs the same way.

Here's how to make these attractive brackets.

Step 1. Cut two pieces of hardwood 1 x 2 slightly longer than the width of the work you plan to display.

Step 2. Set a combination square at 1 inch, and scribe pencil lines across each piece, 1 inch from each end. Reset the square at ¾ inch, and mark the center of each line.

Decorative 1 x 2 brackets, Step 2.

Decorative 1 x 2 brackets, Step 3.

Decorative 1 x 2 brackets, Step 4.

Decorative 1 x 2 brackets, Step 5.

Decorative 1 x 2 brackets, Step 6.

Finished 1 x 2 brackets.

Step 3. Center-punch a drill-starter hole at each spot marked on the 1 x 2s. Then use a ⅜-inch brad-point bit to drill a ⅜-inch-deep hole at each spot, and drill through the center of each hole with a ³/₁₆-inch bit.

Step 4. With a ½-inch straight bit in a router and the router attached to a router table, adjust the unit to cut a rabbet

¼ inch wide and ⅛ inch deep. Then lay each 1 x 2 on the table with large holes up, and cut a rabbet along one inside edge. Turn each piece around, and cut a rabbet into the opposite edge.

Step 5. Replace the straight bit in the router with a ⅜-inch-radius cove bit, and set it for a ⅛-inch depth. Lay a strip of 1 x 2 on the table with rabbets up and one end against the fence. Then run each end of each piece over the bit.

Step 6. Now lay a 1 x 2 on the table with rabbets up and a long edge against the fence. Run it over the bit, turn it around, and run the other edge over the bit. Then do likewise with the other piece to cut coves along all four sides of each piece. (If you want deeper coves, reset the router, and repeat Steps 5 and 6.)

Step 7. Sand brackets, as required, with a pad sander and 120-grit and 220-grit sandpaper. Then apply stain and finish of your choice to them and to four ⅜-inch button plugs.

Step 8. Install the brackets on a wall with #8 wood screws or toggle bolts (in hollow walls). Mount the bottom bracket first, using a spirit level to position it. Use the mounted work to mark guidelines for the top bracket, and position that one allowing an extra ⅛ inch.

15

Framing Calendars

Calendars seem to show up everywhere. Offices and businesses always display them, and I think it's safe to assume they are in most homes. In fact, calendars often show up in several rooms of a house. We have one hanging in the kitchen, and I keep one in my office, another in my studio, and one in the shop. And I'm not even counting the digital calendars and the ones on our watch faces.

As useful, even necessary, as calendars are, and as decorative as so many calendar publishers try to make them, I have never considered them particularly attractive in any environment. To me, a calendar looks like an open magazine nailed to a wall sideways.

In some places this doesn't matter much, if at all. The besmudged calendar hanging on the grimy wall of my mechanic's garage couldn't look much worse, but needn't look any better. The calendar in my workshop is just there to remind me of what day it is, not as a comment on proper shop decor. But in my cedar-walled studio and office, and certainly in our highly visible kitchen, I think calendars should blend with the room's ambiance.

If you have photographs displayed with thumbtacks, and posters taped to the wall, fine. Then go on and nail a calendar right up there with them. But chances are, you have photographs, posters, and artworks tastefully framed and carefully displayed. Perhaps you'll want to give calendars similar attention.

The plans that follow offer two ways to give any calendar special treatment. Inside dimensions of the calendar frame are 14 x 22 inches; the calendar case is 13 x 22 inches. These will accommodate most calendars. If you're accustomed to using larger calendars, you need only alter the dimensions to fit your needs.

In both the frame and case, calendars hang from small decorative hooks or hangers that come in various sizes and configurations. Some are self-adhesive; others attach with nails; still others have nail shafts attached to them. Take your pick, but if you use the last, clip off the nail shaft with wire cutters.

Incidentally, calendars are popular Christmas gifts. Consider what a fine gift a calendar would be inside one of these beautiful frames or cases.

Make a Calendar Frame

This simple, attractive calendar frame offers you several options. Instead of the

Calendar frame, Step 2.

outside corner molding the directions call for, you can substitute any frame molding you like. Or you can skip the molding altogether and let the 1 x 2 frame your calendar unadorned, which was my intention in my original design of this frame.

Although the directions call for decorative rings as hanging hardware, you can attach the frame directly to the wall, if you prefer, with screws into the studs or toggle bolts in any hollow section of the wall. If that's what you want to do, after Step 6 below, before sanding the back panel, drill two 7/32-inch-diameter holes, vertically centered 4 inches from the top and bottom of the back panel. Then skip Steps 13 and 14.

You won't need much in the way of materials for this frame. In fact, you might be able to make do with scraps left over from other woodworking projects. You'll need a 7-foot piece of oak 1 x 2, or two pieces at least 24 inches long and two at least 16 inches long. If you use the ¾ x ¾-inch oak corner molding or similarly narrow frame molding, you can squeak by with a 7-foot strip, but should probably buy an 8-footer. Or you can round up four pieces at least as long as the 1 x 2 sections. The back panel is ¼-inch oak plywood, and you'll need a scrap at least 14½ x 22½ inches.

You will need glue, ¾-inch brads, and wood filler. For hardware, buy a pair of decorative hanging rings or ring pulls, a small decorative picture hanger or hook, and a pair of decorative hangers to mount on the wall.

Here's how this one goes together.

Step 1. From a 7-foot strip or suitable scraps of oak 1 x 2, cut two pieces to 24 inches and two to 16 inches.

Step 2. Tighten a ½-inch straight bit in your router's collet, and adjust the router and table for a ¼-inch-deep, ¼-inch-wide rabbet. Then stand each oak strip on a narrow edge on the router table, and rout a ¼-inch x ¼-inch rabbet along one edge of each piece.

Step 3. Keeping the rabbet on the rear edge, cut off one end of each piece at a 45-degree angle with a miter box and backsaw or power miter saw.

Step 4. Align one end of a yardstick with the inside edge of the miter on each piece, and mark two pieces for cuts at 22 inches and the other two at 14 inches. Then make the second 45-degree cut on each piece.

Calendar frame, Step 4.

Calendar frame, Step 5.

Step 5. Apply wood glue to the mitered ends of the frame sections, and assemble the frame with four corner clamps. Let stand until the glue sets.

Step 6. Lay the frame face down and measure the height and width inside the rabbets. Then cut a piece of ¼-inch oak

Calendar frame, Step 3.

Calendar frame, Step 7.

plywood to ¹/₁₆ inch under those dimensions.

Step 7. Lightly sand the good face of the plywood with 120-grit and 220-grit sandpaper. Run a narrow bead of glue along the inside corner of the rabbet in all sections of the 1 x 2 frame, and lay the plywood panel into the rabbets. Toenail ¾-inch brads through the back panel into the frame sections, and countersink the brads.

Step 8. Use a pad sander and 120-grit sandpaper to sand the face and sides of the 1 x 2 sections. Then use the sander to round over the inside front edges and rear edges of the sections.

Step 9. Cut a piece of ¾ x ¾-inch (outside dimension) oak outside corner molding

with 45-degree angles at the ends, to fit one long edge of the frame. Mix a small amount of five-minute epoxy cement, and apply it to the inside corner of the molding. Clamp the molding to the frame with two or three spring clamps, and let stand until the cement cures.

Step 10. Miter cut a piece of corner molding to fit one of the short frame sections; then cement and clamp it in place. Continue cutting and cementing molding until the face of the calendar frame has been framed with corner molding.

Step 11. Sand the molding, as required, with 120-grit and 220-grit sandpaper, rounding over corners as you sand. Clean the frame to remove dust, wipe it with a tack cloth, and apply the stain and finish of your choice. The frame shown was finished with Watco Medium Walnut Danish Oil Finish.

Step 12. Unless you're using a self-adhesive hook or hanger for the calendar, mix a small amount of five-minute epoxy cement, and apply it to the back of a deco-

Calendar frame, Step 10.

rative hook. Then attach it near the top in the center of the back-panel face.

Step 13. Measure in 2 inches from each top corner, and make marks on the 1 x 2 frame ½ inch from the rear edge. Punch a pilot hole with a hammer and nail set or a scratch awl at each spot, and install a pair of decorative rings.

Step 14. Lay the frame face down on a protected surface, and attach a ¼-inch self-adhesive felt cushion just inside each rear corner.

Build a Calendar Case

You can build a fine-looking calendar case with a little effort and a few scraps of oak 1 x 2, ¾-square, bullnose stop, and ¼-inch plywood. If you don't have suitable scraps on hand, buy one 7-foot piece each of oak 1 x 2, oak ¾-square, and oak ⅜ x 1¼-inch bullnose stop. You will also need a scrap of ¼-inch oak plywood, 13½ x 22½ inches or larger. And that's all the wood you'll need.

For hardware, you'll need two small brass hook-and-strap closures, two brass flat hinges, two 2 x #10 ovalhead wood screws, two #10 finish washers, a small brass knob, a small decorative hook or hanger, glazier's points, and 1-inch brads. If you will be mounting the case on a hollow section of wall instead of directly to the studs, substitute toggle bolts for the ovalhead screws.

You'll find numerous hinges that will work. Make sure the ones you pick are substantial enough to support the weight of the door and to hold up under use, but they should be no wider than two inches. The ones I chose are antique brass, and they're 1½ x 3½ inches.

Calendar frame, Step 13.

Finished calendar frame.

At the glass shop, have a piece of window glass—not picture glass—cut to 12¹⁵/₁₆ x 21¹⁵/₁₆ inches.

When you have gathered these few materials together, you're ready to begin. Here's how.

Step 1. From suitable scraps or the 7-footers you bought, cut two pieces of oak ¾-square to 24 inches and two to 15 inches. Do likewise with the oak bullnose stop.

Step 2. Coat one surface of each strip of ¾-square with glue, and clamp a matching piece of bullnose stop to it with four C-clamps and clamp cushions to form strips of door molding with a beveled lip. Wipe away seeping glue with a damp sponge, and let stand until the glue sets.

Step 3. With a miter box and backsaw set at 45 degrees, cut two pieces of the door molding to 23½ inches and two to 14½ inches, each mitered at both ends. Then stand the oak 1 x 2 on a narrow edge in the miter box, and cut four pieces the same size as the door molding.

Step 4. Set the table-saw fence 1¼ inches from the near teeth of the blade and the blade for a ¼-inch depth. Lay a piece of the mitered 1 x 2 inside broad surface down on the saw table, with a narrow edge against the fence. Then use push blocks to run the piece over the blade. Do likewise with the other three pieces.

Step 5. Move the saw fence to 1⅜ inches from the near teeth of the blade, and run each piece of 1 x 2 over the blade again

Calendar case, Step 2.

Calendar case, Step 3.

Calendar case, Step 4.

Calendar case, Step 6.

to create a ¼ x ¼-inch rabbet in the rear edge of each.

Step 6. Apply glue to the ends of the door molding, and assemble a simple frame with four corner clamps. Wipe seeping glue away with a damp sponge, and let the frame stand until the glue sets.

Step 7. Similarly, apply glue to the ends of the 1 x 2s, and assemble a frame with corner clamps. Wipe excess glue, and let stand until glue sets.

Step 8. When frames are completed, sand them with a pad sander and 120-grit and 220-grit sandpaper, slightly rounding over the front edges of the door frame as you sand. Then clamp the two frames together with C-clamps and clamp cush-

ions, and round over the corners with the pad sander so they will match.

Step 9. Lay the 1 x 2 frame face down, and measure the height and width inside the rabbets. (It should be about 13½ x

Calendar case, Step 7.

Calendar case, Step 10.

Calendar case, Step 11.

22½ inches.) Cut a back panel of ¼-inch oak plywood about 1/16 inch smaller.

Step 10. Scribe a vertical center line down the rear surface of the back panel, and mark for screw holes at 4 inches from the top and bottom edges. Center-punch a starter hole and drill a 7/32-inch-diameter hole at each spot.

Step 11. Sand the face of the back panel with a pad sander and 120-grit and 220-grit sandpaper. Run a narrow bead of glue along the rabbets in the 1 x 2 frame, lay the back panel in place, toe-nail 1-inch brads through the plywood into the 1 x 2, and countersink the brads.

Step 12. Thoroughly clean the partially assembled case to remove all dust, and wipe with a tack cloth. The unit is now ready for the finish of your choice.

Step 13. To duplicate the finish of the case shown, liberally apply Fuller O'Brien Pen-Chrome #640-11 English Oak Stain with a brush. Let it penetrate fifteen min-utes, wipe dry with paper towels, and let stand overnight. Then apply a coat of sanding sealer and two coats of satin-sheen polyurethane, burnishing lightly between coats with 400-grit waterproof sandpaper.

Step 14. When the finish has dried, clamp the two components together at the top and bottom with C-clamps and clamp cushions. Stand the unit on a narrow edge, and position the hinges 2 inches from the top and bottom corners. Use the hinges as guides to mark for screw holes. Punch pilot holes with a hammer and nail set or scratch awl, and attach hinges with the screws provided.

Calendar case, Step 14.

Calendar case, Step 17.

Calendar case, Step 15.

Finished calendar case.

Step 15. Turn the unit over, and position hook-and-strap closures 2 inches from the top and bottom corners. Then mark for and punch pilot holes, and attach closures with the screws provided.

Step 16. Lay the unit face up. Measure down the door frame on the opening side, and make a mark 11¾ inches from the top edge and ½ inch from the outside edge. Center-punch a starter hole, and drill a ½-inch-deep pilot hole slightly smaller in diameter than the knob screw. Then attach the knob.

Step 17. Clean the glass. Open the door, and lay the glass in place. Then secure the glass with equally spaced glazier's points – three each in top and bottom sections, and five each in the side sections.

Step 18. Unless you're using a self-adhesive hook or hanger, mix a small amount of five-minute epoxy cement, and apply it to the back of a decorative hanger. Then attach it near the top in the center of the back-panel face.

Your calendar case is now ready to hang on the wall with screws or toggle bolts. Attach the top screw first, and use a spirit level to make sure the case hangs evenly.

16

Framing Pegboard

Perforated hardboard, more commonly known as perfboard or pegboard, is one of the most useful products there is for various storage and organization projects. It's available at lumber yards, home-improvement centers, and at many discount or department stores. Primarily, it is a functional material, but it can be made attractive. And it's useful anywhere you might want to put it. Most often, it shows up in workshops, garages, basements, kitchens, sewing rooms, hobby rooms, and children's rooms. Since it is inexpensive but easy to work with, homeowners find many applications for it.

When we built the house we currently live in, I covered one 24-foot wall of the garage with pegboard and have since covered nearly every square inch of it with tools, implements, camping gear, cordage, boating equipment, and anything else that will hang from a peg or hook. There, I first put up furring strips and attached the pegboard to the strips to allow the necessary space behind the pegboard for the hooks and pegs. Elsewhere in the house, though, I have taken a different approach.

By building pegboard units that I frame and hang like pictures, I have made the material more attractive, versatile, and useful in other rooms. The methods and materials I use allow me to put up pegboard and move it later, if I wish. In this way, I can take a board down if I'm painting a room. Or if a unit has outlived its usefulness in one room, I can put it to work in another. And if we move to another house, we can take our pegboard units with us.

One of the first boards I built was a 36 x 48-inch vertical unit for the kitchen that houses all sorts of utensils that used to clutter the kitchen cabinets and drawers. On the pegboard, they're always within easy reach. The pegboard not only keeps all these items organized and easy to find, but it looks good too.

There's a 48 x 60-inch board hanging horizontally above a large work table in my studio. I call it my project board, and on it I keep file folders for various writing projects I'm working on, as well as drafting tools, matting and framing tools, and all sorts of other business paraphernalia. Small plastic trays that fit in the pegboard holes hold paper clips, rubber bands, and such. Along the bottom of the board, I have installed a shelf made of 1 x 6 and painted to match the board's molding. My project board keeps me from wasting time looking for items that might get stacked here or there or would be tossed into a desk drawer with a hundred other things.

In my darkroom, I installed a board identical to the kitchen unit, except that this one hangs horizontally. I have two safelights wired into it, and I hang all sorts of photographic gadgets and gizmos on it.

As I write, the finish is drying on two narrow vertical units that will hang on the ends of kitchen cabinets. These small, light-duty boards will make use of wasted space and will hold an assortment of small kitchen utensils that normally get lost in a drawer.

No matter where you might need one of these organizing boards, you'll find the materials readily available and the building techniques simple.

Hooks and Fixtures

Wherever pegboard is sold, you'll find numerous sizes and shapes of hooks, tool holders, and other fixtures and hangers. You can buy them individually or in kits of several different sizes and types. They come in sizes to fit ⅛-inch and ¼-inch pegboard. For starters, buy a kit with a large assortment. Then determine which of these you need more of, and buy them. Be sure to keep extras on hand, as you will gradually find other items to hang until you have completely covered any board.

For small boards, you can usually make a list of the items you plan to hang and take the list when you go shopping for hooks and fixtures. In any event, shop around at several stores to find what's available and what might work best for you.

There are both metal and plastic fixtures. Some are designed to hold tiny objects, others will hold large and heavy items, some hold items under tension, and still others will hold sets or collections of like items. There are also protective plastic tips that fit over the ends of metal hooks to protect any finely finished items you might hang.

No matter what kind of hooks and fixtures you end up buying, I suggest you look for those that are self-stabilizing or buy a packet of little wire clips that you can use with standard hooks and hangers to secure them to the board. Otherwise, you will frequently knock the various hooks and hangers out of their holes, which is definitely a nuisance.

Buying Pegboard and Framing Materials

The standard size for pegboard is a 48 x 96-inch sheet, the same as plywood, paneling, and other sheet stock. At some home-improvement centers and department stores, it is available in smaller sizes, usually 24 x 48 inches and 48 x 48 inches. If you plan to make more than one board, you might need a full sheet or even more, and you will surely find uses for any leftovers.

Pegboard comes in ⅛-inch and ¼-inch thicknesses, either tempered or untempered. Although the ⅛-inch board is suitable for a variety of applications, I prefer the ¼-inch tempered board for most jobs. The thicker board is more rigid and less susceptible to warping. Tempered board is also more warp-resistant than nontempered, is less affected by temperature and humidity fluctuations, looks good when left unfinished, and is the better choice for any board that is to be painted.

For small units, you can use any kind of picture-frame molding that suits you. So you need buy only enough molding to fit the boards you're planning. Or you can make your own table-saw, router, or glued molding.

For larger, heavier-duty units, you will need different materials. Once you have decided how large a piece of pegboard you want to hang, buy enough kiln-dried 1 x 2 common pine or fir (or rip your own) to make a rear framework and an equal amount of 1-inch outside corner molding. For example, for framing a 36 x 48-inch piece of pegboard, you'll need two 8-foot 1 x 2s and the same amount of corner molding.

For small, light-duty boards, you will need only the usual frame-assembly materials and hanging hardware: glue, brads or glazier's points, small screw eyes, picture-hanging wire, and picture hangers. I also put a ¼-inch self-adhesive felt cushion inside each rear corner of the frame on each small board.

For larger, heavy-duty boards, you will need glue and brads, wood filler or spackling paste, and heavy-duty hanging hardware. Use four 1-inch screw eyes— two in the bottom section and one in each side section—for the picture wire, as you would with a large painting. For most boards, standard picture wire will suffice, but if you are building a board larger than 48 x 48 inches and will hang some fairly heavy items on it, use stronger wire. And for safety's sake, hang each heavy-duty board with two 100-pound-capacity picture hangers.

Framing Light-Duty Boards

The small, light-duty boards are the easiest to make, as they go together just like a picture. For that reason, they are simpler to finish, because you can apply the finish to the frame and pegboard separately, any way you wish. If you want, you can stain and polyurethane or lacquer the frame, and leave the pegboard natural. Or you can paint the pegboard. Or you can paint the frame and leave the pegboard natural. Or you can paint everything one color or paint the frame one color and the pegboard another. Do whatever suits you and fits the room's decor.

With these small boards, you can take advantage of any usable space that is going to waste, and if you carefully plan the way to display the items you will store on them, the boards will become attractive additions to any room.

The secret to success with the small boards is to think little. Don't think that you have to hang two dozen items on a board to make it a worthwhile project. If you can fit three, four, or a half-dozen items on one, fine. In the case of small items, you'll not only be able to hang more, but you'll also be organizing the things that are most likely to disappear in a drawer or cabinet.

Also, when you think little, you will begin finding places for these small boards that you never even considered before. If you have a spot where an 11 x 14-inch picture would fit but might look out of place or would be hidden from view, consider an 11 x 14-inch piece of pegboard, attractively framed and storing a few useful items.

When I decided to make the small boards to hang on the ends of our kitchen cabinets, I decided on ⅛-inch pegboard, because I wanted to use the smaller-gauge hooks and fixtures. I also wanted to use the narrowest of moldings, and the ⅛-inch board assured me the proper clearance for the hooks.

I shopped around for a suitable commercial molding, but I found nothing that I liked or would work in the confined spaces where I planned to hang these boards. Ultimately, I decided to make my own molding from oak ¾-square, and this turned out to be an ideal molding for small boards. So I'm sure I will be using more of it in the future.

Of course, you will want to make some boards to fit in specific places, so the dimensions that follow won't work in every case. But these boards will fit in many tight areas, and they will work beautifully with standard kitchen cabinets.

For a pair of these boards, you will need a 24 x 24-inch sheet of ⅛-inch pegboard, two 7-foot strips of oak ¾-square, glue, glazier's points or brads, self-adhesive felt cushions, the usual hanging hardware, and the finishes of your choice. Here's how they go together.

Step 1. Cut the pegboard in half to yield two 12 x 24-inch pieces. Then evenly trim the long edges of each piece to a width of 10 inches (10 x 24 inches overall).

Step 2. Tighten a ⅝-inch straight bit in a router collet, and set the router and table to rout a 5/16-inch-wide, ⅛-inch-deep rabbet. Run the ¾-square over the bit. Reset the router for a ¼-inch depth, and make another pass. Reset the router to take off an additional ⅛ inch, and make the final pass, leaving a ⅛-inch-thick lip on the molding.

Step 3. With a miter box and backsaw set at 45 degrees, cut four pieces of the ¾-square molding to 24⅛ inches inside the rabbets, and four more pieces to 10⅛ inches. Lightly sand the cuts with 120-grit sandpaper to remove any splinters.

Step 4. Apply glue to the ends of the molding, and use corner clamps to assemble two frames, each measuring 10⅛ x 24⅛ inches. Wipe seeping glue away with a damp sponge, and let frames stand for several hours or overnight.

Step 5. Use a pad sander and 120-grit and 220-grit sandpaper to sand the outside surfaces of the frames, slightly rounding

Light-duty board, Step 2.

Light-duty board, Step 4.

Light-duty board, Step 9.

over outside edges and corners as you proceed. Clean frames and boards, and they're ready for finishing.

Step 6. To duplicate the finish of the boards shown, apply a coat of shellac to the pegboard pieces if they are not tempered. Lightly burnish the shellac with 400-grit sandpaper, clean the boards to remove dust, and apply two coats of flat or semigloss latex paint to match the room's decor.

Step 7. Brush a liberal coat of Fuller O'Brien Pen-Chrome #640-11 English Oak Stain onto the frames, let penetrate for fifteen minutes, and wipe dry with paper towels. Then let the frames stand overnight.

Step 8. When stain has dried, apply three coats of Deft Semi-Gloss Clear Wood Finish to all surfaces of the frames, and let dry.

Step 9. Lay frames face down on a protected surface. Lay boards in place inside the frames. Then secure the boards with brads or glazier's points.

Step 10. Install screw eyes in the inside surface of the frame molding so the units will hang flush against the wall or cabi-

nets, and attach picture wire. Then stick a ¼-inch self-adhesive felt pad just inside each rear corner of each frame.

Step 11. Lay boards face up, and arrange the items each will store until you have an eye-pleasing arrangement. Then install the proper hooks and fixtures and hang the boards.

Framing Heavy-Duty Boards

Since pegboard can be affected by temperature and humidity, the large boards require sturdier construction than the lightweight, light-duty boards. The rear framework and face frame keep the board from warping. The directions that follow are for any large board.

Step 1. Once your board is cut to size, lay it face (smooth side) down on a flat working surface. Then use a miter box and backsaw to cut two 1 x 2s the same length as the longest edges of the pegboard.

Step 2. Run a wavy bead of glue along the back of the pegboard near each long edge, lay a 1 x 2 on the glue and flush with the edge, and clamp each strip to the pegboard with C-clamps spaced about 12 inches apart.

Step 3. Measure the distance along the short edges of the pegboard between the 1 x 2 strips, and cut two 1 x 2s to fit. Glue and clamp them to the pegboard, and let stand with clamps in place until the glue sets.

Finished light-duty board.

Step 4. With a miter box and backsaw set at 45 degrees, cut one end off a piece of corner molding. Lay the molding along

Heavy-duty board, Step 2.

Heavy-duty board, Step 4.

one edge of the board, and mark the molding for the second cut. Miter cut the opposite end, apply glue to the inside of the molding, and press it in place on the face of the board. Drive 1-inch brads through the molding into the side edges of the rear frame, and countersink the brads.

Step 5. Miter cut one end of another piece of molding, fit it to an adjacent edge of the board face, and mark it for the second cut. Miter cut the opposite end, and attach the piece as you did the first one. Continue cutting molding and attaching it the same way to the remaining two sides.

Author's project board.

Author's darkroom board.

Masking a board before painting.

Step 6. Fill brad holes with spackling paste if you plan to paint the board or wood filler if you plan to stain and polyurethane or lacquer the board. Let the filler dry; then sand with 120-grit and 220-grit sandpaper. Vacuum the board to remove dust, wipe it down with a tack cloth, and it's ready for installation of hanging hardware and the finish of your choice.

These large boards look best painted, and you can paint the board face one color and frame another, if you wish. Try to coordinate the colors with those of the room where the board will be used. To keep from marring the finish, install screw eyes and hanging hardware before you paint the board.

To give you an idea of how you can coordinate or contrast colors when painting, the board in my studio is painted charcoal black, and the molding is light olive. These colors match the colors of filing cabinets, a desk, and other furnishings in my studio. My darkroom board is gray with blue trim, which matches the primary colors of my darkroom, even my enlarger.

Nontempered pegboard will absorb water from latex paints. So if you use this material, apply a coat of shellac to the board face before painting. Then lightly burnish it with 400-grit waterproof sandpaper before painting, and wipe it with a clean tack cloth.

With tempered board, you can skip the shellac seal. But if you plan to use two colors, run a strip of wide masking tape around the pegboard where it meets the frame. Apply two coats of paint to the frame, remove the tape, and apply two coats of paint to the face. You also have the option of leaving the pegboard face natural.

17

Framing Bulletin Boards

Bulletin boards, like pegboard organizers, are utilitarian objects, but they can also be attractive adjuncts to a room's decor. You can make them any size you want from a variety of suitable and readily available materials. You can hang them anywhere, but you will probably want to give first consideration to the kitchen, workshop, and home office or den. Hang a small one wherever there's a phone. Use several small ones for decorative purposes.

Any bulletin board consists mainly of an underlayment, a covering material, and a frame. The choice of underlayment depends on the design of the board and what it will be covered with. For years, corrugated containerboard has been a popular lightweight underlayment, but I find foamboard a much better choice. For covering materials requiring a rigid underlayment, plywood and hardboard are best.

Burlap and cork are probably the most popular covering materials. With burlap, you have a choice among several colors or natural beige. Cork is available in dark brown, light brown, and a composite of both. It comes in rolls, sheets, and 12 x 12-inch squares, some of which are self-adhesive.

Burlap is a coarse, broad-weave fabric. Although many kinds of adhesives will make burlap stick to an underlayment, some cause the material to become hard and brittle, and others seep through the weave and stain it. You can use fabric adhesives, but those I have checked are comparatively expensive. I prefer 3M Super 77 and Scotch Spra-Ment aerosol adhesives, which are fast, clean, and efficient adhesives for burlap.

Some glues and cements do not work at all with cork. Of the various ones I have tried over the years, several have worked well for me. Panel adhesive and all-purpose construction adhesive—both of which come in cans or in tubes you use with a caulking gun—are good, relatively inexpensive products. Some epoxy cements work with cork, but be sure to read the labels to make certain before buying any. Again, though, I have come to prefer the aerosol adhesives I mentioned above, because they are so easy to work with, and they do a good job.

Of course, you can also use various self-adhesive boards available from Coda, Inc., and Pres-On Products, Inc. (see directory). You can attach burlap to their self-adhesive foamboards and mount cork to their self-adhesive Masonite, Gatorfoam, and codaFoam boards.

Make a Burlap Bulletin Board

Lightweight burlap boards can be used anywhere you need a bulletin board. You can frame them with any commercial molding, or with molding you have made. You can hang these boards with conventional hanging hardware, but because of their light weight, you can also put them up with adhesive foam mounting tape, which makes them ideal for use on hard walls, hollow doors, and anywhere else standard hangers don't work.

Here's how to build a 24 x 36-inch board.

Burlap board, Step 2.

Burlap board, Step 3.

Step 1. Use a straight edge and X-Acto knife to trim a piece of ³/₁₆-inch foamboard to 24 x 36 inches. Then cut a piece of burlap slightly larger.

Step 2. Lay newspapers on your work surface and the foamboard on the newspapers. Then spray an even coat of all-purpose adhesive, such as 3M Super 77, over the entire surface of the foamboard.

Step 3. Carefully set the foamboard aside and remove the newspapers. Spread the burlap on the work surface. Then lay the foamboard on the burlap, adhesive side down, and press the board to the burlap. Turn the board over, and use a roller to press the burlap to the board.

Step 4. Use scissors to carefully trim away excess burlap from the edges of the

Burlap board, Step 4.

Burlap board, Step 3.

board. Then let stand until the adhesive cures.

Step 5. With a miter box and backsaw, cut two pieces of frame molding to 24⅛ inches (inside the rabbets) and two more pieces to 36⅛ inches.

Step 6. Apply glue to one end of a long molding strip, and attach it to a short strip with a corner clamp. Continue connecting strips with glue and corner clamps until the frame is assembled.

Step 7. Drive a 1-inch brad through each corner, and countersink the brads. Fill brad holes with wood filler, and let frame stand with clamps in place until glue and filler cure.

Step 8. Sand the frame, as required, with a pad sander and 120-grit and 220-grit sandpaper. Then apply the stain and finish of your choice.

Step 9. With the frame face down, lay the

Burlap board, Step 9.

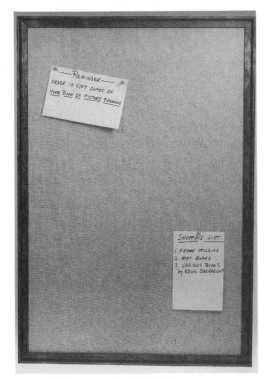

Finished burlap board.

burlap-covered board in place, and secure it with brads or glazier's points.

Step 10. Install two small screw eyes in opposite frame sections, attach picture-hanging wire to them, and the burlap bulletin board is ready to hang.

Make Miniature Cork Boards

The fastest and easiest way to make a cork bulletin board is with self-adhesive cork squares. Of course you can use this material to make boards of any size, but I find them particularly handy for small boards that I put near phones and wherever else they might prove convenient.

Since the squares are 12 x 12 inches, it's best to make underlayments with dimensions divisible by 12: 12 x 24 inches, 24 x 24 inches, 12 x 36 inches, and so on. You can cut the cork, if you must, but it's much easier and neater to make the underlayment fit the cork than vice versa.

The miniature boards can be displayed alone or in eye-catching groupings. For example, instead of one large bulletin board, you might prefer to hang an arrangement of small boards.

For underlayment you can use any suitably rigid material, such as tempered ¼-inch hardboard and ¼-inch or ½-inch plywood. For small boards, ¼-inch plywood will work, but you must make sure the material is flat. I prefer ½-inch plywood for these boards, no matter the size, as it provides a rigid foundation, and I needn't worry about it warping later.

To make the 12 x 24-inch board shown, you will need a scrap of ½-inch plywood that size or larger, an 8-foot clear fir 1 x 2 (or suitable scraps), two 12 x 12-inch self-adhesive squares, glue, brads, wood filler, hanging hardware, and the finish of your choice. When you've gathered your materials, follow these simple construction steps.

Step 1. Trim a piece of ½-inch plywood to 12 x 24 inches. Lightly sand the edges with 120-grit sandpaper to remove any splinters left by the saw blade.

Step 2. Clean the board to remove dust, and wipe it down with a tack cloth. Peel the release paper from two cork squares, and press them to the plywood board. Use a roller to firmly seat the cork squares.

Step 3. Use a radial-arm saw, table saw, or router and router table to turn the 1 x 2 into a simple box molding (see Chapter 8).

Step 4. With a miter box and backsaw set at 45 degrees, cut two frame sections from the box molding to 12⅛ inches and two to 24⅛ inches.

Step 5. Apply glue to the frame-section ends, and use four corner clamps to assemble a frame that's 12⅛ inches by 24⅛ inches.

Step 6. Drive two 1¼-inch brads at each corner of the frame, and countersink the brads. Fill the holes with wood filler, and let the frame stand with clamps in place until glue and filler set.

Miniature cork board, Step 2.

Miniature cork board, Step 6.

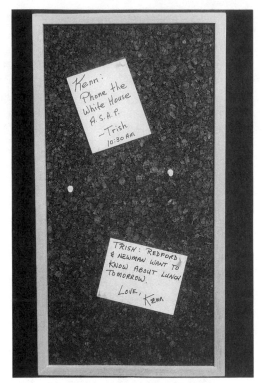

Finished miniature cork board.

Step 7. Sand the frame with a pad sander and 120-grit and 220-grit sandpaper, slightly rounding over sharp edges and corners as you proceed. Clean the frame, wipe it with a tack cloth, and it's ready for the finish of your choice.

Step 8. When the finish dries, lay the frame face down on a protected surface. Then lay the cork board in place in the frame, and secure it with brads or glazier's points.

Step 9. You can hang the board vertically or horizontally. So install two small screw eyes on the inside surface of the appropriate frame sections, and attach picture-hanging wire.

Step 10. With the board face down, attach a ¼-inch self-adhesive felt cushion just inside each rear corner of the frame. Then hang the board with a standard picture hanger.

Build a Big Cork Board

The board shown here is the heavy-duty one I built to hang in my shop. I made it mostly from scraps left over from other projects, but had to buy the cork.

For the rear frame you will need two 6-foot 1 x 2s or suitable scraps: two 3-footers and three 2-footers. You will also need a 24 x 36-inch piece of ¼-inch plywood, cork to cover it, and two 6-foot pieces of 1-inch outside corner molding. Glue, brads, wood filler, and hanging wire complete the list.

Follow these construction steps to build an identical board for your shop or elsewhere.

Step 1. Trim a piece of ¼-inch plywood to 24 x 36 inches with a table saw or circular saw and guide. Then use a straight

Big cork board, Step 1.

edge and X-Acto knife to trim a sheet of cork to the same dimensions.

Step 2. Cut two strips of 1 x 2 to 36 inches each. (If you aren't using scraps, cut one piece from each of two 6-footers.) Stand them on their narrow edges, and run a bead of glue down the top edge of each. Lay the plywood on them, attach it with 1-inch brads, and countersink the brads.

Step 3. Measure the distance between the 1 x 2s (should be about 22½ inches), and cut three pieces of 1 x 2 to fit.

Step 4. With plywood face up, measure down each long edge, and make marks at 18 inches. Then align a yardstick with these marks, and scribe a pencil line across the plywood.

Step 5. Run a bead of glue along one narrow edge and both ends of a piece of 1 x 2, and press it in place between the two attached strips at one end of the assembly. Drive two 1½-inch brads through each of the attached strips into

Big cork board, Step 4.

Big cork board, Step 2.

Big cork board, Step 5.

Big cork board, Step 6.

the ends of the 22½-inch strip. Secure the plywood to it with 1-inch brads, and countersink the brads. Attach another strip the same way at the opposite end of the plywood.

Step 6. Lay the assembly face down, and make guide marks at the center of each long strip of 1 x 2. Apply glue to the remaining piece of 1 x 2, align it with the guide marks, and drive 1½-inch brads into the ends. Lay the assembly face up, drive 1-inch brads along the guideline scribed in Step 4, and countersink the brads.

Step 7. Cover the sides of the assembly with masking tape. Lay the unit face up

Big cork board, Step 6.

Big cork board, Step 7.

on newspapers, and apply a liberal coat of an all-purpose adhesive, such as 3M Super 77.

Step 8. Lay the cork sheet atop the plywood, align it with the edges, and firmly press it in place. Then use a roller to set the cork in the adhesive, and let stand until the adhesive cures.

Step 9. After removing the masking tape, use a miter box and backsaw to cut a piece of 1-inch outside corner molding, with 45-degree miters at each end, to fit each edge of the unit. Run a bead of glue along the inside corner of each piece of molding, and attach it with 1-inch brads,

Big cork board, Step 9.

Big cork board, Step 8.

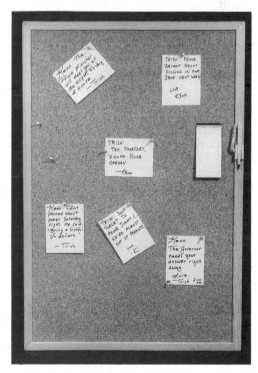

Finished big cork board.

driven through the sides into the 1 x 2 strips. Countersink the brads.

Step 10. Fill all brad holes with wood filler. When the filler dries, lightly sand it, as required, with a pad sander and 120-grit and 220-grit sandpaper.

Step 11. This board was designed to hang vertically. Lay it face down, measure 12 inches down each vertical 1 x 2, and attach screw eyes on the inside surface of the 1 x 2s. Attach picture-hanging wire to them.

Step 12. Attach a ½-inch self-adhesive cork or felt cushion just inside each rear corner of the 1 x 2 framework, and your bulletin board is ready to hang.

18

Making Shadow-Box Frames

Three-dimensional objects pose some problems for the framer, most of which are easily solved by the use of shadow-box frames. Commercially manufactured shadow-box frames are available through some retail outlets, but they are usually meant for two-dimensional pictures and require modification before you can display three-dimensional objects in them. And those I have seen aren't the best quality.

I have done some shopping around for shadow-box frames and moldings at the usual outlets and haven't found anything useful. Although some commercially made moldings can be adapted for use in making shadow boxes, they require more work than I can justify; it's as easy to make my own moldings from scratch.

Shadow-box frames offer aesthetic and practical advantages. The deep frame walls add a subtle visual appeal to the subject by casting shadows that change with the viewer's position—hence, the name *shadow box*. The frame walls also provide the extra depth that three-dimensional objects require.

The variety of items suitable for display inside shadow-box frames is endless. You might want to give such treatment to certain carvings, ceramics, needlework, and any deep-relief artwork. You can use shadow boxes to frame medals, ribbons, and other awards. Use them for artifacts and collections of all kinds.

There aren't any rules when it comes to framing three-dimensional objects. I have seen them attached to placques and simple slabs of wood and displayed against backgrounds of every imaginable material.

The use of glass is a matter of personal choice. Its main function is to keep dust off the object being framed. So if what you're framing might be harmed by dust (some fabrics, for example) or simply might be a nuisance to keep clean (anything intricate), then you'll probably want to frame it behind glass.

Mounting Three-Dimensional Objects

Before you build a shadow-box frame for any three-dimensional object or collection of objects, you need to give some thought to how the items should be mounted. In fact, you will probably want to see to any necessary matting and mounting before you build the frame.

Some objects should be wired to mount boards or background boards or attached with monofilament fishing line, but most can be attached with some kind of adhesive. Epoxy cement is an excellent mounting adhesive, because it will work with so many different kinds of materials. You will find two-part (resin and hardener) epoxy kits that cure in several hours or overnight and others that will set in four or five minutes. Take your pick.

Epoxy cement should be considered a permanent adhesive. If you are mounting anything of value or potential value and want to use a reversible adhesive, use silicone glue and seal, which cures to a rubbery consistency and can be peeled off with some effort.

You can mount most items directly to mat board or to mat board, hardboard, foamboard, or plywood that has been covered with any appropriate material. Some popular coverings are burlap, linen, vinyl, leather, acrylic, cork, plastic sheeting, and wallpaper. Naturally, heavy objects should be mounted to a substantial board, and if the board is covered, the covering material should be durable and permanent.

Shadow-Box Frame with Glass

To make a shadow-box frame for displaying items behind glass, I designed a frame molding that goes together as simply as any frame and requires none of the usual inserts commonly used with box molding to make shadow-box frames. The molding looks simple, but is a bit more complicated than some. Nevertheless, it's easy to make if you just take your time and follow the directions.

When this molding is made from 1 x 2, as the directions stipulate, there will be a 1-inch clearance between the frame lip and the rear rabbet. Allowing for the thickness of the glass and mat, you can display items up to ¾ inch thick. If you want to display thicker items, use stock wider than 1 x 2, and adjust saw-blade settings as necessary.

Use picture glass with this frame, not nonglare glass, which would distort the items being framed because of the distance between the glass and the mount board.

Unlike other frames in which your glass, mats, and mount board are all cut to identical dimensions, with this frame, your mount board and backing will be larger than the glass and mats. In an 8 x 10-inch frame, such as the one shown, the dimensions inside the rear rabbets are 8½ x 10½ inches. So for this frame, I cut the mount board and hardboard backing to 8⅜ inches x 10⅜ inches.

To make an 8 x 10-inch frame, you'll need a 4-foot 1 x 2 (I used oak for the frame shown), a scrap of ⅛-inch hard-board, glue, glass, and the usual hanging hardware. Here's how it goes together.

Step 1. Set the table-saw fence ¼ inch from the *near* teeth of the blade and the blade for a ¼-inch depth. Lay a 1 x 2 broad side down on the saw table with a narrow side against the fence, and run it over the blade.

Step 2. Stand the 1 x 2 on the narrow side farthest from the groove cut in Step 1, with the ungrooved broad surface against the fence. Then run the piece over the blade to create a groove in a narrow side.

Step 3. Set the fence ¼ inch from the *far* teeth of the blade and the blade for a ½-

Shadow-box frame, Step 3.

inch depth. Then lay the 1 x 2 grooved broad side down on the saw table with the grooved narrow side against the fence, and run the piece over the blade to create a ¼ x ½-inch rabbet in one narrow side of the piece.

Step 4. Reset the blade for a 1¼-inch depth. Stand the 1 x 2 molding on the saw table with the rabbeted edge down and the grooved broad side against the fence. Now run the piece over the blade to create a rabbet in the broad side with a ¼-inch lip at the face edge of the molding. This completes the shadow-box molding.

Step 5. To make an 8 x 10-inch shadow-box frame, use a miter box and backsaw set at 45 degrees to cut two sections to 8⅛ inches and two to 10⅛ inches inside the miters. Sand the inside surfaces between the front lip and rear rabbet with 120-grit sandpaper to remove saw-blade marks. Then assemble the frame with

Shadow-box frame, Step 2.

Shadow-box frame, Step 4.

Shadow-box frame, Step 5.

glue and clamps, and let the frame stand until the glue sets.

Step 6. Sand the frame with a pad sander and 120-grit and 220-grit sandpaper, slightly rounding over the front outside edges and corners as you proceed. Clean the frame to remove dust, and wipe it with a tack cloth. The frame is now ready for the finish of your choice.

Step 7. To duplicate the finish of the frame shown, apply a coat of Fuller O'Brien Pen-Chrome #640-11 English Oak Stain, let penetrate for ten to fifteen minutes, and wipe dry with paper towels. Let stand overnight, and apply three coats of Deft Semi-Gloss Clear Wood Finish.

Step 8. Lay the frame face down on a protected surface. Clean the glass, and lay it in place on the lip of the frame. Next, lay the mat or mats against the glass, and secure everything with glazier's points.

Step 9. Check the rear dimensions of the frame, and cut the mount board slightly undersize to fit. Mount the three-dimensional object on the mount board with epoxy cement or silicone glue and seal. (Let the latter stand for twenty-four hours before proceeding.)

Step 10. Cut a piece of ⅛-inch hardboard the same size as the mount board to fit the rear of the frame. Lay the mounted work in place in the rabbet at the rear of the frame. Then run a narrow bead of silicone glue and seal around the rear edge of the frame, press the hardboard in place, apply more silicone if necessary, and let stand for twenty-four hours.

Shadow-box frame, Step 9.

Finished shadow-box frame.

Step 11. Attach a sawtooth hanger to the rear of the frame near the top center. Attach self-adhesive felt or foam weather-stripping cushions near the bottom corners, and the framed work is ready for hanging.

Glassless Shadow-Box Frame

In designing the molding for a glassless shadow box, I came up with one that has proved to be a favorite and one I will be using on many projects in the future, for both three-dimensional and two-dimensional works. It's an easy molding to make, and the frames made from it are quite attractive.

To make the 8 x 10-inch frame shown, all you need is a 4-foot strip of oak 1 x 2, a 4-foot strip of oak ¾ x ¾-inch cove molding, glue, and hanging hardware.

My original plan was to make a box molding, glue the cove molding to it, and make my frames from this. Then I decided to experiment with my router and router table, and I routed a cove into the outside corner of the molding, and that's what turned a simple, handsome molding into an elegant one. You might want to experiment with other bits to see what effects you can achieve. Try ogee and beading bits for starters.

With this frame, cut mats and mount boards to identical outside dimensions, as you would with most frames.

To build the frame, follow these steps.

Glassless shadow-box frame, Step 3.

around the molding about every 12 inches.) Let stand until the cement cures.

Step 4. Tighten a ⅜-inch-radius cove bit in the router collet. Set the router and table for a ⅛-inch depth. Then lay the molding face down on the router table and rout a cove into the outside corner. Make as many more passes as necessary to achieve effects you like. Two passes at ⅛-inch increments sufficed for the molding shown.

Step 5. To make an 8 x 10-inch frame, use a miter box and backsaw to cut a piece of molding to 10⅛ inches and another to 8⅛ inches, inside the rabbet. Use those pieces to mark two more sections, and cut them. Then assemble the frame with glue and corner clamps, and let stand until the glue sets.

Step 6. The frame should require little sanding. Use a pad sander on flat surfaces and an abrasive sponge on areas difficult to sand. Clean the frame, wipe it

Step 1. Set the table-saw fence 1¼ inches from the *far* teeth of the blade and the blade for a ¼-inch depth. Lay a 1 x 2 broad side down on the saw table and run it over the blade.

Step 2. Reset the fence ¼ inch from the *far* teeth of the blade and the blade for a 1¼-inch depth. Then stand the 1 x 2 on a narrow edge on the saw table with the grooved surface against the fence, and run the piece over the blade to create a basic box molding.

Step 3. Cut ¾ x ¾-inch cove molding the same length as the 1 x 2. Mix enough five-minute epoxy cement to coat one flat edge of the cove molding, and apply a thin coat to it. Press it in place behind the lip of the box molding, and secure it with spring clamps. (If you don't have enough clamps, tightly wrap masking tape

Glassless shadow-box frame, Step 4.

Glassless shadow-box frame, Step 5.

Finished glassless shadow-box frame proves ideal for this fish fossil.

with a tack cloth, and it's ready for the finish of your choice.

Step 7. To duplicate the finish of the frame shown, brush on a coat of Fuller O'Brien Pen-Chrome #640-11 English Oak Stain, let it penetrate ten to fifteen minutes, wipe dry with paper towels, and let stand overnight. Then apply three coats of Deft Semi-Gloss Clear Wood Finish.

Step 8. Lay the frame face down on a protected surface, and lay the mounted and matted piece in the frame. Secure it with brads or glazier's points.

Step 9. Install two small screw eyes on the inside surfaces of the left and right frame sections so the frame will hang flat against the wall, and attach picture-hanging wire. Then stick a ¼-inch self-adhesive felt cushion just inside each rear corner of the frame.

19

Building Collector Frames

If you or someone in your household is a collector, you will probably want to build frames to house and display your collections. You can make such frames in a variety of sizes and designs to accommodate all sorts of collectible items: carvings, models, dolls, shells, bottles, china and glassware, ceramics, tools, and various antiques.

You needn't be an avid collector, however, to find uses for collector frames. In children's rooms such frames are useful for storing toys in an attractive way. A large frame will hold potted plants. Use one to display a chess set, or in a kitchen you can fill one with spice jars. Simple, unadorned collector frames are useful in workshops and hobby rooms for holding containers of hardware and small parts.

The two frames featured in this chapter can be put to use in a number of ways,

and by building them you will learn the basics of collector-frame construction. But the most useful frames will be the ones you design yourself for specific uses and collections.

Designing Collector Frames

The first step in designing any collector frame is to assemble all the items you plan to store in it. Lay them out on the floor and arrange them as you might in a collector frame to get an idea of how much wall space you will need. Once you have decided on rough dimensions, you might find it helpful to cut a scrap of cardboard, mat board, or foamboard to size, and lay that on the floor with your collection arranged on it.

When you have achieved a pleasing arrangement, sketch it roughly on a sheet of paper. Then rearrange the items to find other possibilities, and sketch them. Try horizontal and vertical displays. If your collection is large, you might want to house it in several frames.

The widest item in your collection will determine the width that all shelves must be. Objects of similar height can be put on a shelf together. Anything taller than the other items might look best in a compartment by itself. If you have two or three such items, make a single space for them, or design separate spaces. Try it both ways, and pick the design that looks best.

There are several materials you will find useful for shelves and uprights. In the smallest frames, you can use ¼-inch-thick lattice. Micro Wood, which comes in 3 x 24-inch strips of ⅛-inch and ¼-inch hardwood, can be ripped into shelves and uprights of various sizes. For larger units, you should look for ½-inch stock available in several different species at many lumber outlets. For example, the lumber company where I do most of my business stocks clear fir in 8-foot strips that measure ½ x 3½ inches, which is what I used to build a large collector frame that covers just over 12 square feet of wall and holds all the spices and many other items that once cluttered our kitchen cabinets.

Another material I plan to use for a similar frame is oak of the same dimensions as the fir, but this material has one beveled edge. It is used for splashboard on oak counters and is ideal as shelving for large oak collector frames.

Plywood is the best and most useful material for back panels. You can also use plywood for the top, bottom, sides, shelves, and uprights if you take measures to conceal the laminations in the edges of the material. If you will be painting the unit, you can use a putty knife to spread spackling paste on the plywood edges; then sand it smooth when it dries. With hardwood plywood, you can use edging tape or various moldings that fit.

Another useful material to keep in mind for collector frames of all sizes is ¼-inch plate glass. This excellent shelving material slides into ¼-inch dadoes and needs no gluing. Find a glass shop that reclaims plate glass from damaged store windows, as this salvaged glass is much cheaper than new glass. Once you've settled on a design for any frame, determine the number and dimensions of the glass shelves you will need, order them cut to those dimensions, and ask to have one long edge of each shelf seamed or beveled. This will take the sharp edges off. Use the seamed edges as the fronts of your shelves.

Once you have decided on the dimensions and chosen your materials, it's a good idea to make a scale drawing on graph paper. This will enable you to determine how much of each material you will need, and it will also be an aid in the shop when you're building your frame.

Miniature Collector Frame

Here's a little frame that is easy to build and goes together quickly with a few inexpensive materials. It can hold a collection of small items. Several will hold a larger collection. Use it in a kid's room for Matchbox cars, or put one in the kitchen to hold spice containers, or make one to display chessmen.

Of course, you can alter dimensions to fit your needs. But to make the frame shown, you will need a 3-foot pine or fir 1 x 4, a 5-foot piece of ¼ x 1⁵⁄₁₆-inch lattice, a scrap of ¼-inch plywood at least 12 x 14½ inches, glue, brads, and hanging hardware.

To make the frame a bit fancier, you can attach screen molding, corner molding, decorative molding, or frame molding to the front edges. If that's your preference, you'll need a 6-foot strip.

Here's how to put this one together.

Step 1. With a miter box and backsaw set at zero degrees, cut a piece of 1 x 4 to 15 inches.

Step 2. Set the table-saw blade for a ¼-inch depth. Set the fence 3¼ inches from the *near* teeth of the blade. Lay the 1 x 4 broad side down on the saw table, and cut a ¼-inch-deep dado in it 3¼ inches from one end. Move the fence to 3½ inches from the *far* teeth of the blade, and widen the dado to ¼ inch.

Step 3. Set the fence 6 inches from the *near* teeth of the blade, and run the 1 x 4 over the blade again. Reset the fence at 6¼ inches from the *far* teeth of the blade,

and run the piece through the saw again to create a second dado 2½ inches from the first.

Step 4. Set the fence 8¾ inches from the *near* teeth of the blade, and start another dado. Reset the fence at 9 inches from the *far* teeth, and widen that dado to ¼ inch.

Step 5. To cut the last dado, set the fence 11½ inches from the *near* teeth for the first pass and 11¾ inches from the *far* teeth for the second pass.

Step 6. Set the blade for a ½-inch depth and the fence 3½ inches from the *far* teeth. Lay the 1 x 4 dadoed side down on the saw table with one narrow side against the fence, and run it over the blade to create a ⅛-inch-wide, ½-inch-deep rabbet. Rotate the piece, and cut a rabbet into the opposite edge. Do the same with a scrap of 1 x 4 that's at least 13 inches long. Reset the fence 3¼ inches from the *near* teeth, and widen the rabbets in each piece to ¼ inch.

Step 7. Install the blade guard on the saw.

Miniature collector frame, Step 2.

Miniature collector frame, Step 5.

Miniature collector frame, Step 6.

Set the fence 1⁹/₁₆ inches from the *near* teeth of the blade. Lay the dadoed 1 x 4 broad side down on the saw table with a narrow side against the fence, and rip a strip from the piece. Rotate the piece and rip another strip from the opposite edge. Then rip two strips from the other 1 x 4 the same way.

Step 8. With a miter box and backsaw set at 45 degrees, cut the ends off the dadoed pieces for an overall outside length of 15 inches. From the other strips, miter cut two 13-inch pieces.

Step 9. Use glue and corner clamps to assemble a 13 x 15-inch frame from these four sections. Drive two 1-inch brads at each corner, and countersink the brads. Let the frame stand with clamps in place until the glue sets.

Step 10. Measure the height and width inside the rabbets in the rear of the frame, and cut a piece of ¼-inch plywood slightly smaller to fit. Sand the face of the plywood with a pad sander and 120-grit and 220-grit sandpaper. Run a narrow bead of glue along the corner of the rabbet on all four sides of the frame. Lay the

Miniature collector frame, Step 9.

Miniature collector frame, Step 10.

Miniature collector frame, Step 12.

Step 13. Fill brad holes and any other holes or imperfections with wood filler (if unit will be finished naturally) or spackling paste (if unit will be painted), and let stand until filler sets. Then sand face and sides with a pad sander and 120-grit and 220-grit sandpaper. (If you plan to add molding to the face, you can skip the 220-grit sanding there.)

Step 14. Use a miter box and backsaw set at 45 degrees to cut four pieces of screen molding, decorative molding, frame molding, or 1-inch outside corner molding to fit the frame face. Then attach the molding with glue and ¾-inch brads. If you're using decorative molding or an intricate frame molding, you might prefer attaching it with five-minute epoxy cement and clamps.

Step 15. Vacuum the frame to remove dust, and wipe all surfaces with a tack cloth. The frame is now ready for the finish of your choice. Although you should be able to brush on a stain without any trouble, make sure your final coat—lacquer, polyurethane, enamel—is an aerosol, which will enable you to coat all surfaces neatly.

rear panel in place, secure it with toe-nailed ¾-inch brads, and countersink the brads.

Step 11. Carefully measure the distance between each pair of dadoes, and use a miter box and backsaw set at zero degrees to cut four strips of lattice to fit. Cut these for a snug fit. If you own a belt-and-disk sander or a Black & Decker Finishing Machine, cut the strips about ¹/₁₆ inch longer than you need, and gradually sand the ends until they fit perfectly.

Step 12. Mix a small amount of five-minute epoxy cement, and apply a tiny bit to the inside of each dado. Then slide lattice shelves into the dadoes, and let stand until the cement cures.

Miniature collector frame, Step 14.

Finished miniature collector frame.

Step 16. When the unit is finished, install two sawtooth hangers inside the top rear corners, or two decorative rings in the top of the frame, 2 inches from the corners and ½ inch from the rear edge. If you use sawtooth hangers, attach two ¼-inch-thick foam weather-stripping pads inside the bottom rear corners. With decorative rings, use ¼-inch-wide self-adhesive felt cushions inside all four rear corners.

Oak Collector Frame

Here's a frame that can hold a variety of objects and will look good in any room. By building this one, you will also learn some techniques that will serve you well when you design your own collector frames.

You will need a 7-foot piece of oak 1 x 4, a 7-foot strip of oak screen molding, a 7-foot strip of oak panel molding, two ¼ x 3 x 24-inch strips of oak Micro Wood, a 15 x 19-inch piece of ¼-inch oak plywood, glue, brads, and the usual hanging hardware.

To build this attractive frame, just follow these easy steps.

Step 1. Set the table saw or bandsaw fence 2¾ inches from the *near* teeth of the blade, and rip the oak 1 x 4 to that width. Reset the fence 2½ inches from the *near* teeth, and rip the oak Micro Wood to that width.

Step 2. With a miter box and backsaw set at 45 degrees, cut two vertical frame sections from the ripped 1 x 4 to a length of 18 inches inside the miters (19½ inches overall) and two horizontal sections to 14 inches inside the miters (15½ inches overall).

Step 3. Remove the blade guard from the table saw. Set the fence 2¾ inches from the *far* teeth of the blade and the blade for a ½-inch depth. Lay one of the frame sections inside surface down on the saw table, with the face surface against the fence. Run the piece over the blade to cut

Oak collector frame, Step 3.

a ⅛-inch-deep, ½-inch-wide rabbet in the rear edge. Do the same with the remaining three frame sections. Then reset the fence 2½ inches from the *near* teeth, and run each piece over the blade again to create a ¼-inch-deep, ½-inch-wide rabbet in each piece.

Step 4. Use a pencil to mark the four frame sections: *top, bottom, left,* and *right.* Lay the bottom section inside surface up. Measure from the left inside edge of the miter, and make marks at 4 and 4¼ inches. Then use a combination square to scribe parallel lines across the piece at those marks. Turn the piece so it stands on its rear edge, and scribe identical lines across the face surface.

Step 5. Lay the vertical sections inside surface up. Measure down each from the inside edges of the top miters, and make marks at 5¼ and 5½ inches. On the right vertical only, make marks 6¼ and 6½ inches from the inside edge of the bottom miter. Then use a combination square to scribe parallel lines at these marks across the inside and face surfaces of the vertical sections.

Step 6. Set the table-saw blade for a ¼-inch depth. Lay the bottom frame section inside surface down on the saw table,

and use the miter gauge to move it over the blade to remove the material between the parallel lines scribed in Step 4, creating a ¼-inch-wide, ¼-inch-deep dado in the piece. Do the same on the inside surfaces of the left and right vertical sections.

Step 7. Apply glue to the ends of the frame sections, and construct a 15½ x 19½-inch frame with four corner clamps. If necessary, draw the miter joints together at the rear edges of the frame with a pair of bar clamps. Then let the frame stand until the glue dries.

Step 8. Check the height and width of the rear of the frame, inside the rabbets. Then cut a piece of ¼-inch oak plywood ¹/₁₆ inch smaller. Sand the face of the plywood back panel and the inside surfaces of the frame with a pad sander and 120-grit and 220-grit sandpaper.

Step 9. Mix a small amount of five-minute epoxy cement and apply it sparingly to the rear of the frame, being careful to avoid the inside edge of the frame. Lay the back panel in place in the rabbets, and clamp with four bar clamps, or place a heavy object on it until the cement cures.

Oak collector frame, Step 5.

Oak collector frame, Step 6.

Oak collector frame, Step 7.

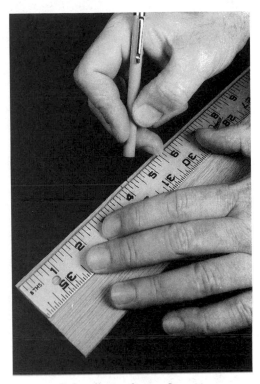

Oak collector frame, Step 11.

Step 10. Measure the distance between the top dadoes in the frame vertical sections (should be about 14½ inches). Use a miter box and backsaw set at zero degrees to cut the top shelf from a piece of the 2½-inch-wide oak Micro Wood to fit.

Step 11. Lay the shelf top side down, measure from the left, and make marks on the underside at 4¼ and 4½ inches. Use the marks as guides to scribe two parallel lines with a combination square. Then mark the face surface of the shelf the same way.

Step 12. Set the table-saw blade for a ⅛-inch depth. Lay the shelf face up on the saw table, and use the miter gauge to move it over the blade, as in previous steps, to cut a ¼-inch-wide, ⅛-inch-deep dado.

Step 13. Measure the distance between the dado in the shelf underside and the dado in the frame bottom section. Then cut a vertical piece of Micro Wood to fit.

Step 14. Measure from the bottom of the Micro Wood vertical and make marks on the right broad surface at 6½ and 6¾ inches. Using the marks as guides, scribe parallel lines across the right and face surfaces with a combination square. Then cut a ¼-inch-wide, ⅛-inch-deep dado between the lines.

Oak collector frame, Step 16.

Oak collector frame, Step 18.

Step 15. Slide the Micro Wood vertical into the appropriate dadoes, and measure the distance between the dado in the Micro Wood and the one in the right frame section. Then cut a piece of Micro Wood to fit.

Step 16. After checking for fit, remove all the Micro Wood pieces from the frame, and sand them with a pad sander and 120-grit and 220-grit sandpaper. Mix a small amount of five-minute epoxy cement, and apply a tiny amount to the inside of each dado with the tip of a toothpick. Then put small tacking spots of cement along the back edge of each piece, and slide them into place, starting with the top shelf.

Step 17. Sand the face of the frame with a pad sander and 120-grit sandpaper. Then vacuum the frame to remove dust.

Step 18. With a miter box and backsaw, cut one end off of a strip of screen molding at a 45-degree angle. Lay the strip along one face edge of the frame, and use the frame as a guide to mark the strip for the second cut. Cut the piece to fit, and dry clamp it to the frame with two bar clamps. Cut pieces to fit the other three edges, and dry clamp them to check for fit. Mark the pieces *left, right, top,* and *bottom.*

Step 19. Mix a small amount of five-minute epoxy cement, and apply a thin coat to the right face surface of the frame, near the outside edge. (Keep cement about ¼ inch away from the inside edge so it won't seep there. Seepage along the outside edge won't matter.) Clamp the right strip of screen molding to the glued right face with two bar clamps or edge

Oak collector frame, Step 19.

Finished oak collector frame.

clamps. Attach the left piece the same way. Then apply cement to the top and bottom face edges, and press the remaining strips of screen molding in place. Let the frame stand until the cement cures.

Step 20. When the cement dries, remove clamps and use a sharp knife to trim away the cement that seeped from the screen molding. Then sand the left, right, top, and bottom surfaces of the frame with a pad sander and 120-grit and 220-grit sandpaper.

Step 21. Use the miter box and backsaw to cut four pieces of panel molding to fit the four sides of the frame. Mix a small amount of five-minute epoxy cement, and attach the molding, one strip at a time, with cement and two spring clamps per piece. (When applying the cement, avoid the front edge to prevent seepage onto the frame face.) Let the frame stand with clamps in place until the cement sets.

Step 22. Do any necessary sanding with 120-grit and 220-grit sandpaper. Vacuum the frame, and wipe all surfaces with a tack cloth, and the frame is ready for the finish of your choice.

Step 23. To duplicate the finish of the frame shown, brush on a coat of Fuller O'Brien Pen-Chrome #640-11 English Oak Stain, let penetrate for ten to fifteen minutes, and wipe dry with paper towels. Let the frame stand overnight, and apply three coats of Deft Semi-Gloss Clear Wood Finish.

Step 24. Lay the frame face down on a protected surface, and attach a sawtooth hanger inside each top rear corner. Then attach a 1-inch piece of ¼-inch-thick foam weather-stripping tape inside each bottom rear corner. Use two wire nails to hang the unit.

20

Framing as a Business

By now, you certainly must realize that doing your own mounting, matting, and framing can save you a tremendous amount of money and will keep saving you money in the years to come. If you have entertained the notion of getting into framing as a business, perhaps you should think more seriously about it and start making plans and moving in that direction. Framing is a relatively easy business to get into and one that requires little in the way of overhead.

What's more, framing is a business you can approach gradually and on one or more of several levels. You can keep it a hobby. You can turn enough of a profit on your hobby to pay for your materials and tools. You can work at framing as a part-time job, or you can make it a full-time business. You can specialize or generalize. You can work in a garage or base-ment workshop, or set up business in a commercial building. The choices are yours.

It's probably best to start out slowly. After all, you might find a particular niche you don't want to go beyond. By moving toward your goals gradually, you should be able to avoid the pitfalls and risks that often cause small-business failure.

In the beginning, you might want only to do framing jobs for friends and others on a limited part-time basis. Then, as you gain confidence in your skills and realize that you can, indeed, make substantial profits, you can seek more business.

Think Deductible

Taxes are necessary nuisances in every business. You will probably have to register your business with some state or local bureaucracy to get a license to work, which usually means a license for the bureaucracy to take a portion of your earnings. And, of course, the feds will want their cut. There's no getting around it, but by being aware of what you will face you can take advantage of all the deductions that are rightfully due you.

Think *deductible*. From the very beginning, think *deductible*. In every aspect of your business, think *deductible*. When you go shopping, think *deductible*. When you travel on business, think *deductible*. When you buy a tool for mounting, matting, or framing, and when you buy framing materials, think *deductible*. When you have letterhead stationery and business cards printed, think *deductible*. When you buy $1,000 worth of oak that you will turn into molding for resale, and when you pay 49¢ for a container of brads you will use making frames for customers, think *deductible*.

Practically everything you buy and every service you pay for that is related to your framing business is deductible in some way. But you must be able to prove that you did indeed pay for an item or service before you can take the deduction. So, from the start, keep receipts on everything.

You will undoubtedly use a vehicle in your business. You will haul wood from lumber yards, and you will transport glass, mat boards, and other materials. You might deliver mats and moldings to various customers. You will drive to the office-supply store, the print shop, and the post office in connection with your business. And you will no doubt use your vehicle in a number of other business-related ways.

The IRS allows deductions for such uses of a vehicle, but you must be able to prove how much you used the family flivver in your business. So put a notebook in your car, and call it your *Business Mileage Log*. The first time you use the vehicle for business purposes, record the date and the odometer reading. Then, for every business trip you take—whether it's to a frame shop two blocks away or a lumber mill two states away—list the date, destination, starting odometer reading, ending odometer reading, and total miles. It's then an easy matter at the end of the year to determine the total miles driven and the portion of the total that was for business.

Whether you prepare your own tax return or have a professional prepare it for you, good records are essential. So you must keep track of every financial transaction. In addition to the receipts you must keep as a record of how much you have spent on your business, you must also keep accurate records of your income. One of the best ways is with a simple invoice system. You will find two-part invoice forms at any local office-supply outlet, or you can order them from Quill Corporation (see directory). Whenever you sell anything to anyone, make out an invoice. If you sell two dozen mats to the One Stop Photo Shop, make out an invoice. If you sell 120 feet of molding to the Fancy Frame Shop, make out an invoice. When your neighbor hands you a $20 bill for a framing job you did, make out an invoice. Give your customer the original invoice, and keep the copy for your records.

It's also a good idea to become familiar with the way small businesses are taxed. There are tax guides available at any bookstore, and you would do well to buy and read one. Also, the Internal Revenue

Service will send you, on request, a copy of Publication 334, *Tax Guide for Small Business.*

Getting Your Name Known

Well before you're ready to open your own framing shop you will need to consider advertising and allied activities as a way of getting your name established. The first step in that direction is to think up a name for your service or company and get letterhead stationery and business cards made. You might want to design some sort of logo, in which case a competent printer or graphic artist can be of tremendous help.

Next, contact your local phone company and get the name and number of the person you should talk to about a listing in the Yellow Pages. This is an inexpensive bit of advertising that will last a year and could shove a lot of business your way.

Go to every local art exhibit and craft show, and pass out business cards to all who will take them. You might even want to rent booth space for a display of your mats, moldings, and frames.

Get in touch with the local chapters of major fund-raising organizations, such as Ducks Unlimited, that stage annual banquets and auctions. Artworks of all sorts are popular at such events, and often these organizations have difficulty getting donated works matted, mounted, and framed in time for their festivities. Talk to the chapter chairman about doing some framing for them. You can offer your work at reduced prices, or you might even consider framing several items for the cost of the materials and donating your labor in exchange for the publicity you can gain.

Make no mistake: people are going to see your work. But you must make sure that as often as possible when they see your work they will also see your name, address, and phone number.

Supplier Accounts

As soon as the ink dries on your business cards, pay visits to local businesses that might supply you with the various materials you need to run your business. Use the Yellow Pages to help you make a list of office-supply outlets, frame shops, lumber companies, glass shops, and any other suppliers you might buy from.

Talk to the sales managers or owners of these companies, and ask to set up accounts with them. Also inquire about professional discounts. Most will offer discounts of 10 to 30 percent or more, which can go a long way toward keeping your costs down.

Once you are established with these various suppliers and they get to know you and your work, they will often refer potential customers to you.

Building Your Framing Business

You can build your business without risking capital, taking out a second mortgage, or hocking your watch. You can make mats, mount photographs, sell frames, manufacture moldings, do custom framing, or all of the above and then some.

You can let leftovers from various mounting and matting jobs accumulate in oddball sizes of mat board, or you can do as I do now and turn most of these scraps into standard-sized mats and mount boards. These standard-sized boards are much easier to store and to sell. When you have built up your stock of them, start looking for customers.

You can try the frame shops, but chances are, the folks there are already turning their scraps into standard mats and selling them. However, if your prices are low enough, you might make sales there.

You're better off to try the local photo shops. If they sell mats, chances are they're buying them from commercial sources whose prices you might be able to beat. If they aren't selling mats, tell them why they should be. Likewise with local artist-supply shops and department stores. You might even try home-improvement centers, gift shops, and galleries.

Once you have lined up your customers, you can start turning out mats on a production basis. A single 32 x 40-inch sheet of mat board will yield eight 8 x 10-inch mats, and you can use much cheaper material (chipboard or card stock) for mounting boards. Of course, you will need to make larger and smaller mats, but remember that you can use leftovers from large mats to make smaller mats. Just determine how many mats you can turn out in an hour and how much you must make as an hourly rate. If the figures are compatible, you're in business.

You can make moldings and sell them through various outlets. Pick several attractive moldings that you can make at a good pace and low cost with readily available materials, and frame several small items you can carry with you as samples. Then visit local lumber yards, home-improvement centers, department stores, artist-supply stores, and frame shops with your samples and an order book.

If you can work in your garage or basement turning out molding at a rate of 100 feet an hour, at a cost of 25¢ a foot, then sell it for 50¢ a foot, your gross income will be $25 an hour. Of course, you must spend time selling and seeing to other related chores, but you will still end up with a tidy profit.

Ah, but you have to persuade others to buy your product, right? Show your potential customers an attractive molding they can buy for 50¢ a foot and resell for $1 a foot, and they won't be potential much longer. That's a 100 percent markup for the retailer.

Still skeptical? Well, when was the last time you saw top-quality frame molding for a buck a foot? But you're probably wondering if you can, in fact, produce frame molding at a rate of 100 feet an hour and at a cost of only 25¢ a foot. Let me remind you that I buy pine 1 x 4 at 10¢ a foot that I then rip into 1 x 2, which I then turn into a basic, rustic box molding at a cost of 5¢ a foot. And I am able to turn this molding out at a rate of 200 feet an hour. So 100 feet an hour at a cost of 25¢ a foot was a deliberately conservative example.

Visit art galleries and get the names of local artists. Then show the artists how they can save money buying mats and moldings from you. Chances are, you will find some artists who consider matting and framing a nuisance and an intrusion on their creativity. They might gladly turn over all such work to you.

When you have saturated all the local markets, take your show on the road. Combine business with pleasure by taking a few days to see sights and visit potential customers outside your immediate vicinity.

When your framing income matches

or exceeds the income from your full-time job, that might be the time to take the plunge and make framing your profession. If you begin cautiously and proceed gradually, you should be able to avoid the hazards associated with operating a small business. With some planning, effort, and a little luck, you should be able to turn this interesting hobby into an enjoyable career.

Directory of Manufacturers and Suppliers

Alto's EZ/Mat
607 West 3rd Ave.
Ellensburg, WA 98926
(509) 962-9212
(800) 225-2497

Mat cutters, mat-cutting systems, oval templates, and round templates.

American Machine & Tool Company
Fourth Ave. and Spring St.
Royersford, PA 19468
(215) 948-0400

Power and hand tools for all phases of woodworking.

Black & Decker (U.S.), Inc.
U.S. Power Tools Group
10 North Park Dr.
P.O. Box 798
Hunt Valley, MD 21030
(301) 683-7000

Black & Decker and Elu woodworking tools.

Boone Supply
5330 SW Lower Dr.
Lake Oswego, OR 97034
(503) 635-9428

Matsushita saw blades.

Brookstone Company
127 Vose Farm Rd.
Peterborough, NH 03458
(603) 924-9541

Framing and woodworking tools.

C.E.I., Inc.
P.O. Box 1300
Ellensburg, WA 98926
(509) 962-8282

CustoMat pressure-sensitive adhesive mat boards.

Coda, Inc.
196 Greenwood Ave.
Midland Park, NJ 07432
(201) 444-7755

Adhesives, adhesive mount boards,
print rollers, presses, standouts.

Craftsman Wood Service Co.
1735 West Cortland Ct.
Addison, IL 60101
(312) 629-3100

Framing and woodworking tools, picture frame moldings.

Crescent Cardboard Company
P.O. Box XD
100 West Willow Rd.
Wheeling, IL 60090
(312) 537-3400

Complete line of mat and mount boards.

Diamond Machining Technology, Inc.
85 Hayes Memorial Dr.
Marlborough, MA 07152
(617) 481-5944

Diamond hones and files.

Doran Enterprises, Inc.
2779 South 34th St.
Milwaukee, WI 53215
(414) 645-0109

Premier brand mounting adhesives,
rollers, and cutters.

Eubank Frame, Inc.
P.O. Box 425
Salisbury, MD 21801
(301) 546-3331

Eubank frame, Uni-Frame.

Falcon Safety Products, Inc.
1065 Bristol Road
Mountainside, NJ 07092
(201) 233-5000

Mounting, matting, and trimming
tools and materials.

The Fine Tool Shops
170 West Rd.
Portsmouth, NH 03801
(800) 533-5305

Framing and woodworking tools.

Jerry's Artarama
P.O. Box 1105
New Hyde Park, NY 11040
(516) 328-6633

Mounting, matting, and framing tools
and materials.

Lee Valley Tools, Ltd.
1080 Morrison Dr.
Ottawa, Ontario K2H 8K7 Canada
(613) 596-0350

Framing and matting tools.

Leichtung Workshops
4944 Commerce Pkwy.
Cleveland, OH 44128
(216) 831-2555 (Ohio residents)
(800) 321-6840

Miter boxes, mat cutters, and other
tools for framing and woodworking.

Leonard Products Co.
Box 240211
8107-Q Arrowridge Blvd.
Charlotte, NC 28224
(704) 527-5261

EZ Mount adhesive mount boards.

Light Impressions Corp.
439 Monroe Ave.
P.O. Box 940
Rochester, NY 14603
(716) 271-8960
(800) 828-6216

Mounting, matting, and framing tools and materials. Complete line of archival-quality materials

Lineco, Inc.
P.O. Box 2604
Holyoke, MA 01041
(413) 533-4387

Archival-quality materials for conservation framing.

Meisel Photochrome Corp.
9645 Webb Chapel Rd.
Dallas, TX 75220
(214) 350-6666

Complete photo lab services, mounting, ultraviolet protection.

Michael Business Machines Corp.
145 West 45th St.
New York, NY 10036
(212) 997-1700

Kutrimmer cutters and trimmers.

Mr. Frame Inc.
7208 Centreville Rd.
Manassas, VA 22111
(703) 361-2179

Picture frame moldings and supplies.

NuArc Co., Inc.
6200 West Howard St.
Niles, IL 60648
(312) 967-4400

Vacuum presses.

Premier Division
Martin Yale Industries, Inc.
500 North Spaulding Ave.
Chicago, IL 60624
(312) 826-4444

Paper trimmers and cutters.

Pres-On Products, Inc.
1020 South Westgate
Addison, IL 60101
(312) 543-9370

Adhesive-coated mount boards of various materials and all sizes.

Product Marketing International
P.O. Box 297
Ellicott City, MD 21043
(301) 997-5244

Rotary cutters and accessories.

Quill Corporation
100 South Schelter Rd.
Lincolnshire, IL 60069
(312) 634-4800

Complete line of office supplies and furnishings, and matting and framing supplies.

RBI Industries, Inc.
National Sales/Marketing Office
40 Westpark Rd.
Dayton, OH 45459
(800) 535-8665

Framing and woodworking tools.

Russell Harrington Cutlery, Inc.
44 River St.
Southbridge, MA 01550
(617) 765-0201

Dexter mat cutters and blades.

The Saunders Group
21 Jet View Dr.
Rochester, NY 14624
(716) 328-7800
(800) 828-6214

Dry-mounting and pressure-sensitive mounting materials and RotaTrim rotary cutters and accessories.

Seal Products, Inc.
550 Spring St.
Naugatuck, CT 06770
(203) 729-5201

Dry-mounting, vacuum, and pressure-sensitive mounting materials and presses.

3M Commercial Tape Division
3M Center
P.O. Box 33600
St. Paul, MN 55144
(612) 736-1360

Mounting tissues, aerosol adhesives, adhesive transfer applicators, vacuum and pressure-sensitive mounting presses.

Trend-lines
375 Beacham St.
Box 6447
Chelsea, MA 02150
(617) 884-8882
(800) 343-3248

Framing and woodworking tools.

University Products, Inc.
P.O. Box 101
Holyoke, MA 01041
(413) 532-3372
(800) 628-1912

Mounting adhesives, mount boards, mounting equipment, mat boards. Complete line of archival-quality materials.

Woodcraft Supply
41 Atlantic Ave.
P.O. Box 4000
Woburn, MA 01888
(617) 935-9278
(800) 225-1153

Framing and woodworking tools and materials.

The Woodworkers' Store
21801 Industrial Blvd.
Rogers, MN 55374
(612) 428-2899 (Customer service)
(612) 428-2199 (Orders)

Framing and woodworking tools and materials, Micro Wood, finishing products.

Woodworker's Supply
5604 Alameda Place, N.E.
Albuquerque, NM 87113
(505) 821-0500

Framing and woodworking tools.

XYLO Inc.
2000 Louisville Rd.
P.O. Box 8062
Savannah, GA 31412
(800) 627-5040

Unfinished wood moldings and lacquered exotic hardwood moldings.

Index

Acrylic frames, 103–5
Alto's (Alto Albright), 265
   deluxe mat cutter, 29
   EZ/Mat, 25, 27, 29, 44–46, 74
   oval templates, 74–76, 79
   standard mat cutter, 27
American Machine & Tool Company, 265
Archival corrugated board, 20, 21

Base shoe molding, 117
Beaded molding, 128
Beveled molding, 122, 131–32
Black & Decker (U.S.), Inc., 265
   Dustbuster, 33
   Finishing Machine, 254
   routers and tables, 122
   Workmate, 33, 98, 100, 123
Boone Supply, 265
Borders, mat, 43–45, 63
Box molding, 118–19, 123
Boyne Mat Corner Marker, 25, 77
Brackets, making your own, 209–12, 214
Brick molding, 117–18
Brookstone Company, 265
Bulletin boards, framing, 233–42
Bullnose stop molding, 117
Butt-joint frames, 195–99

C.E.I., Inc., 87
   CustoMat, 86
Calendars, framing, 215–22, 224
Chipboard, 35, 52, 59, 186, 263
Coda, Inc. (Cold-Mount products), 266
   codaFoam, 52, 186, 204, 234

Galerie kits, 52
   Mural-Mounts, 52
   roller, 52–53
   Stand-Outs, 52
Collector frames, 250–59
Color, selecting, 39–42, 50, 63–64, 76–77, 103
Conservation mounting and matting
   cost of, 36–38, 39
   Materials for, 20–21, 35, 36, 37–39
   reasons for, 36–39
Con-Tact, 80, 85
Corners
   cropping, 31
   mat-sample, 30–31
   special treatments for, 62, 67–71, 73
Corrugated container board, 20–21, 39
Coved molding, 127–28
Cove molding, 117
Covering mats, 80–82, 85, 87
Craftsman Wood Service Co., 266
Crescent Cardboard Company, 266
   mat and rag boards, 21, 30, 41, 42
   mat-sample sheet, 41
CustoMat, 87
Cutout mats, 62, 64–65

Dap Wood Dough, 140–41
Decorating mats, 76–80
Decorating moldings, 132–36, 138
Deft wood finishes, 90, 146, 148, 230, 246
Design of frames, 18–19
Dexter knives and mat cutters, 27
Diamond Machining Technology, Inc., 206–7, 266
Displaying and hanging, tips on, 171–74

Doran Enterprises, 266
  Gallerie-Mount, 51
Drip cap molding, 117
Dry mounting, 49
Dry-mount presses, 54
Dust-Off, 32–33
Dust seals, attaching, 160–63

Elmer's Professional Carpenter's Wood Glue, 89
Elu woodworking tools, 98, 122
Eubank Frame, Inc., 266
  Uni-Frame, 206–9

Falcon Safety Products, Inc., 266
  Perma/Mount, 51, 61
  Print Positioner, 25–26, 46, 55–56, 58
  Print Trimmer, 53–54
Filets, 109–10
Fine Tool Shops, The, 266
Finishing wood frames, 139–40
  clear finishes, 90, 146, 148, 230, 246, 249, 259
  filling and patching, 140–42, 232, 242
  painting, 147–48, 193, 198–99, 227, 232, 254
  removing finishes, 148–49
  rustic wood frames, 185
  sanding and preparing, 142–43, 147, 191, 197, 198,
    202, 218, 221, 222, 228–29, 232, 235, 238, 242,
    245–46, 248–49, 254, 259
  shellacking, 38, 90, 140, 141–42, 147, 185, 192,
    198, 232
  staining, 89, 144–47, 185, 188, 191, 198, 202, 218,
    222, 227, 229–30, 232, 235, 246, 249, 254, 259
Flat molding, 119–21, 124
Floater fixtures, 186–88
Floater frames, 188–94
Foamboard, 20, 21, 50, 52, 59, 207–8, 210, 235
Frames
  for bulletin boards, 233–42
  for calendars, 215–22, 224
  design of, 18–19
  filets for, 109–10
  functions of, 17–18
  liners for, 109–10
  for pegboard, 225–32
  tips for building, 110–11
  types of
    butt-joint, 195–99
    collector, 250–59
    floater, 188–94
    lap-joint, 199–200, 202
    metal and acrylic, 102–5
    ready-made, 102–5
    rough-edge box, 180–81
    rustic system, 183–85
    rustic wood, 175–85
    shadow-box, 243–49
    wane, 181–83
Framespace, 158

Framing
  basics of, 13–19
  as a business, 260–64
  getting into, 19
  making your own moldings for, 112–25, 127–36,
    138, 175–85
  materials for, 88–90
    best woods, 113–15, 136, 176–78
    commercial wood moldings, 105–11, 175–76
    construction moldings, 115–18
  objects suitable for, 15–17
  safety tips for, 9–11
  savings potential in, 14–15, 209
  tools for, 90–96, 98, 100–101, 178–79
  without frames, 203–12, 214
  without miters, 195–200, 202
  See also Finishing wood frames
Fuller O'Brien Pen-Chrome stains, 144, 145–46, 188,
    202, 222, 229–30, 246, 249, 259

Gatorfoam, 50, 52, 186, 204, 234
Glazing, 90, 150–53
  tools and techniques for, 153–57
Grooved molding, 121–22, 124–25, 127, 132

Hanging and displaying, tips on, 171–74
Hardboard, 20, 50–51, 204, 210
Hardware, hanging, 90, 105
  installing, 165–69
  making an adjustable picture-wire jig, 169–71
Heat mounting, 21
Hinges, 22, 42, 43, 47–48
How to Make Your Own Picture Frames, 139–40

Indented-corner mats, 70–71
Insta-Hinge, 22, 42, 47–48
Installing
  hanging hardware, 165–69
  mounted works, 157–60
  oils, acrylics, batiks, 163–65
Intercraft frame products, 103
  Frameless Frame, 205–6
Intermediate mounting and matting, 34
IRS (Internal Revenue Service), 261–62

J-molding, 123
Jerry's Artarama, 266

Lap-joint frames, 199–200, 202
Lattice molding, 116–17
Lee Valley Tools, Ltd., 266
Leichtung Workshops, 25, 267
Leonard Products Company, 267
  EZ Mount, 51
Light Impressions Corp., 174, 267
Lineco, Inc., 267
Liners, 109–10

Masonite, 50, 52, 186, 189, 234

Mat board, standard, 20, 21, 37, 186
  neutralized wood-pulp, 21, 36, 37–38
  precut versus, 35–36
Mat cutters/cutting guides
  description of, 25, 27, 29, 53–54, 73–74
  high-speed, 73
  razor blades for, 31–32, 53
  using, 31–32, 44–46, 65, 67–71, 73–76, 82
Materials
  color of, 39–42, 50, 63–64, 76–77, 103
  framing, 88–90
  manufacturers and suppliers of, 265–68
  matting, 20–24, 34–42, 86
  mounting, 20–24, 34–42, 50–52
  texture of, 42, 64
Mat-sample corners, 30–31
Mats
  borders of, 43–45, 63
  covering, 80–82, 85, 87
  decorating, 76–80
  functions of, 17–18
  types of
    for conservation mounting, 20–21, 35, 36–39
    with cutouts, 62, 64–65
    indented-corner, 70–71
    multiple, 63–64
    notched, 62, 64–65, 71, 73
    notched-corner, 71, 73
    octagonal, 65, 67
    oval-windowed, 73–76
    precut, 35–36
    with special corner treatments, 62, 67–71, 73
    zag-corner, 67–69
Matsushita saw blades, 101
Matting
  advanced, 62–65, 67–71, 73–82, 85, 87
  basic, 42–48
  cropping corners, 31
  cutting windows, 43, 63, 64–76
  materials for, 20–24, 34–42, 86
  positioning, 25–26, 46–47, 55–56, 58
  safety tips for, 9–11
  sample corners, 30–31
  tools for, 24–27, 29–33
  See also Mat cutters/cutting guides
Meisel Photochrome Corp., 151, 267
Metal frames, 103–5
Michael Business Machines Corp., 267
Micro Wood, 136, 169–71, 210, 255–58
  brackets, 211–12
Miter boxes
  selecting, 90–92
  using, 100, 107–8, 110, 190, 196–97, 220, 228, 230–31, 235, 237, 241, 252, 253, 255–59
Miters, framing without, 195–200, 202
Moldings, picture-frame
  basic description of, 88–89
  best woods for, 113–15, 136, 176–78
  decorating, 132–36, 138

making your own, 112–25, 127–36, 138, 175–85
  types of
    base shoe, 117
    beaded, 128
    beveled, 122, 131–32
    box, 118–19, 123
    brick, 117–18
    bullnose stop, 117
    commercial wood, 105–11, 175–76
    construction, 115–18
    cove, 117
    coved, 127–28
    drip cap, 117
    flat, 119–21, 124
    grooved, 121–22, 124–25, 127, 132
    J-, 123
    lattice, 116–17
    metal and acrylic, 102–11
    ogee stop, 117
    outside corner, 117
    parting bead, 116
    ready-made, 102–5
    Roman ogee, 128–29, 132
    rounded, 129–30
    router, 122–25, 127–32, 136
    rustic wood, 175–85
    saw, 118–22, 136
    shingle, 117
    ¾-square, 116
Mounting
  basic, 42–48
  bench for, 33
  conservation, 20–21, 35, 36–39
  dry, 49
  heat, 21
  intermediate, 34
  installing mounted works, 157–60
  materials for, 20–24, 34–42, 50–52
  modern methods of, 58–59, 61
  of photographs and posters, 49–56, 58–59, 61
  positioning, 25–26, 46–47, 55–56, 58
  safety tips for, 9–11
  tools for, 24–27, 29–33, 52–55
  vacuum, 50
  wet, 49–50
Mounting boards/sheets, adhesive, 51–52, 80, 82, 85, 87
Mr. Frame Inc., 267
Multiple mats, 63–64
Museum board, 20, 36

Neutralized wood-pulp mat board, 21, 36, 37–38
Nielsen frames, 104
Notched mats, 62, 64–65
  notched-corner, 71, 73
NuArc Co., Inc., 267

Octagonal mats, 65, 67
Ogee stop molding, 117

Outside corner molding, 117
Oval-windowed mats, 73–76

Painting
   brackets, 210
   frames, 147–48, 193, 198–99, 227, 232, 254
Parting bead molding, 116
Pegboard, framing, 225–32
Photographs and posters, mounting of
   basic description of, 49–50
   materials for, 50–52
   tools for, 52–55
Picture Framing and Wall Display, 41
Plastic Wood, 140
Positioning, 25–26, 46–47, 55–56, 58
Precut mats, 35–36
Premier Division, Martin Yale Industries, Inc., 267
Pres-On Products, Inc., 234, 267
   Hi-Tack, 52
   Low-Tack, 52
   Pres-On thermo adhesive, 52
Presses, 54–55, 58
Product Marketing International, 267

Quill Corporation, 261, 268

Rag board, 20, 21, 36, 37
Razor blades, 31–32, 46, 53
RBI Industries, Inc., 268
Ready-made frames and moldings, 102–11
Reinhardt, Ed, 139
Rogers, Hal, 139
Rollers, 52–53, 59, 61, 81
Roman ogee molding, 128–29, 132
Rough-edge box frames, 180–81
Rounded molding, 129–30
Router moldings, 122–25, 127–32, 136
Russell Harrington Cutlery, Inc., 268
Rustic system frames, 183–85

Safety tips, 9–11
Saunders Group, The, 268
   RotaTrim, 54
Savings potential in framing, 14–15, 209
Saw moldings, 118–22, 136
Scotch
   Adhesive Transfer Tape, 48
   Magic Tape, 23
   Mounting Adhesive, 51–52
   Photo Mount, 51
   Removable Magic Tape, 23
   752 ATG Adhesive Transfer Applicator, 23–24, 162
   Spra-Ment, 51, 233
   See also 3M Company
Seal Products, Inc., 268

Sears
   Craftsman miter box, 91–92
   routers and tables, 122
Shadow-box frames, 243–49
Shellac Sticks, 140, 141–42
Shellacking, 38, 90, 147, 185, 192, 198, 232
Shingle molding, 117
Sporty's Tool Shop, 268
Staining
   brackets, 210, 214
   frames, 89, 144–47, 185, 188, 191, 198, 202, 218,
      222, 227, 229–30, 232, 235, 246, 249, 254, 259
Standouts, 51, 52

Tax Guide for Small Business, 262
Texture, selecting, 42, 64
3M Company, 173, 268
   Super 77 Spray Adhesive, 51, 81, 233, 235, 241
   See also Scotch
¾-square molding, 116
Tools
   framing, 90–96, 98, 100–101, 178–79
   glazing, 153–57
   manufacturers and suppliers of, 265–68
   matting, 24–27, 29–33
   mounting, 24–27, 29–33, 52–55
   safety tips when using, 9–11
Trend-lines, 268
Tyvek tape, 23

University Products, Inc., 268

Vacuum mounting, 50
Vacuum presses, 54, 58

Wane frames, 181–83
Watco wood-finishing products, 145–46, 185, 218
Wet mounting, 49–50
Windows, mat, 43, 63
   oval, 73–76
Woodcraft Supply, 268
Woodworkers' Store, The, 268
Woodworker's Supply, 268

X-Acto
   knives, 26–27, 44, 61, 78, 134, 161–62, 207, 235,
      239
   mat cutters, 27
XYLO Inc., 268

Zag-corner mats, 67–69
Zar Wood Patch, 140